Artificial Intelligence in Accounting and Auditing

Mariarita Pierotti · Anna Monreale · Federica De Santis

Artificial Intelligence in Accounting and Auditing

Accessing the Corporate Implications

palgrave macmillan

Mariarita Pierotti
Department of Computer Science
University of Pisa
Pisa, Italy

Anna Monreale
Department of Computer Science
University of Pisa
Pisa, Italy

Federica De Santis
Department of Economics
and Management
University of Pisa
Pisa, Italy

ISBN 978-3-031-71370-5 ISBN 978-3-031-71371-2 (eBook)
https://doi.org/10.1007/978-3-031-71371-2

This Palgrave Macmillan imprint is published by the registered company Springer Nature Switzerland AG
The registered company address is: Gewerbestrasse 11, 6330 Cham, Switzerland

Acknowledgements

Research partly funded by PNRR—M4C2—Investimento 1.3, Partenariato Esteso PE00000013—"FAIR—Future Artificial Intelligence Research"—Spoke 1 "Human-centered AI", funded by the European Commission under the NextGeneration EU program

This work has been supported by SoBigData.it that receives funding from European Union—NextGenerationEU—National Recovery and Resilience Plan (Piano Nazionale di Ripresa e Resilienza, PNRR)—Project: "SoBigData.it– Strengthening the Italian RI for Social Mining and Big Data Analytics"—Prot. IR0000013—Avviso n. 3264 del 28/12/2021; and by the NextGenerationEU program under the funding schemes PNRR-PE-AI scheme (M4C2, investment 1.3, line on AI) FAIR (Future Artificial Intelligence Research).

Contents

List of Figures

List of Tables

CHAPTER 1

The New Corporate Data Ecosystem

Federica De Santis

1.1 Introduction

Since we shifted from an industrial economy to an information economy during the late 1960s, scholars and practitioners clearly recognized the central role information plays in conducting and controlling business (Bertini, 1990; Galbraith, 1968; McGee et al., 1993). In an information economy, what you know determines your success far more than what you own, and competition is mainly based on companies' "ability to acquire, manipulate, interpret, and use information effectively" (McGee et al., 1993, p. 1). Nowadays, the fruits of the "knowledge era" or "information society" are easy to see, as every device is online, sensors are ubiquitous and generate continuous streams of data, and the utter volume of data produced and consumed on the Internet will increase by orders of magnitude (Cavanillas et al., 2016; Mayer-Schönberger & Cukier, 2013).

Such a growing "datafication" of the world (Lycett, 2013) where technological advancements offer new opportunities to extract value from the so-called data deluge (Cavanillas et al., 2016) led to the emergence of the concept of Big Data (Gandomi & Haider, 2015). Big Data can be defined as "high-volume, high-velocity and high-variety information assets that demand cost-effective, innovative forms of information processing for enhanced insights and decision-making" (Gartner IT Glossary).

Currently, the sheer annual volume of data and information generated is approximately 120 zettabytes and it is expected to increase by over

M. Pierotti et al., *Artificial Intelligence in Accounting and Auditing*,
https://doi.org/10.1007/978-3-031-71371-2_1

150% to 181 zettabytes by 2025 (Acciarini et al., 2023). Organizations from almost every industry have the opportunity to collect and use Big Data by means of advanced technologies such as data analytics, artificial intelligence, and machine learning (Acciarini et al., 2023; Akter et al., 2016; Erevelles et al., 2016) to generate knowledge (de Camargo Fiorini et al., 2018; Lee, 2017; Zaitsava et al., 2023). However, several commentators underline that many companies are struggling to manage this knowledge generation potential (Chen & Xiaotong, 2014; Gandomi & Haider, 2015; Zaitsava et al., 2023).

This chapter, therefore, introduces the reader to the key concepts related to the new corporate data ecosystem and lays the groundwork for understanding how data is collected, stored, managed, and utilized within an organization. We will also highlight the importance of data ecosystems in driving business decisions, innovation, and competitive advantage by focusing on both opportunities and challenges related to the use of Big Data and related technology to drive and control businesses.

1.2 The Data Deluge: How the Corporate Data Ecosystem Is Expanding

Nowadays, the data explosion combines with unprecedented advancements in computing power and connectivity, thus allowing for an increasing amount of Big Data to be analyzed anytime, anywhere (Cappa et al., 2021; Zillner et al., 2021). Big data analytics has the potential to transform the way businesses compete, as they can extract hidden patterns from a set of raw data for making correct decisions, increasing productivity, generating knowledge, and upgrading innovations (Maroufkhani et al., 2020).

Big data as a research field finds its roots in practice, rather than in academia (Manyika et al., 2017) since practitioners first recognized the relevance of Big Data in driving business innovation, due to its ability to provide information about customers' preferences, feedback about firms' products and services, and insights about emerging trends (Cappa et al., 2021; George et al., 2014; Mazzei & Noble, 2017; Vecchio et al., 2018). Over the last fifteen years, scholars have increasingly paid attention to Big Data and business analytics by investigating their potential to revolutionize the way we work, live, and conduct business (Chen et al., 2012; George et al., 2014; Mikalef et al., 2020). From that moment on, researchers have attempted to explore the phenomenon of Big Data and business analytics and to understand how organizations can create and capture value from their data resources (Cappa et al., 2021; Cavanillas et al., 2016; Mikalef et al., 2020).

The Emergence of Big Data: Definition and Evolution

The most widespread definition of Big Data can be referred to as the so-called Vs framework, that stems from the recognition of its distinctive characteristics. The seminal work of Laney (2001) firstly proposed the 3Vs model, focusing on Big Data's volume, velocity, and variety. Starting from the 3Vs model, scholars and practitioners described other key features of Big Data, so that the original interpretive framework has evolved to include also Big Data value, veracity, and data variability (Gandomi & Haider, 2015).

Volume is conceived as a purely quantitative dimension, which refers to the magnitude of Big Data in terms of the amounts of available data, that either consumes huge storage capability or consists of a large number of records. Therefore, "big" only reflects the size of the dataset (Chen & Xiaotong, 2014; Gandomi & Haider, 2015; George et al., 2014). A dataset indeed is considered "Big" only if it pushes traditional information systems' limits, thus requiring advanced capturing and storage tools and, way more importantly, advanced data processing capabilities (Vasarhelyi et al., 2015).

Variety is conceived as the qualitative dimension of Big Data that "makes big data really big" (Sagiroglu & Sinanc, 2013, p. 43), as it reflects the structural heterogeneity of a dataset and the Big Data's ability to provide granular precision by means of a great variety of data sources (Günther et al., 2017; Yoo, 2015; Zaitsava et al., 2023). In today's information society, data is generated from a great variety of sources and formats, and contains multidimensional fields (Russom, 2011). Variety, therefore, relates to the richness of data representation, that enables a distinction between structured, semi-structured, and unstructured data (Kaisler et al., 2013). Challenges arise due to the differing nature of structured and unstructured data. Structured data, which resides in fixed fields (e.g., in relational databases or spreadsheets), can be managed with conventional technological solutions. However, structured data constitutes less than 20% of the existing Big Data. The remainder consists of semi-structured data, which does not conform to fixed fields but includes tags and markers to separate data elements (such as XML or HTML-tagged text), and unstructured data, which lacks fixed fields and includes freeform text (e.g., books, articles, email bodies) as well as untagged audio, image, and video data (Manyika et al., 2011).

The challenging aspect of such attribute lies in the conceptual difference between data and information[1] and its consequences on information production processes. Data indeed is the raw material of the information production process, by means of which data is classified and organized in a unique "elementary message" that is aimed at reducing the inherent uncertainty of decision-making processes, thus increasing its effectiveness. As a consequence, information is the output of the information production process that is thus aimed at adding value to rough data (Marchi, 2003). To transform data, both structured and unstructured, into valuable information and exploit its potential, appropriate analytics tools and techniques are required. However, significant challenges exist in finding analytics and data management technologies that can effectively derive valuable insights from these vast volumes of unstructured data (De Santis, 2018; Gandomi & Haider, 2015).

The velocity attribute captures the speed at which a company processes and analyzes data (Akter et al., 2019; Günther et al., 2017; Sivarajah et al., 2017; Zaitsava et al., 2023). Velocity is challenging for organizations because it contributes to the Big Data's complexity. Companies must harness vast amounts of data that is continuously flowing and fast-generated (De Santis, 2018). Such fast data must be analyzed and acted upon close to real time in order to create value and allow companies to gain a competitive advantage. Strictly related to the velocity attribute is Big Data's variability, that refers to the fluctuations of the data flow rate, which is subject to periodic peaks and troughs (Gandomi & Haider, 2015).

Big Data's Veracity refers to how predictable, reliable, and accurate the data and the related analytics are (Ohlhorst, 2012). Therefore, this attribute identifies the credibility or trustworthiness of the output generated (de Camargo Fiorini et al., 2018; Zaitsava et al., 2023). Reliability issues with Big Data mostly emerge because data can be extracted from many different sources, either internal or external to the organization,

[1] For an in-depth examination of the new data-information-knowledge paradigm, see Chapter 2.

either traditional or new at a constantly increasing pace. Veracity, therefore, emphasizes the need to be aware of data quality (Erevelles et al., 2016).

The last attribute, Big Data Value, measures the usefulness of data in making decisions (Kaisler et al., 2013). Big Data's Value is characterized by a certain degree of ambiguity as it relates both to the extent to which Big Data generates economically worthy insights for decision-making (Fosso Wamba et al., 2015), and to the relatively "low value density" as compared to large volumes of available data. Useful information that provides leverage for decision-making within a problem space is often hidden among huge amounts of non-traditional data received in the original form (Gandomi & Haider, 2015). The challenge here is in the form of a "needle-in-a-haystack problem," which consists in understanding what data is worth acquiring and what is worthless, and then transforming and extracting that data for analysis (Kaisler et al., 2013; McGuire & Ladd, 2014). In this respect, some authors also added a further attribute, namely the "decay" of Big Data, to underline the declining value of data over time and the need for timely information processing and real-time data-driven actions (Lee, 2017).

To summarize, Lee (2017, pp. 294–296) proposed an integrated view of Big Data as reported in Fig. 1.1. According to the author, the three edges of the integrated view of Big Data represent the three Big Data's dimensions that were first listed by Laney (2001): i.e., volume, velocity, and variety. Inside the triangle Lee (2017) listed five further Big Data's dimensions that are affected by the growth of the three triangular dimensions: veracity, variability, complexity, decay, and value. Moreover, the relationship between the initial 3Vs with the additional dimensions is explained. That is to say that all the five further dimensions but veracity are positively impacted by the growth of the three triangular dimensions.

In such representation of Big Data, traditional data that mostly consists in structured data such as ERP and legacy data represents a subset of Big Data with the same three dimensions, although the scope of each dimension is much smaller than that of Big Data.

In this regard, Moffitt and Vasarhelyi (2013) proposed a representation of the expanding corporate data ecosystem, as depicted in Fig. 1.2.

This view also suggests that, though scholars and professionals use to define Big Data by referring to its characteristics, one must consider Big Data as a moving, rather than static, target (Kaisler et al., 2013). Big Data's Volume is a dynamic attribute that varies across time and space.

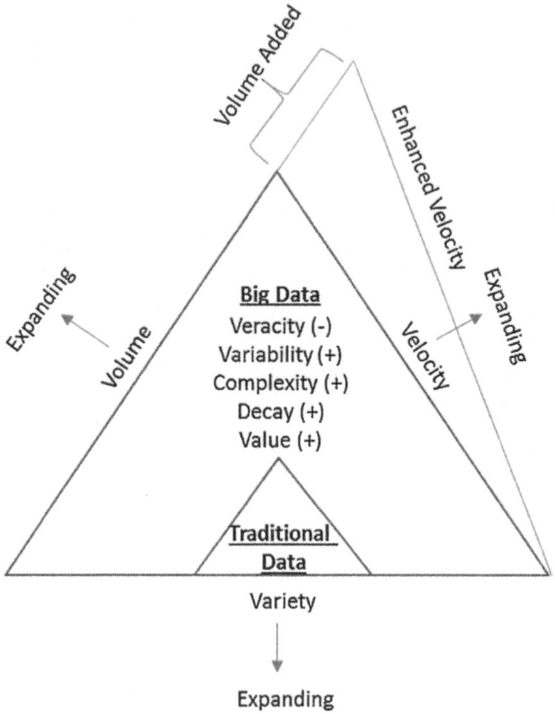

Fig. 1.1 An integrated view of Big Data (*Source* Lee [2017]. Big data: Dimensions, evolution, impacts, and challenges. *Business Horizons, 60*, p. 295)

What qualifies as Big Data today may not meet future "high-volume" thresholds due to continuous advancements in storage capabilities. Similarly, two datasets of the same size might require different data management technologies, meaning one might not meet the characteristics of Big Data (Gandomi & Haider, 2015). Therefore, the term "Big Data" implies that the data volume is at or beyond the limits of what a company's information system can store, manage, and process efficiently (Vasarhelyi et al., 2015).

Although the quantities of data available today are undeniably large, volume alone cannot define this new data ecosystem (Boyd & Crawford, 2012). The term "big" can be misleading, as it directs researchers' and practitioners' attention to the dataset size rather than to the insights it can

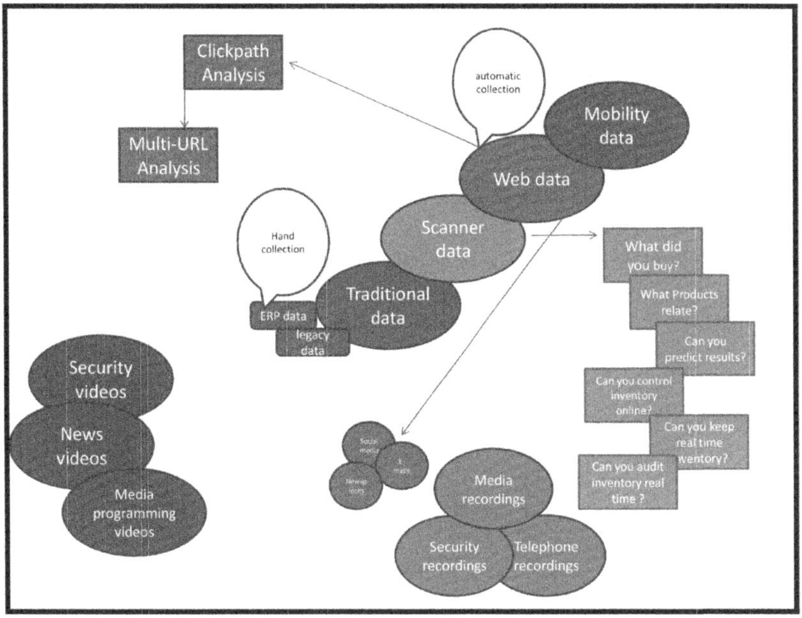

Fig. 1.2 The expanding corporate data ecosystem (*Source* Moffitt and Vasarhelyi [2013]. AIS in the age of Big Data. *Journal of Information Systems, 27*(2), p. 10)

provide. The defining parameter of Big Data thus becomes its granularity, shifting the focus from the number of records to the detailed information each record contains, i.e., how smart the data is (George et al., 2014).

Moreover, Big Data is "worthless in a vacuum." Its potential value is unlocked only when leveraged for decision-making. To enable evidence-based decision-making, organizations need efficient processes to turn high volumes of fast-moving and diverse data into meaningful insights (Gandomi & Haider, 2015, p. 140). This involves understanding the relationship between data, information, and knowledge, with the assumption that "data is a record, information is a message, and knowledge is a model of how something works" (Bhimani & Willcocks, 2014, p. 471). Big data should not only be collected, extracted, cleansed, and integrated; it must also be modeled using advanced analytic tools and interpreted by decision-makers to deliver business value.

The Sources of Big Data

We know that Big Data represents the cornerstone of the business environments' digitalization because, when combined with appropriate analytics tools, it provides companies with the ability to extract intelligence from data and translate that into business advantage, so that managers can decide based on evidence rather than intuition (McAfee et al., 2012). Further, Big Data is everywhere since there is a smartphone in every pocket and a computer in every backpack (McGee et al., 1993). As many authors underline, not only we are "awash with more information than ever before, but that information is growing faster" (Mayer-Schönberger & Cukier, 2013, p. 6).

Big Data is generated by a wide variety of sources and can be classified as follows, depending on how it is owned and managed (Cappa et al., 2021; George et al., 2014):

1. Public data
2. Open data
3. Private data
4. Data exhaust
5. Community data
6. Self-quantification data.

Public data is typically generated by individuals and used by public entities such as governments, governmental organizations, and local communities. This data category includes data collected from free Wi-Fi access in public areas or public transportations by municipal organizations and can be used for a wide-ranging business and management applications or for several research purposes by public entities. Public data also includes data related to energy use, and health care, that must be accessed under certain restrictions in order to protect individuals' privacy. Open data, instead, is usually not tradable as it is freely accessible to anyone interested. This data includes data collected by large international organizations about global trends or phenomena, such as the data collected by the World Bank about the global economic and institutional trends. Open data is usually provided as aggregate data, thus lacking any connection to specific individuals so that data users are not required to confront privacy and ethical concerns.

Private data are generally created and owned by firms, non-profit organizations, and individuals and reflect private information. Companies typically collect private data by means of proprietary platforms such as the company's Enterprise Resource Planning (ERP) or Customer Relationship Management (CRM) system, website, or social networks accounts. This category also includes consumer transactions, radio-frequency identification (RFID) tags used by supply chains, movements of companies' goods and resources, and data collected through mobile application (mostly interactions with customers).

Data exhaust refers to data passively collected from the general environment in which the company operates. That data, in its original form, has little or zero value for the collector as it is usually collected for other purposes, but it can be combined with other data sources to create new sources of value. As a way of example, data exhaust comprises data that individuals passively generate during their daily activities such as when they make purchases, or access healthcare services, or when they interact with others on Internet. Individuals also generate data exhaust with their information-seeking behavior via Internet or by phone. Companies can use such data to infer people's preferences or to predict consumers' behavior.

That labeled as community data mostly consists in unstructured data (i.e., text, images, video, etc.) that is generated by means of social networks, blog, and the like. Typical community data includes social networks' feeds, consumers' reviews on product and services, voting buttons associated with consumers' sharing, scoring, and reviewing systems (e.g., the "Like" button on Facebook or "I found it useful" on Amazon).

Finally, we consider self-quantification data as data generated by individuals when they quantify personal actions and behavior, such as that data generated via sensors on common wearables (e.g., a smartwatch or a wristband) used to monitor exercise and movement, or that collected by sensors installed on home automation accessories (e.g., energy consumption). That data becomes of interest when it is collected via mobile applications, aggregated, and then tracked for psychology, marketing, or public policy purposes.

Over time, scholars have proposed other potential classifications of Big Data sources, such as the one proposed by Baesens et al. (2016), who distinguished data sources among the following categories:

1. Large-scale enterprise systems, that include companies' most widespread transactional information systems such as ERP systems, CRM, and Supply Chain Management (SCM) platforms. These sources usually generate structured data.
2. Online social graphs, i.e., the social networks within which people interact each other and all the digital platforms through which people access media content.
3. Mobile devices, since they are maybe the today's most widespread gateway to the Internet, with 5 billion handsets worldwide, that allow to track and potentially geotag every action taken by a user.
4. Internet of things (IoT), that relates to the vast types of sensors connecting objects one another and with humans.
5. Open data/public data, that comprises data about topics including weather, traffic, maps, environment, and housing.

Broadly speaking, within the information society, where everything happens in the physical world can be recorded and thus turned into data, new sources of data usually emerge because of the interactions that occur through a web-based connection. Based on this consideration, we can group all the possible sources of Big Data according to the "Internet of Events" paradigm (van der Aalst, 2014), as reported in Fig. 1.3.

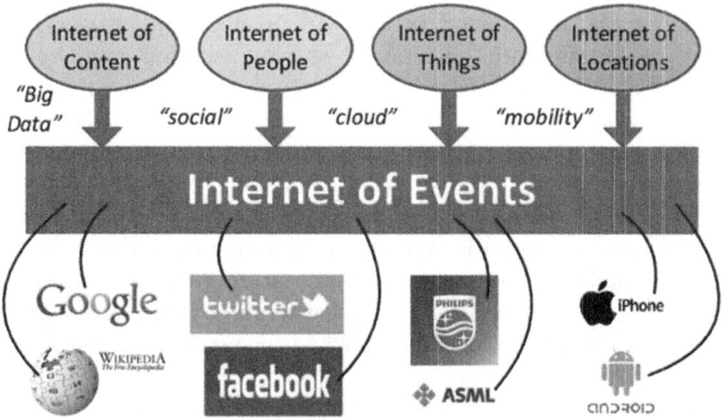

Fig. 1.3 Internet of Events and new sources of Data (*Source* van der Aalst, W. [2014]. Data scientist: The Engineer of the Future)

1.3 Big Data and Artificial Intelligence: Opportunities for Decision-Making and Control Processes

In today's complex and dynamic business environment, the ability to explore data to understand customer behavior, segment customer bases, offer customized services, and gain insights from multiple data sources is crucial for achieving a sustainable competitive advantage (Assunção et al., 2015). Since digitalization has made the use of data crucial for companies (Lull et al., 2024), many firms are investing in Big Data to find innovative ways to differentiate themselves from their competitors (Ghasemaghaei & Calic, 2020). In the current marketplace, organizations need for more advanced data analyses, scenario planning, and predictive capabilities to face higher complexity and uncertainty in the external environment (Visani, 2017). Big Data and advanced analytics tools can be particularly helpful in dealing with such new challenges. Whether the emergence of Big Data has impacted on how managers collect, process, and use data to achieve business goals (Warren et al., 2015), advanced analytics tools such as data analytics, data mining, machine learning, and artificial intelligence provide companies with the ability to investigate, discover, and create questions. Specifically, the use of Big Data analysis and the development of artificial intelligence techniques stimulate more questions, more complex questions and, most importantly, have the power to answer these questions (Cokins, 2016, pp. 4–5).

Both academics and professionals unanimously recognize that a proficient use of digital technology can lead to reducing costs and improving efficiency and innovation (Zhang & Li, 2024). Big Data has the potential to positively impact on the effectiveness of business strategy and on organizational performance in almost every industry and business function (de Camargo Fiorini et al., 2018; Lull et al., 2024) by facilitating process standardization, streamlining operational activities, and improving customer interactions (Betti et al., 2024).

To effectively respond to the changes occurred in the marketplace and gain competitive edge, companies are increasingly required to carefully monitor product and service quality, time-to-market, as well as flexibility in the production processes, which have become critical corporates' value drivers. This means that the scope of task-level decisions and control activities has enlarged to encompass all the processes that compose the company's value chain (D'Onza, 2008).

The rapid advancement of emerging technologies, such as cloud computing, the IoT, Big Data, and artificial intelligence (AI), is transforming the paradigm of advanced manufacturing toward the so-called cognitive manufacturing, which bases on robust data collection and utilizes this data to extract actionable insights (El Kalach et al., 2024; Wang et al., 2021). Specifically, cognitive manufacturing "not only integrates the physical and digital worlds but also allows for flexible, reconfigurable, and adaptive production" (El Kalach et al., 2024).

Moreover, the increasing deployment of IoT, Big Data, and other AI-based technologies allows companies to use real-time data throughout the entire product lifecycle, from "the inception of an intangible concept,through the recycling of a finished product" (Wang et al., 2021). As a way of example, by conducting advanced market analysis via data mining, firms are able to gain valuable insights on how to develop the product's conceptual design, then they can collect data from sensors to track parts, monitor machinery, and optimize operations. The use of IoT and AI algorithms enables companies to exploit real time, highly granular data to enhance procurement, supply, and production processes. This kind of data, in fact, allows ubiquitous process control and optimization to reduce waste and maximize yield or throughput (Manyika et al., 2011; Wang et al., 2021).

To enhance overall customer satisfaction, Big Data derived from customer interactions can inform product development decisions. As technology advances, embedding sensors in products to generate data on utilization, usage patterns, and performance is increasingly feasible. The availability of such real-time granular data provides manufacturing companies with unprecedented opportunities to identify emerging product defects, enabling immediate adjustments to the production process and informed product development planning. Additionally, leveraging large datasets in marketing, sales, and after-sales service activities presents numerous opportunities. Companies can develop monetization models based on post-sales services priced according to usage, rather than solely on product purchases (Manyika et al., 2011; Wang et al., 2021).

Scholars also underlined that Big Data and AI can significantly impact on supporting managerial control activities, since managers are now able to combine traditional accounting data with new data sources (e.g., GPRS, RFID, sensors, and the like) to improve planning and decision-making processes, by focusing more on assessing the emerging trends within the competitive environment, than on purely historical data

(Appelbaum et al., 2017; Bhimani & Willcocks, 2014; Cokins, 2016; Krahel et al., 2012). Advancements in statistical forecasting algorithms, combined with the opportunity to access vast amounts of data from multiple sources, also improve managers' ability and accuracy in making predictions about customers' demand and resource use, thus enhancing the budgeting process (Manyika et al., 2011; Warren et al., 2015).

The exploitation of the new corporate data ecosystem offers the opportunity to capture transactions before they can be officially recorded in the company's accounting system. For example, inventory movements can be recorded way earlier than their actual receipt or delivery by using IoT technology, to enhance procurement and supply processes, as well as to accurately monitor time-to-market. Further, the use of Big Data and AI is also impacting the nature and structure of internal reporting, that is becoming increasingly frequent, detailed, and digital, thus allowing managers to promptly access huge dataset by means of smart visualization tools and dashboards (Chowdhury, 2023; Krahel & Vasarhelyi, 2014).

With a focus on the opportunities that Big Data and AI open up in the Management Control Systems' domain, researchers also refer to the possibility to discover and measure behaviors that are connected with the company's goal outcomes, that fosters the creation of tailored and inductively determined performance measures (e.g., measure the time employees spend at the phone in order to track their productivity). Organizations can integrate traditional financial data with different types of data collected from their wider ecosystem to infer new and more representative measures of firm's and individual performance (De Santis, 2018). Companies, in fact, can exploit the wide variety of data sources (e.g., mobile devices, IoT, social networks, etc.) to monitor how employees behave and use the firm's resources to identify correlating data points and develop a performance-explaining model (Sundström, 2024). As a consequence, the focus of management accountants will shift from keeping records to analyzing patterns in data in order to gather useful insights for decision-making, budget development, and performance monitoring.

Finally, current hypercompetition is forcing companies to create new ways for differentiate themselves from their competitors (Ghasemaghaei & Calic, 2020). Business models are becoming increasingly replicable by potential competitors, but the knowledge base created by means of a proper understanding and exploitation of Big Data and AI technologies can be a valuable resource that is not easily imitated or substituted by competitors, thus representing a way to create entry barriers in the marketplace (Cappa et al., 2021; De Santis, 2018; Rikhardsson & Yigitbasioglu, 2018).

Nowadays, strategic decisions increasingly stem from the analysis and interpretation of vast amounts of unstructured data exhaust and community data that comes from a variety of channels, such as social media, smartphones, online searches, and so on (George et al., 2014). Data used for decision-making purposes is challenging traditional paradigms in a variety of ways, because of the deep changes occurred both in data sources and in the modes of data collection. Relevant data to strategic intelligence is now far more granular, defined, and highly specific, as well as more aggregate, raw, and amorphous (Bhimani, 2015). Therefore, the emergence of the new corporate data ecosystem has blurred the boundaries between operational, managerial, and strategic decisions-making and control processes (Anthony, 1965, 1988). Following this path, the assumption according to which someone in the organization is appointed to make decisions, while someone else is engaged in action is becoming less and less representative for companies involved in the Big Data environment (Bhimani & Willcocks, 2014, p. 480).

1.4 Big Data and Artificial Intelligence: What Are the Challenges for Contemporary Organizations

Despite the wide range of opportunities the use of Big Data with AI offers to businesses operating in almost every industry, the realization of such benefits should not be merely assumed (Ghasemaghaei & Calic, 2020). As with any disruptive innovation, Big Data presents multiple challenges to adopting firms (Lee, 2017). Understanding and addressing these challenges is crucial for companies seeking to leverage these technologies to improve performance and gain a competitive edge.

The Nature and Complexity of Big Data

Organizations must recognize that Big Data is not merely an increase in the volume of data, but rather it encompasses different types of data and necessitates diverse analytical techniques (Kaisler et al., 2013). This distinction implies that management accountants and decision-makers need to expand their skillsets to include advanced statistical capabilities and a deep understanding of business processes (Krahel & Vasarhelyi, 2014). While the speed, accuracy, breadth, and affordability undeniably benefit from advanced data collection and analysis, it is also extremely important that accountants develop specific capabilities to define rules for exception reporting and data aggregation to maintain these benefits.

The Black-Boxing Effect and Data Quality Issues

The use of advanced software for data capture can lead to a "black-boxing" effect in business decision and control processes, where data is processed and presented without thorough scrutiny of its quality. This means that data is used as mere inputs of decision-making process, and the exercise of human judgment now begins at the point where data has been already packaged and made available for consumption. In other words, data is now "given" to decision-makers, who are formally and substantially excluded from their manufacture. This situation can diminish the role of human judgment in the decision-making process, thus making it less wise (Quattrone, 2016).

In a Big Data environment, it is also easy to fall in the "the more is better" trap, due to the fact that data collection is way easier than information extraction (De Santis, 2018; Kaisler et al., 2013). As Big Data is mostly unstructured and collected from a wider array of sources, the quality of data tends to decline. Furthermore, the assumption that Big Data is inherently more valuable than smaller datasets is misleading. Automated data collection tools can exacerbate issues related to data inaccuracies, errors, and structural changes over time, thereby compromising data quality (Bhimani & Willcocks, 2014).

Data quality is critical in a Big Data environment, where ensuring the accuracy of each data item can be impractical due to the sheer volume of data, but managers also need timely information to assume effective business decisions (De Santis, 2018). Nevertheless, a robust data quality control process is essential to develop quality metrics, repair erroneous data, and balance the costs and benefits of quality assurance (Lee, 2017). The challenge here lies in managing the "quality vs. quantity" dilemma, where the focus should be on acquiring high-quality data rather than merely increasing data volume (Kaisler et al., 2013; Kitchin, 2014).

Privacy and Security Concerns

The extensive collection of personal data through Big Data technologies raises serious privacy and security concerns for individuals, firms, and governments. Protecting privacy is often at odds with enhancing service quality and reducing costs, necessitating a balance between data use and privacy protection. The appropriate balance varies depending on the service type, customer demographics, data type, and regulatory environment.

Weak security and privacy protection measures can lead to financial loss, damage to a firm's reputation, and user resistance to Big Data adoption. While protecting privacy is often counterproductive to both firms and customers, as Big Data is a key to enhanced service quality and cost reduction, effective mechanisms in these domains are essential to prevent the inadvertent transmission of confidential information to unintended parties (Randolph-Seng et al., 2024).

Interpretability and Bias in Artificial Intelligence

The second wave of the machine age introduces new risks, particularly regarding the interpretability of AI algorithms. These algorithms often exhibit low transparency, making it difficult for humans to understand how decisions are made. This lack of interpretability can embed hidden biases in the data used to train the systems, perpetuating discrimination based on race, gender, ethnicity, or other factors.

Additionally, AI systems, which rely on statistical rather than literal truths, may not guarantee consistent performance across all scenarios, particularly those not represented in the training data. This lack of verifiability is a significant concern in mission-critical applications. Moreover, diagnosing and correcting errors in AI systems can be challenging due to the complex underlying structures, such as those of artificial neural networks (Brynjolfsson & McAfee, 2017).

Organizational Barriers to Analytics

Market research indicates that inadequate staffing and skills, lack of business support, and issues with analytics software are substantial barriers to effective analytics implementation in corporations (Assunção et al., 2015). To overcome these challenges, organizations must invest in building analytical capabilities, securing executive support, and ensuring the availability of robust analytics tools. Specifically, the skills of both management accountant and decision-makers in the organization must expand both in scope and adaptability.

In conclusion, while Big Data and AI offer transformative potential for businesses, they also pose significant challenges. Addressing these challenges involves ensuring data quality, balancing privacy and security concerns, enhancing the interpretability of AI systems, and overcoming organizational barriers to analytics. By strategically managing these issues, companies can harness the power of Big Data and AI to drive innovation and improve performance.

1.5 Conclusions

The emergence and expansion of the corporate data ecosystem, driven by advancements in Big Data and AI, have revolutionized the way organizations operate, compete, and make decisions. This chapter has introduced the foundational concepts of Big Data and its significance in the contemporary business landscape. The explosive growth of data, coupled with advanced analytics and AI, presents unprecedented opportunities for organizations to derive value and gain competitive advantages. However, the potential of Big Data also comes with considerable challenges that need careful management.

The book's subsequent chapters delve deeper into these concepts and their practical applications. Chapter 2 explores the critical transition from data to informed corporate decision-making, emphasizing the processes and tools that facilitate this transformation. Chapter 3 provides a comprehensive introduction to artificial intelligence, laying the groundwork for understanding its various facets and capabilities. The necessity of trustworthy AI is discussed in Chapter 4, where the focus is on ensuring reliability, transparency, and ethical considerations in AI implementations.

In Chapter 5 , the application of AI in supporting business decisions is examined, highlighting how AI can enhance strategic, tactical, and operational decisions. Chapter 6 discusses the role of AI in risk management, providing insights into how predictive analytics and machine learning models can identify and mitigate risks. The integration of AI into financial accounting is covered in Chapter 7, showcasing its impact on financial reporting, fraud detection, and compliance.

Managerial accounting, with its focus on internal decision-making and performance evaluation, is the subject of Chapter 8. This chapter illustrates how AI tools can streamline processes, provide real-time insights, and improve efficiency. Chapter 9 addresses the use of AI in auditing, where AI techniques are employed to enhance audit accuracy, detect anomalies, and ensure compliance.

Finally, Chapter 10 presents a collection of case studies demonstrating the practical application of AI in various business contexts. These real-world examples provide valuable lessons on the successful implementation of AI technologies and their tangible benefits to organizations.

In conclusion, while the corporate data ecosystem offers immense potential for innovation and competitive advantage, organizations must navigate the associated challenges effectively. The insights provided in this book aim to equip businesses with the knowledge and strategies necessary to harness the power of Big Data and AI, ultimately driving better decisions, fostering innovation, and maintaining a competitive edge in the evolving digital landscape.

References

Acciarini, C., Cappa, F., Boccardelli, P., & Oriani, R. (2023). How can organizations leverage big data to innovate their business models? *A Systematic Literature Review. Technovation, 123*, 102713. https://doi.org/10.1016/j.technovation.2023.102713

Akter, S., Bandara, R., Hani, U., Fosso Wamba, S., Foropon, C., & Papadopoulos, T. (2019). Analytics-based decision-making for service systems: A qualitative study and agenda for future research. *International Journal of Information Management, 48*, 85–95. https://doi.org/10.1016/j.ijinfomgt.2019.01.020

Akter, S., Wamba, S. F., Gunasekaran, A., Dubey, R., & Childe, S. J. (2016). How to improve firm performance using big data analytics capability and business strategy alignment? *International Journal of Production Economics, 182*, 113–131. https://doi.org/10.1016/j.ijpe.2016.08.018

Anthony, R. N. (1965). *Planning and Control Systems: A framework for analysis*. Harvard University Press.

Anthony, R. N. (1988). *The management control function*. Harvard Business School Press.

Appelbaum, D., Kogan, A., Vasarhelyi, M., & Yan, Z. (2017, April). Impact of business analytics and enterprise systems on managerial accounting. *International Journal of Accounting Information Systems, 25*, 29–44. https://doi.org/10.1016/j.accinf.2017.03.003

Assunção, M. D., Calheiros, R. N., Bianchi, S., Netto, M. A. S., & Buyya, R. (2015). Big data computing and clouds: Trends and future directions. *Journal of Parallel and Distributed Computing, 79–80*, 3–15. https://doi.org/10.1016/j.jpdc.2014.08.003

Baesens, B., Bapna, R., Marsden, J. R., Vanthienen, J., & Zhao, J. L. (2016). Transformational issues of big data and analytics in networked business. *MIS Quarterly, 40*(4), 807–818.

Bertini, U. (1990). *Il sistema d'azienda*. Giappichelli Editore.

Betti, N., DeSimone, S., Gray, J., & Poncin, I. (2024). The impacts of the use of data analytics and the performance of consulting activities on perceived internal audit quality. *Journal of Accounting & Organizational Change, 20*(2), 334–361. https://doi.org/10.1108/JAOC-08-2022-0125

Bhimani, A. (2015). Exploring big data's strategic consequences. *Journal of Information Technology, 30*(1), 66–69. https://doi.org/10.1057/jit.2014.29

Bhimani, A., & Willcocks, L. (2014). Digitisation, Big data and the transformation of accounting information. *Accounting and Business Research, 44*(4), 469–490. https://doi.org/10.1080/00014788.2014.910051

Boyd, D., & Crawford, K. (2012). Critical questions for big data: Provocations for a cultural, technological, and scholarly phenomenon. *Information Communication and Society, 15*(5), 662–679. https://doi.org/10.1080/1369118X.2012.678878

Brynjolfsson, E., & McAfee, A. (2017, July 18). The business of artificial intelligence. *Harvard Business Review*. https://hbr.org/2017/07/the-business-of-artificial-intelligence

Cappa, F., Oriani, R., Peruffo, E., & McCarthy, I. (2021). Big data for creating and capturing value in the digitalized environment: Unpacking the effects of volume, variety, and veracity on firm performance*. *Journal of Product Innovation Management, 38*(1), 49–67. https://doi.org/10.1111/jpim.12545

Cavanillas, J. M., Curry, E., & Wahlster, W. (2016). The Big Data Value Opportunity. In J. M. Cavanillas, E. Curry, & W. Wahlster (Eds.), *New horizons for a data-driven economy: A roadmap for usage and exploitation of big data in Europe* (pp. 3–11). Springer International Publishing. https://doi.org/10.1007/978-3-319-21569-3_1

Chen, H., Chiang, R. H. L., & Storey, V. C. (2012). Business intelligence and analytics: From big data to big impact. *MIS Quarterly, 36*(4), 1165–1188.

Chen, X.-W., & Xiaotong, L. (2014). Big data deep learning: Challenges and perspectives. *IEEE, 2*, 514–525.

Chowdhury, E. K. (2023). Integration of artificial intelligence technology in management accounting information system: an empirical study. In M. Z. Abedin & P. Hajek (Eds.), *Novel financial applications of machine learning and deep learning* (Vol. 336, pp. 35–46). Springer International Publishing. https://doi.org/10.1007/978-3-031-18552-6_3

Cokins, G. (2016). The top seven trends in management accounting. *Edpacs, 53*(4), 1–7. https://doi.org/10.1080/07366981.2016.1148957

de Camargo Fiorini, P., Seles, B. M. R. P., & Chiappetta Jabbour, C. J., Barberio Mariano, E., & de Sousa Jabbour, A. B. L. (2018). Management theory and big data literature: From a review to a research agenda. *International Journal of Information Management, 43*, 112–129. https://doi.org/10.1016/j.ijinfomgt.2018.07.005

De Santis, F. (2018). *Auditing and management control systems in the age of big data*. Franco Angeli.

D'Onza, G. (2008). *Il sistema di controllo interno nella prospettiva del risk management*. Giuffrè editore.

El Kalach, F., Yousif, I., Wuest, T., Sheth, A., & Harik, R. (2024). Cognitive manufacturing: Definition and current trends. *Journal of Intelligent Manufacturing*. https://doi.org/10.1007/s10845-024-02429-9

Erevelles, S., Fukawa, N., & Swayne, L. (2016). Big data consumer analytics and the transformation of marketing. *Journal of Business Research, 69*(2), 897–904. https://doi.org/10.1016/j.jbusres.2015.07.001

Fosso Wamba, S., Akter, S., Edwards, A., Chopin, G., & Gnanzou, D. (2015). How 'big data' can make big impact: Findings from a systematic review and a longitudinal case study. *International Journal of Production Economics, 165*, 234–246. https://doi.org/10.1016/j.ijpe.2014.12.031

Galbraith, J. K. (1968). The new industrial state. *Science and Society, 32*(2).

Gandomi, A., & Haider, M. (2015). Beyond the hype: Big data concepts, methods, and analytics. *International Journal of Information Management, 35*(2), 137–144. https://doi.org/10.1016/j.ijinfomgt.2014.10.007

George, G., Haas, M. R., & Pentland, A. (2014). Big data and management. *Academy of Management Journal, 57*(2), 321–326. https://doi.org/10.5465/amj.2014.4002

Ghasemaghaei, M., & Calic, G. (2020). Assessing the impact of big data on firm innovation performance: Big data is not always better data. *Journal of Business Research, 108*, 147–162. https://doi.org/10.1016/j.jbusres.2019.09.062

Günther, W. A., Mehrizi, M. H. R., Huysman, M., & Feldberg, F. (2017). Debating big data: A literature review on realizing value from big data. *Journal of Strategic Information Systems, 26*(3), 191–209. https://doi.org/10.1016/j.jsis.2017.07.003

Kaisler, S., Armour, F., Espinosa, J. A., & Money, W. (2013). Big data: Issues and challenges moving forward. *Proceedings of the Annual Hawaii International*

Conference on System Sciences, 995–1004. https://doi.org/10.1109/HICSS.2013.645

Kitchin, R. (2014). Big data, new epistemologies and paradigm shifts. *Big Data & Society, 1*(1), 205395171452848. https://doi.org/10.1177/2053951714528481

Krahel, J. P., Moffitt, K., & Vasarhelyi, M. A. (2012). The route to digital accounting. *Interactive Business Reporting, 2*(4), 16–19.

Krahel, J. P., & Vasarhelyi, M. A. (2014). AIS as a facilitator of accounting change: Technology, practice, and education. *Journal of Information Systems, 28*(2), 1–15. https://doi.org/10.2308/isys-10412

Laney, D. (2001). 3D data management: Controlling data volume, velocity and variety. *META Group Research Note, 6*(70), 1.

Lee, I. (2017). Big data: Dimensions, evolution, impacts, and challenges. *Business Horizons, 60*(3), 293–303. https://doi.org/10.1016/j.bushor.2017.01.004

Lull, J. J., Cervelló-Royo, R., & Galdón, J. L. (2024). Crossroads between big data and entrepreneurship: Current key trends. *International Entrepreneurship and Management Journal*. https://doi.org/10.1007/s11365-024-00986-2

Lycett, M. (2013). "Datafication": Making sense of (big) data in a complex world. *European Journal of Information Systems, 22*(4), 381–386. https://doi.org/10.1057/ejis.2013.10

Manyika, J., Chui, M., Brown, B., Bughin, J., Dobbs, R., Roxburgh, C., & Hung Byers, A. (2011). *Big data: The next frontier for innovation, competition, and productivity*. http://dln.jaipuria.ac.in:8080/jspui/bitstream/123456789/14265/1/mgi_big_data_full_report.pdf

Manyika, J., Chui, M., Miremadi, M., Bughin, J., George, K., Willmott, P., & Dewhurst, M. (2017). A future that works: AI, automation, employment, and productivity. *McKinsey Global Institute Research Technical Report, 60*, 1–135.

Marchi, L. (2003). *I sistemi informativi aziendali*. A. Giuffrè Editore.

Maroufkhani, P., Tseng, M.-L., Iranmanesh, M., Ismail, W. K. W., & Khalid, H. (2020). Big data analytics adoption: Determinants and performances among small to medium-sized enterprises. *International Journal of Information Management, 54*, 102190. https://doi.org/10.1016/j.ijinfomgt.2020.102190

Mayer-Schönberger, V., & Cukier, K. (2013). *Big data: A revolution that will transform how we live, work, and think*. Houghton Mifflin Harcourt Publishing Company. https://doi.org/10.1093/aje/kwu085

Mazzei, M. J., & Noble, D. (2017). Big data dreams: A framework for corporate strategy. *Business Horizons, 60*(3), 405–414. https://doi.org/10.1016/j.bushor.2017.01.010

McAfee, A., Brynjolfsson, E., & Dearstyne, B. W. (2012). Big data's management revolution. *Harvard Business Review, 90*(12), 16–17.

McGee, J. V., Prusak, L., & Pyburn, P. J. (1993). *Managing information strategically: Increase your company's competitiveness and efficiency by using information as a strategic tool* (Vol. 1). Wiley.

McGuire, S., & Ladd, B. (2014). Big data and human capital management. *Workforce Solutions Review, 5*(2), 30–31.

Mikalef, P., Pappas, I. O., Krogstie, J., & Pavlou, P. A. (2020). Big data and business analytics: A research agenda for realizing business value. *Information & Management, 57*(1), 103237. https://doi.org/10.1016/j.im.2019.103237

Moffitt, K. C., & Vasarhelyi, M. A. (2013). AIS in an age of big data. *Journal of Information Systems, 27*(2), 1–19. https://doi.org/10.2308/isys-10372

Ohlhorst, F. J. (2012). *Big data analytics: Turning big data into big money.* Wiley

Quattrone, P. (2016). Management accounting goes digital: Will the move make it wiser? *Management Accounting Research, 31*, 118–122. https://doi.org/10.1016/j.mar.2016.01.003

Randolph-Seng, B., Atinc, Y., Bui, S., & Malik, Z. (2024). Big data and the disillusioned employee: Inside the ethical internet of things. *Technological Forecasting and Social Change, 201*, 123271. https://doi.org/10.1016/j.techfore.2024.123271

Rikhardsson, P., & Yigitbasioglu, O. (2018). Business intelligence & analytics in management accounting research: Status and future focus. *International Journal of Accounting Information Systems, 29*(April), 37–58. https://doi.org/10.1016/j.accinf.2018.03.001

Russom, P. (2011). *Big data analytics* (TDWI Best Practices Report, Fourth Quarter, 6).

Sagiroglu, S., & Sinanc, D. (2013). Big data: A review. *International Conference on Collaboration Technologies and Systems (CTS), 2013*, 42–47. https://doi.org/10.1109/CTS.2013.6567202

Sivarajah, U., Kamal, M. M., Irani, Z., & Weerakkody, V. (2017). Critical analysis of big data challenges and analytical methods. *Journal of Business Research, 70*, 263–286. https://doi.org/10.1016/j.jbusres.2016.08.001

Sundström, A. (2024). AI in management control: Emergent forms, practices, and infrastructures. *Critical Perspectives on Accounting, 99*, 102701. https://doi.org/10.1016/j.cpa.2023.102701

van der Aalst, W. (2014). *Data scientist: The engineer of the future.*

Vasarhelyi, M. A., Kogan, A., & Tuttle, B. M. (2015). Big data in accounting: An overview. *Accounting Horizons, 29*(2), 381–396. https://doi.org/10.2308/acch-51071

Vecchio, P. D., Mele, G., Ndou, V., & Secundo, G. (2018). Creating value from Social Big Data: Implications for smart tourism destinations. *Information Processing & Management, 54*(5), 847–860. https://doi.org/10.1016/j.ipm.2017.10.006

Visani, F. (2017). Applying business analytics for performance measurement and management. The case study of a software company. *Management Control, 2*, 89–123. https://doi.org/10.3280/maco2017-002006

Wang, L., Liu, Z., Liu, A., & Tao, F. (2021). Artificial intelligence in product lifecycle management. *The International Journal of Advanced Manufacturing Technology, 114*(3–4), 771–796. https://doi.org/10.1007/s00170-021-06882-1

Warren, J. D., Moffitt, K. C., & Byrnes, P. (2015). How big data will change accounting. *Accounting Horizons, 29*(2), 397–407. https://doi.org/10.2308/acch-51069

Yoo, Y. (2015). It is not about Size: A Further thought on Big Data. *Journal of Information Technology, 30*(1), 63–65. https://doi.org/10.1057/jit.2014.30

Zaitsava, M., Marku, E., Di Guardo, M. C., & Shahgholian, A. (2023). A fine-grained perspective on big data knowledge creation: Dimensions, insights, and mechanism from a pilot study. *Journal of Management and Governance, 27*(2), 547–573. https://doi.org/10.1007/s10997-022-09659-0

Zhang, C., & Li, W. (2024). *Big data quantification for complex decision-making* (p. 328). Scopus. https://doi.org/10.4018/979-8-3693-1582-8

Zillner, S., Gomez, J. A., García Robles, A., Hahn, T., Le Bars, L., Petkovic, M., & Curry, E. (2021). Data economy 2.0: From big data value to AI value and a European data space. In E. Curry, A. Metzger, S. Zillner, J. C. Pazzaglia, & G. Robles (Eds.), *The elements of Big Data value: Foundations of the research and innovation ecosystem* (pp. 379–399). Springer International Publishing. https://doi.org/10.1007/978-3-030-68176-0_16

CHAPTER 2

From Data to Corporate Decision-Making Process

Mariarita Pierotti

2.1 From Data to Knowledge

It is widely recognized that all resources are essential in an organization, but the importance of information resources has been undervalued. In the Fordist era, for example, producing the required amount of products was possible, and the only factor that determined competitive advantage was price, regardless of human and organizational capital. However, with the economy becoming increasingly globalized, dynamic, complex, and fast-paced, and with the advent of information technology and communication, price alone is no longer enough to compete in the market. Therefore, the centrality of information resources has grown in managerial activity, leading to the emergence of the "information society."

From the 1950s, Herbert A. Simon introduced a new perspective on decision-making that differed from the traditional concept of the "economic man" as being rational and having access to all the necessary information. Simon's model, known as the "administrative man," recognizes that individuals within an organization do not have complete knowledge of all the available alternatives, nor do they know the potential outcomes of each alternative (Simon, 1957).

Despite this, managers spend significant time gathering as much information as possible to analyze the economic, technological, political,

M. Pierotti et al., *Artificial Intelligence in Accounting and Auditing*,
https://doi.org/10.1007/978-3-031-71371-2_2

and social environments to make informed decisions. These decisions should align with the company's goals and be as rational as possible. Therefore, information flows and their purposes are crucial for successful decision-making.

Organizational actors are still adjusting to dealing with information-related topics. Information plays a crucial role in corporate organizations, and the systems responsible for generating this information are called Corporate Information Systems. The relevance of these systems lies in the fact that decision-making, when combined with the intuition of the decision-maker, becomes more rational when relevant information is available. Information is fundamental to companies, businesses, and organizations, as it forms the basis of knowledge and experience. There is no single meaning of information, and different disciplines approach the concept differently. However, comparing concepts such as data, information, knowledge, and wisdom has successfully reduced ambiguity in the professional academic literature. A conceptual scheme can be used to understand the relationship between these concepts and make strategic decisions.

The DIKW hierarchy is a central model for information management, information systems, and knowledge management. However, while there has been significant debate over the years about related issues, such as the nature and definition of information, little direct discussion has been had about the DIKW hierarchy and its meaning. Additionally, there has been limited discussion of the nature of wisdom and even less discussion of the organizational processes that contribute to its cultivation.

As information is fundamental to our existence, it has been considered by many disciplines, such as communications theory, library and information science, information systems, cognitive science, and organization science. This has generated multiple perspectives on the nature of information.

Floridi suggests that information is currently one of the most important, most used, and least understood mundane and technical concepts. In this scholar's approach, there are six different ways to define information: the communication theory approach, the probabilistic approach, the modal approach, the systemic approach, the inferential approach, and the semantic approach.

In recent years, there has been a renewed interest in this field due to the development of the philosophy of information as a new discipline. Information philosophy aims to critically examine information's fundamental principles and conceptual nature, including its dynamic attributes such as computation and information flow. However, there is still a lack of agreement on the definition of the term "information" among scholars, with various writers attributing different meanings to the word.

Debates about the nature of knowledge are equally long-standing and have gained momentum in recent years with the development of the knowledge management discipline. Knowledge management, like the philosophy of information, has been influenced by various disciplines, including philosophy, cognitive science, social science, management science, information science, knowledge engineering, artificial intelligence, and economics.

Kakabadse et al. (2001) propose five different perspectives of knowledge management, each of which takes a different position on the nature of knowledge and knowledge processes. These perspectives include philosophy-based, cognitive, network, community, and quantum.

In summary, the literature on the philosophy of information and knowledge management is extensive and provides numerous viewpoints on defining information and knowledge. Some contributions also delve into the nature of data and wisdom. However, most of the discussion centers on only one element of the DIKW hierarchy instead of examining all of the elements and their interrelationships (Fig. 2.1).

Several scholars have expanded on the DIKW hierarchy, with Ackoff (1989) being one of the most notable contributors. He introduced understanding as a distinct element and a transitional level between knowledge and wisdom in his elaboration.

Ackoff's article is not the only early mention of the hierarchy. Cleveland (1987) mentions the hierarchy early, which can be found in the information science literature. Around the same time as Ackoff, Zeleny

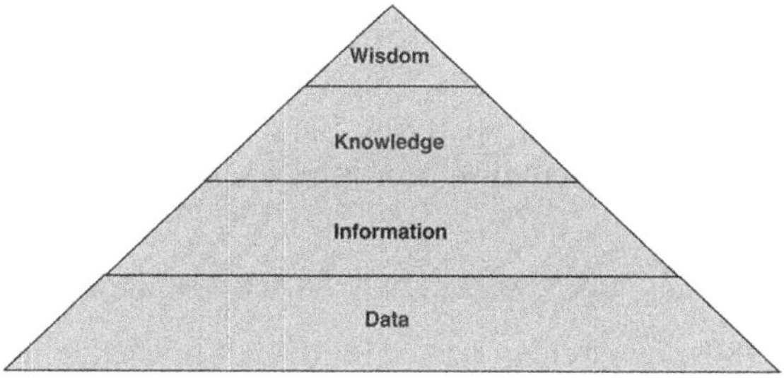

Fig. 2.1 The DIKW hierarchy Rowley (Rowley, 2007)

(1987) also discusses the DIKW hierarchy and proposes an additional level, enlightenment, at the top. Enlightenment is not only answering or understanding why (which he defines as wisdom) but going further and attaining the sense of truth, the sense of right and wrong, and having it socially accepted, respected, and sanctioned. Also, Cooley (1987) builds the DIKW hierarchy during his discussion of tacit knowledge and common sense.

According to Ackoff, data, information, knowledge, and wisdom have distinct definitions and transformation processes.

Data are symbols that represent properties of objects, events, and their environment. They are the products of observation, but they are of no use until they are in a usable (i.e., relevant) form. The difference between data and information is functional, not structural.

Information is contained in descriptions and answers to questions that begin with words such as who, what, when, and how many. Information systems generate, store, retrieve, and process data. Information is inferred from data.

Knowledge is know-how and is what makes possible the transformation of information into instructions. Knowledge can be obtained either by transmission from another who has it, by instruction, or by extracting it from experience.

Intelligence is the ability to increase efficiency.

Wisdom is the ability to increase effectiveness. It adds value, which requires the mental function that we call judgment. The ethical and aesthetic values that this implies are inherent to the actor and are unique and personal.

More recently, Bellinger et al. (2004) have elaborated further on Ackoff's exposition, suggesting that understanding is not a separate level but rather that understanding supports the transition from one stage to the next. They suggest that moving from data to information involves "understanding relations," moving from information to knowledge involves "understanding patterns," and moving from knowledge to wisdom involves "understanding principles."

2.2 Knowledge Management

In the late 1980s, researchers started studying knowledge more comprehensively. However, it was in the mid-1990s that the "knowledge boom" happened, leading to numerous theoretical contributions focused on various aspects of the subject (Quagli, 2001). This resulted in a wide range of research papers covering different academic and operational orientations. It was a challenge to define knowledge and understand how it's created and disseminated (Gabrielli, 2006; Profili, 2004; Quagli, 2001). A new theory, the knowledge perspective or knowledge-based view of the firm, emerged, interpreting the dynamics and existence of a firm concerning the management of knowledge resources. This theory offers a unified approach to interpreting the diverse and specific aspects of corporate knowledge studies (Quagli, 2001).

The Resource-Based View (RBT) theory explains that a company's competitive advantage is sustainable by controlling scarce resources and optimally utilizing them. By combining resources, a company can focus on its organizational competencies, which become the most significant levers for gaining competitive advantage. This leads to strategic behavioral conduct known as leveraging (Chiucchi, 2004; Profili, 2004).

In an unpredictable business environment, it's essential to consider the available resources when defining the strategic identity of a company. Intangible resources are crucial, as they're based on knowledge and trust accumulated over time. These resources are difficult to replicate or transfer and offer a competitive advantage that can be maintained over time. Accumulating resources in a company takes time, but it helps develop implicit knowledge and skills related to specific production processes.

Competence-based theory emerged alongside the resource-based view in the early 1990s. This theory suggests that resources, whether tangible or intangible, aren't enough to create a competitive advantage on their own. Instead, it's crucial to focus on developing and managing key competencies deliberately. Core competencies play a significant role in achieving a competitive advantage (Stalk et al., 1992).

Capabilities are the results achieved by the joint action of multiple resources that interact through organizational processes. Companies need to develop distinctive capabilities to adapt to dynamic external environments. Having an endowment of resources, skills, and capabilities is identified as a fundamental requirement for achieving a competitive position (Nonaka & Takeuchi, 1998; Stalk et al., 1992).

Teece, Pisano, and Shuen have introduced the concept of dynamic capabilities which refers to an enterprise's ability to restructure and renew its core competencies. They emphasize that an enterprise's growth is dependent not only on the quality and quantity of its existing resources but also on the evolutionary potential of its initial assets which are provided by dynamic capabilities. According to Vicari (2008) and Nonaka and Takeuchi (1998), companies can gain and maintain their competitive advantage through the constant development of their resources when the environment is unstable and unpredictable. Teece et al.'s theory states that firms with dynamic capabilities are proactive, as they continuously change the basis of their competitive advantage by anticipating the direction of change (Teece, 1998).

There has been a growing interest in the concept of knowledge and an awareness of the limitations of existing theories on this subject. This has led to various research works converging toward the Knowledge-Based View (KBV), which represents the coming together of numerous perspectives. The KBV focuses on analyzing knowledge as a resource and the processes involved in generating, developing, transferring, and utilizing it to create value (Profili, 2004).

Many authors believe that the current understanding of this topic is not yet a complete and consistent theory but rather a collection of various contributions that do not fit perfectly. Some of these authors include Kaplan et al. (2001).

Knowledge is a valuable resource that is difficult to replicate and transfer. It is also scarce and gives rise to complex problems regarding its appropriateness. In the Resource-Based View (RBV), the content of the resources accumulated within the company plays a fundamental role, while in the Knowledge-Based View (KBV), the processes that enable the company to accelerate the diffusion of resources, skills, and competencies within the company become decisive.

The Knowledge-Based Theory (KBT) redefines the concept of organizational learning and knowledge assets. It examines the organizational conditions for the creation and management of knowledge and attributes to the firm, the characteristic of distinguishing itself from the market for the learning processes that take place within it. KBT places greater emphasis on the activity of the individual in the creation and preservation of knowledge by assigning the organization the primary role of applying knowledge rather than creating it.

The Organization Knowledge Creation approach, developed by Nonaka and Takeuchi, places the problem of knowledge creation by the business organization as a whole at the center. The interest in knowledge accumulation processes underlying knowledge-based theory stems from several considerations. Firstly, the need to oversee and activate knowledge development is an essential reason behind the existence of companies. The organizational context creates the necessary conditions for developing a shared language, a climate of cooperation, and relationships of a social nature that allow the integration of individual knowledge and experience to create organizational competencies that increase the company's value. Moreover, organizational forms guarantee more excellent protection of management-relevant knowledge than the market, both by the existence of a common objective and the existence of rules and standards of behavior established by top management (Tardivo, 2008).

Numerous studies have been conducted to create theories on developing and disseminating knowledge. These theories are based on two fundamental concepts: the differentiation between tacit and explicit knowledge and the assumption that individual knowledge is the foundation of organizational knowledge. Some of the notable studies include Demsetz (1997), Kogut and Zander (1993), Wiig (1997), Nonaka and Takeuchi (1998), Spender and Grant (1996), Foss (1996), Conner and Pralahad (1996), Dosi (2009), Teece (1998, 2000), Davenport and Prusak (1998), Foray (2000), Rullani (2004), and Mokyr (2006).

The knowledge-based view of an enterprise is built on the following pillars: Firstly, the accumulation and application of knowledge at a collective level is the primary source of value for an enterprise. In today's context, where competition is boundless, and innovation rates are high, knowledge has become a resource that businesses must invest in to achieve a sustainable and long-lasting competitive advantage.

Secondly, the creation of new knowledge and the dissemination of innovation takes place at different times and in different ways, not only in firms that belong to the same sector and use the same technology but also in different units of the same organization. Therefore, knowledge is not evenly spread within organizations, different enterprises, or economies.

Moreover, knowledge is created by individuals who need specialization to be efficient in the creation and accumulation of this resource. The acquisition of knowledge requires more specialization than that required for its utilization, as production requires the coordinated effort of individuals holding different knowledge. Consequently, managers should recognize and value the process through which knowledge is created and utilized within organizations.

Spender and Grant (1996) argue that the main problem in business theory is to investigate the role of organizations, rather than just individuals, in possessing and developing knowledge. They also suggest that learning, i.e., the acquisition of knowledge, is crucial as it is the group that learns, not just the individual. Therefore, it is essential for businesses to develop organizational learning capabilities.

The term "knowledge" has multiple connotations and countless definitions in the literature, making it a complex concept that is difficult to define. Knowledge bears numerous nuances and paradoxes, and scholars have proposed several definitions that we will present below.

Davenport and Prusak describe knowledge as a "fluid mix of framed experience, values, contextual information, and expert insight that provides a framework for evaluating and incorporating new experiences and information." Knowledge is generated and applied in the minds of knowers, and in organizations, it often becomes embedded not only in documents or repositories but also in organizational routines, processes, practices, and norms.

According to Alberto Quagli, knowledge is "a system of information learned and distributed in the company in different ways and correlated with each other by functional links. This allows operators to interpret various external and internal environmental situations in a way that is appropriate to the economic conditions of the productive combination and to orient their judgments of convenience accordingly."

It is difficult to define knowledge in a univocal and synthetic manner, as various authors have defined it in multiple ways. However, all definitions of knowledge share the commonality that it is a cognitive process. Knowledge is created by individuals and disseminated throughout the organization's knowledge network. It is the integration of information according to logical-functional connections that occur in our minds.

It is necessary to emphasize that data, information, and knowledge are not interchangeable concepts. Although knowledge is related to data and information, it does not coincide with either of them. Data is the essential raw material for creating information and can be a number, a characteristic associated with a specific phenomenon, or a measure of the state of a system. However, data alone cannot provide a judgment or interpretation.

Information is a message transmitted from a sender to a receiver. It refers to one or more datasets and is related to a specific problem context. Information, in a broader sense, provides answers to questions.

Knowledge represents something more profound than the concepts of data and information. It is a combination of information, the organization's intangible values, present skills, experience, and know-how that provide a frame of reference for evaluating and assimilating new experience and information. It, therefore, refers to people's cognitive and logical resources and is, by its very nature, at different times an input and an output of a combinatory process that is difficult to encode and memorize as it is the cause and effect of values, visions, ideas, perceptions, mental schemes of those who process them in order to make decisions and perform actions.

Knowledge is a valuable resource that is different from data and information. It is a combination of intangible values, present skills, experience, and know-how that provide a frame of reference for evaluating and assimilating new information. Knowledge is a complex asset that is unique and challenging to manage because it is embedded chiefly in people and is thus difficult to codify or measure (Bellandi, 2009).

Economic analysis indicates that managing knowledge is a complex task due to the unique nature of the asset being managed (Tronti, 2015). Knowledge is an intangible economic asset that is mainly embedded in people, making it difficult to quantify or measure. In the modern economy, it is more important to recognize and classify the quality and coherence of the process that knowledge is integrated into rather than simply measuring its quantity.

The relationship between data, information, and knowledge is not linear, meaning that processing and producing new information requires applying knowledge. This activity almost always involves human intervention and the use of individual knowledge, also known as tacit knowledge (Rullani, 2004). Knowledge is not a commodity and has properties that are incompatible with the classical notion of commodities.

Knowledge is heterogeneous and embedded in people's thoughts and actions. It becomes explicit when expressed or written down, or when a property right is associated with it. Tacit knowledge is continually reconstituted, and there is a vast, perpetually invisible world (Foray, 2000).

Knowledge is the only resource that does not deteriorate but grows and enhances through sharing. It can be used limitlessly without running out, and the more it is shared, the more abundant it becomes. This characteristic gives rise to decreasing marginal costs as the scale of production increases. Knowledge is not a scarce resource because its uses are not competing with each other, and economic agents are not rivals in its use (Rullani, 2004).

Knowledge is neither excludable nor divisible since it is not possible to deprive others of knowledge through copying, imitation, or learning. In this sense, it generates advantages for those who possess it and externalities for third parties who can obtain it at little or no cost. A company has much more difficulty controlling its knowledge than its machinery: The opportunities for leaks are countless. Knowledge can, therefore, spread uncontrollably.

In the past, much more than today, knowledge conferred a special status on those who possessed it, one of exclusivity concerning its possession. The diffusion of knowledge found obstacles in the personal attitude of those who were aware of this status, as well as in the costs of the uncertainty associated with its transmission: those who possessed knowledge could only be willing to share it under special conditions, not necessarily monetary. Today, knowledge is increasingly a non-excludable good, as the spread of information and communication technologies makes it much easier for consumers to use it, even if they cannot ensure its exact understanding and often cannot even indicate its actual quality (Foray, 2000; Rullani, 2004; Tronti, 2015).

Knowledge, therefore, has a cumulative and progressive character as it can give rise to new ideas and open new research avenues. At the same time, by its "tacitness," knowledge is dispersed and fragmented (Foray, 2000).

Knowledge is not instrumental, as cognitive processes also act on the ends and identities of the subjects involved, but reflexive, as it propagates itself by modifying its premises; thus, it is a joint product, i.e., a product that requires the connected contribution of all participants, no one excluded, and, in this sense, knowledge creation is increasingly a collective process (Rullani, 2004). Rullani points out how knowledge is locally bounded and not very persistent. New knowledge is usually of little value to the community because it is not absolute and must always be defined in a specific context. The process leading to the generalization of knowledge is complex and challenging. Moreover, knowledge is not very persistent because it undergoes deterioration and eventually obsolescence when it is no longer useful (Foray, 2000; Rullani, 2004).

The concept of knowledge remains evasive and elusive, so it is also worth reflecting on the critical components of this resource. According to Davenport and Prusak, the foundational elements of knowledge are the following (Davenport & Prusak, 1998):

- Experience: Knowledge develops over time, through experience. The word experience comes from the Latin ex-prior, "to put to the test," and is defined as knowledge that is gained through use or practice. Experience allows us to gain a historical perspective with which to interpret new events or realities;
- Ground truth: Ground truth is a term borrowed from military vocabulary, which is used to describe the truth of reality, as opposed to the reality postulated by general theories. It is "ground truth," which means knowing what works and distinguishing it from what does not work;
- Complexity: The importance of experience and "ground truth" are essential indicators of knowledge's ability to deal with complexity. Knowing "more" can seem misleading because it confronts us with the complexity of the decision, and clarity and simplicity are often preferred at the expense of comprehensive knowledge. The need for clear information often leads to being both sure and wrong simultaneously.
- Judgment: While data and information do not have an evaluative component, knowledge provides a framework for evaluating and assimilating new experience and new information in the light of what is already known and can, therefore, improve itself. Knowledge is a system and, as such, grows, changes, and also interacts with the external environment.
- Rules of thumb and intuition: Knowledge works by following general rules, i.e., flexible guidelines that have developed through trial, experience, error, and observation;
- Values and beliefs: People's values and beliefs have a powerful impact on organizational knowledge. Indeed, it is people who make organizations, and these people act according to their values and beliefs. Therefore, values and beliefs are integral to knowledge and largely determine what the knowledge holder sees, absorbs, and concludes from his or her observations. People with different values see different things and organize their knowledge according to their values.

As explained above, knowledge management is undoubtedly an interdisciplinary field of research (Hansen et al., 1999; Kuhn & Abecker, 1997; Van Heijst et al., 1997); for this reason, different approaches exist in the literature. To limit the scope and to facilitate the discussion, only the economic-managerial literature will be considered. Specifically, when analyzing the research in this subject area, there are two main views called: knowledge as a product (o content-centered) and knowledge as a process (process-centered) (Mentzas et al., 2003).

In the knowledge as a product approach, knowledge is treated as a product, which can be managed and manipulated independently of the object itself. The primary assumption is that all business information can be captured, distributed, managed, and manipulated. According to this view, the only information to be processed by the KM system will be structured knowledge and information that can be easily converted into objective values. The information object, in this case, will be disconnected from the context and the person who created and used it.

In contrast, following the second line of research (knowledge as a process), the emphasis is on how knowledge creation is proposed, encouraged, and guided. This negates the idea of being able to capture, manage, and distribute it within the organization. The tendency is to associate KM with a valuable system for increasing collaboration and coordination. In contrast to knowledge as a product, in the latter case, information cannot be disconnected from the (producer) person and the environment. To stimulate the process of knowledge distribution, a whole series of processes must be developed to favor human interactions since the exchange is person-to-person. In the first approach, ICT tools are used to foster information storage/reuse, while in the second, they are used to foster information sharing. Figure 2.2 briefly summarizes the main features of the two approaches (Mentzas et al., 2003).

In the course of the discussion, the first of the presented approaches (-KM as a product) will be used, focusing mainly on organizational knowledge and the methodology of Business Process Management (BPM) and Business Process Reengineering (BPR).

Starting from an assumption of Nonaka (Nonaka, 1991), the knowledge management process can be decomposed into seven different phases

- mapping and identification of the information present in the company;
- definition of the domain of knowledge, the domain is the type of information that is actually to be managed;
- valorization of present information and support of valuable actions for the development of new knowledge;
- saving present and future knowledge;

	Product-centric approach	Process-centric approach
Focus	Knowledge is represented as objects. The emphasis is on capturing, organizing and sharing knowledge objects. Utilization of products and systems that contain codified knowledge	Knowledge is associated with the individual that owns it. Knowledge sharing is accomplished through human contacts and relations
Strategy	Exploitation of organized, codified and easily reusable knowledge. Linking of people with systems that capture and disseminate knowledge	Exploitation and empowerment of individual and team knowledge. Development of networks for linking people, promotion and facilitation of discussions so that tacit knowledge can be shared
Human resources	Employment of professionals who are well suited to the reuse of knowledge. Training is facilitated passively (through courses, presentations and computer-based courses). Rewarding focuses on using and contributing to the organization's knowledge base	Employment of highly creative professionals who work in teams. Training is facilitated through on-the-job learning, group brainstorming sessions and one-to-one mentoring. Rewarding focuses on group performance and knowledge sharing between professionals
Information technology	Heavy investment in IT. Tools include document repositories, search and retrieval tools	Moderate investment in IT. Tools include discussions databases, real-time communication and collaboration tools, net conferencing and push technologies

Fig. 2.2 The approaches: —KM as a product|| e —KM as a process (Mentzas et al., 2003)

- utilization of present knowledge within the organizational memory;
- maintenance of the information memory, meaning the updating, modification or deletion of the values present within the business administration;
- preparation/transformation and dissemination of acquired knowledge.

Nonaka's model just outlined was then reworked by various authors (Dieng, 2000; Dieng et al., 1999; Kuhn & Abecker, 1997), who combined the research present within the discipline of computer science with organizational and managerial research.

The literature includes several reworkings of Nonaka's original model; however, the one depicted in Fig. 2.3 best summarizes all the research on KM (Dieng et al., 1999).

The knowledge distribution establishes how information is disseminated within the organization. To do this, one can choose to use the passive form of knowledge dissemination or the active form (Van Heijst

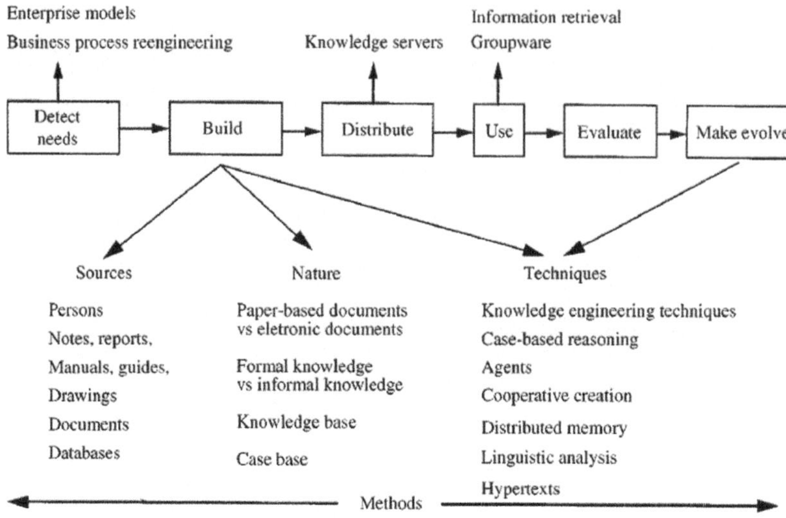

Fig. 2.3 Reworkings of Nonaka's original model (Dieng et al., 1999)

et al., 1997). This discrimination strictly depends on how the information in the organizational memory is accessed. If the information sent by the KM system to the users occurs independently of their needs, we are dealing with an active distribution. In contrast, if, on the other hand, the system sends knowledge to the user only after receiving a request from the user, then the distribution is termed passive.

Resource utilization, which coincides with the fifth phase of the model, is closely related to distribution and the detect needs' phase. Each user may have different access to information in quantity, the number of documents that can be analyzed, and quality, which can be indicated as the amount of information visible for each document. An organizational actor may have access to all or part of the content in a document. This limitation in the quality or quantity of manageable information depends directly on the role assumed by the user within the organization. Some data may be accessible by some people and not by others, but not only that, the type of access may also be different. In some cases, the user can read the information passively (which he/she has the right to access) and supplement, modify, or delete it. This will define both the rules of access and the mode of utilization of corporate values.

Taking up the analyses conducted by Kuhn and Abecker (Kuhn & Abecker, 1997), subsequently reworked by Macintosh (Macintosh et al., 1999), knowledge management is not only used to manipulate knowledge assets but also to manage processes that act directly and indirectly on organizational memory. These may include, for instance, developing, sharing, communicating, and securing knowledge (Macintosh et al., 1999 (refer to Fig. 2.4).

Thus, knowledge management manages all corporate knowledge and processes helpful in creating a competitive advantage. Therefore, KM should be considered the essential macro-process to support all the characteristic activities of enterprises (Gnoato & Roveda, 2008). In managerial practice, there is often a tendency to consider KM as a computer application (usually software) for document management. This is a very restrictive and inaccurate view since ICT tools are the tool rather than the methodology.

As pointed out earlier, human resources are the input variables for the KM system and represent the main component for creating new knowledge. The task assigned to knowledge management will be to foster the development of a working environment to develop knowledge creation and sharing. Specifically, the roles and competencies of individual workers will be established, identifying the key person for each business process (process owner). In addition, it will also be necessary to limit, if not eliminate, the communication barriers within the organization and try to retain

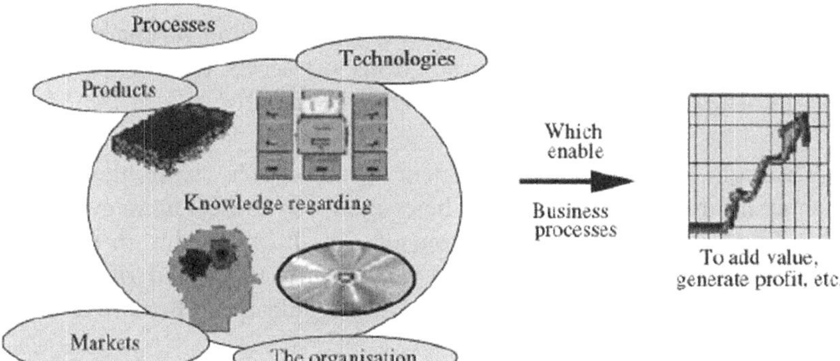

Fig. 2.4 The impacts of KM on the corporate structure (Macintosh et al., 1999)

the individual worker since the loss of a human resource negatively affects the quality and quantity of information in the organizational memory.

Although companies are structured according to a functional type of logic (e.g., R&D, logistics, administration, sales, etc.), in management reality, they function by processes (Mintzberg, 1979). Following the definition proposed by Hammer and Champy (Champy, 2009), the process is a set of activities that, through inputs of different natures, produces an output, which is the value for the customer. The process is not a mere succession of activities but a flexible sequence of actions directed and guided by the purpose to be pursued (Beretta, 2002). Within the management of business processes, the KM system ensures a better circulation of information, thus favoring the strengthening of relationships in the - Ba||. Through the re-engineering of business processes, it will be possible to connect knowledge producers with users, thus reducing management costs and information retrieval times. Lastly, technology can be used to support all the aspects described above, thus enabling:

- more incredible speed in sharing information;
- a high standard of security in information management (e.g., encryption, user restriction, information access modes, etc.);
- to digitally encode all corporate information, 'normalising' it and making it immediately available to all systems;
- the representation of information in different formats (reports, graphs, tables, etc.), in order to be more understandable to end users;
- maximum customization of data, since depending on the role, task, etc., each user will have restrictions on access to and use of the information (read-only, write-only, or read/write).

Through knowledge management technologies, it is possible to manage information from various heterogeneous sources at an ever-lower cost. The processing and translation of overall knowledge in time and space make it possible to improve the quality and speed of decision-making processes inside and outside the organization (Bordin & Selva, 2002).

Summarizing all the research analyzed so far, a second definition of Knowledge Management Systems (abbreviated as KMS) can be arrived at, according to which it can be understood as a system composed of people, technologies, and knowledge (-organizational memory||) that interact in order to create new knowledge, subsequently making it available to users within the organization (Gallupe, 2001).

Feedback and control processes, in general, are those that ensure the optimal functioning of the KM system (Gallupe, 2001).

The ability to exploit all available information is a critical component for the success of modern enterprises. As the volume of information increases, internal and external to the company, this challenge becomes more difficult. This problem is further exacerbated by the fact that many companies are becoming increasingly "knowledge-centered." Therefore, a more significant number of employees need access to a greater variety of information to be effective.

2.3 The Problem-Solving Perspective

The decision-making process involves a series of steps: intelligence, design, choice, and implementation. During the intelligence phase, people observe their surroundings for any indications of the need for new actions. This means that problem recognition must come before problem-solving or decision-making, as others have also suggested.

Mintzberg and Waters (1990) suggest a multistage decision-making process that begins with an identification phase, similar to Simon's intelligence phase. However, they break it down further into two routines: decision recognition and diagnosis. Decision recognition occurs when certain stimuli reach a minimum threshold of importance to a decision-maker, leading them to believe that action is necessary. Before receiving such stimuli, individuals are not aware of the need for any specific action.

Berthon et al. (2001) describe the first stage of decision-making as problem perception and suggest that it involves the processes of scanning, noticing, and constructing meaning about environmental changes. Kiesler and Sproull also frame the process similarly, distinguishing between noticing, interpreting, and incorporating stimuli.

Several authors agree with the idea that there should be a distinction between problem recognition and problem-solving. For example, Schneider and Shiffrin make this distinction in their discussion of information-processing modes. Problem-solving involves a conscious and effortful control of attention as an individual seeks to understand a problem or opportunity.

On the other hand, problem recognition involves an automatic or default processing mode wherein decision-makers spread their attention across various inputs, making it challenging to distinguish an issue from its environmental background. The literature on environmental scanning has also made a similar distinction.

The process of problem-solving involves two key stages: problem recognition and diagnosis. Various authors have highlighted the importance of separating these two stages. Schneider and Shiffrin (1977), for example, discuss information-processing modes and note that problem-solving aligns with the controlled mode, where individuals consciously focus their attention to gain an understanding of a specific issue. In contrast, problem recognition aligns with the automatic or default processing mode, where decision-makers scan a range of inputs, making it harder to distinguish a particular problem from its background. The literature on environmental scanning often highlights this same distinction.

The concept of problem recognition before problem-solving, or decision-making, is widely discussed. For instance, Mintzberg and Waters (1990) propose a multistage decision-making process that begins with an identification phase. This phase is similar to Simon's intelligence phase, but Mintzberg and Waters (1990) break it down further into two routines: decision recognition and diagnosis. Decision recognition occurs when certain stimuli reach a minimum threshold of importance in the view of a decision-maker, leading them to believe that action is necessary.

El Sawy and Pauchant (1988) classify managers' information acquisition patterns into two categories: reactive and proactive. The critical difference between these patterns is whether or not the manager is aware of a specific problem that needs to be solved. Similarly, Zmud (1984) identifies three types of managers on a continuum of problem-awareness: scanners, trackers, and probers.

Vandenbosch and Higgins (1996) make a distinction between scanning and focused searches. They differentiate between recognizing the existence of a problem or opportunity, on the one hand, and taking purposeful actions to solve a problem or exploit an opportunity, on the other hand. This distinction forms the basis of one dimension of their research model.

It is reasonable to assume that no organization exists without both potential and actual problems and opportunities. Therefore, organizations could benefit from implementing practices that support their members' problem-recognition and problem-solving efforts.

The vertical axis of the research model distinguishes between organizational practices that support problem-solving and those that support problem recognition.

Organizations today operate in a highly competitive and complex global market, which makes it crucial for them to make quick decisions that can help them stay ahead of the competition (Aguilar, 1967; Porter, 1980). With the advent of the Internet, the amount of information that needs to be managed has increased significantly. To achieve the desired results within a specified timeframe, it is essential to provide each worker with the right tool (Quagini, 2004). The software component of a Knowledge Management System (KMS) is the application tool that marks the final stage of implementation. However, technology is only one of the three components that need to be analyzed.

When analyzing the application systems present in Knowledge Management (KM), it is imperative to consider the concept of Business Intelligence (BI). According to Quagini (2004), Turban et al. (2008), and Sharda et al. (2014), BI is a system that retrieves "useful" information to achieve a company's strategy. The term Business Intelligence was coined by the consultancy firm Gartner Group in the 1990s. There are different definitions of BI in the literature and managerial practice (Gilad & Gilad, 1985; Quagini, 2004; Raisinghani, 2004; Turban et al., 2008).

For instance, Raisinghani (2004) proposed a definition that Turban (Turban et al., 2008) expanded. According to this definition, Business Intelligence is a macro-category that includes methodologies, applications, databases, tools, and architectures. The primary purpose of BI is to provide different data to different people, and the information is entirely disconnected from the context (Turban et al., 2008).

The proposed definition of BI is derived from the company's practice. It is defined as a complex system of rules, skills, and tools aimed at converting information into knowledge. The goal is to improve the performance and decision-making processes of line managers and top management (Quagini, 2004). We will analyze only the most important applications in the following paragraphs.

The Data Warehouse

The term Data Warehouse (DWH) literally means "data warehouse or warehouse." There are many definitions of the topic in the literature, but from an IT point of view, this system represents a platform where data from various company areas (such as administration, marketing, sales, production) and from outside sources (like the Internet portal or CRM) are integrated and archived. Simply put, it is a database that stores current and historical data that company managers may find useful (Laudon & Laudon, 2003). By having all the data available, it is possible to carry out a whole series of data analysis, projection, and reporting operations. The DWH could be referred to as a second-level KMS system specializing in decision support within the three-level model. This tool is usually used by a limited number of users, in most cases, managers, or top management.

Inmon (2000) coined the concept of data warehouse and defined its main characteristics. There are four fundamental characteristics, which include:

- Decision-oriented system: Unlike transactional systems, DWH is not oriented toward production but toward supporting the decision-making process. An integrated collection of data. It represents one of the fundamental requirements of a DWH. Data from multiple transactional systems and external sources flow into the Data Warehouse; the goal of integration can be achieved by following different paths. We could, for example, use the uniform coding method or the semantic homogeneity methodology of all variables, etc. As a rule, the optimization of the normalization process previously carried out by the ETL Extraction, Transformation, Loading (ETL) system is also carried out within the DWH.
- Subject oriented: The DWH system is oriented toward company-specific topics rather than applications or functions. In a DWH, data is stored so that users can easily read or process it. The objective, therefore, is no longer to minimize redundancy through normalization but to provide data with a structure capable of promoting the production of information. We move from functional design to data modeling to allow a multidimensional vision of the same.
- Time variant: The data stored within a DWH is very detailed and has a much longer time horizon than that stored in an operational system (from 2 to 5 years). It, however, means that the data contained in a DWH is updated up to a specific date, which in most cases is before the user queries the system. In other words, the data present within the system represents a snapshot of the system and cannot in any way be updated in real time. This characteristic turns out to be

opposed to that present in transactional systems in which the data always corresponds to a constantly updated situation.

- Not volatile: This characteristic indicates the non-modification of the data contained in the DWH, which allows read-only access. It also involves greater design simplicity than a relational database supporting a transactional application.

In addition to the characteristics mentioned earlier, a data warehouse has some unique features that make it stand out. One of these is its architecture, which includes specialized procedures for accessing and loading data, known as ETL (Extraction, Transformation, and Loading). In addition, it is essential to define the internal representation of the data structure, including choosing the reference model (relational or multidimensional), deciding on the level of detail for data normalization (Golfarelli et al., 2006; Quagini, 2004), and determining the percentage of redundancy accepted (Inmon, 2000; Turban et al., 2008). These decisions impact the precision and reliability of the decision-making system. Finally, the update frequency is another critical feature that affects the accuracy and reliability of the decision-making system.

The Data Mart

The Data Mart is a system that contains a specific set of data from the larger DWH system. This data is designed to cater to the unique needs of different business departments such as sales, quality, R&D, and marketing. Essentially, the Data Mart provides a specialized DWH system for each department for more efficient analysis. To analyze the data, commonly used tools include OLAP, DSS, reporting systems, and Data Mining. Compared to the DWH system, the Data Mart is less complex and has a smaller size, which enables faster and more in-depth analysis.

The ETL System

The ETL (Extract, Transform, Load) system is an application that is used to extract, transform, and load data into the Data Warehouse (DWH). It is one of the tools in the Knowledge Management System (KMS) that is cataloged in the first level. The ETL system takes internal and external information and reconciles it. This process checks for inconsistencies, errors, redundancies, and other issues with the data and then corrects, cleans up, or converts it to a format that is compatible with the DWH's data structure.

Initially, the information is normalized and standardized, meaning it is converted into one or more values that are compatible with the DWH's data structure. After that, the system checks the data, makes necessary corrections, and loads it into the Data Warehouse. Due to the large amount of heterogeneous data, the ETL process can take a long time, usually about 6–8 hours in large organizations. As a result, data is usually uploaded once a day. Users can then perform their analysis operations on the historical data.

The OLAP Systems

OLAP, which stands for Online Analytical Processing, is a system that can analyze data subsets, also known as "info cubes" in a multidimensional manner. These cubes are usually sourced from a Data Warehouse or Data Mart (Laudon & Laudon, 2003). OLAP is a powerful tool that processes information quickly, is flexible, and can be customized by the end-user. With OLAP, users can conduct statistical analyses and market research on a virtually infinite number of variables.

To get started, the OLAP system searches for the relevant information requested by the user within the DWH or Data Mart. Once the data is found, the system generates the requested info cube. For example, if a manager wants to perform statistical analyses on products and customers within a certain time period, they can query the DWH through OLAP. The system then searches for all the information requested by the user and creates an info cube in which each face contains information relating to customers and products sold for the time period considered.

The cube is a tool that allows users to manipulate data by performing various operations such as sorting, filtering, drilling down, or rolling up the data. These operations enable users to derive insights from the data and make informed decisions based on the results (Kimball & Ross, 2016; Turban et al., 2008).

One of the operations that can be performed on the cube is the "slice and dice" technique. When we slice the cube, we resize it by sectioning it according to a specific dimension. This means that some variables within the cube will need to remain constant. For instance, if a user wants to view only the sales data for product X, by customer and time period, they can set the product variable to the desired value.

On the other hand, when we dice the cube, we resize it by limiting the range of values of all the variables.

The operations listed below can be utilized on a data cube to alter its dimensions and gain various perspectives on the information:

- Slice and dice: This operation involves resizing the cube by sectioning it through a dimension. Certain variables within the cube must remain constant. For instance, to view only the sales of product X by customer and time period, you need to set the product variable to a specific value. Conversely, the dice operation allows you to limit the range of values of all the variables. For example, you can resize the cube to look for sales from 2023 to 2024 of products with a cost higher than a certain amount.
- Roll-up: This function aggregates data by eliminating a level of detail from a hierarchy. By removing the customer variable, you can view the sales divided by a single product in the desired time frame, increasing the level of detail of the information.
- Drill down: Unlike roll-up, this function decreases the aggregation of data by introducing a further level of detail in a hierarchy. You can analyze sales divided by products in a certain area in different periods.
- Pivoting is an operation that enables to analyze the same information from different perspectives without altering the dimensions of the cube. By rotating the cube to reorganize the cells, we can gain new insights and have three distinct views of the data.

In the literature, various OLAP architectures exist, but in managerial practice, only three are commonly utilized: ROLAP, MOLAP, and HOLAP.

The ROLAP model, short for Relational OLAP, stores information from the Data Warehouse or Data Mart in relational databases. However, the resulting cubes only have two dimensions, requiring multiple tables to be connected in order to create a multidimensional cube. This reliance on relational data is why it's called a relational model.

One advantage of ROLAP is its direct correlation to relational data, but it comes at the cost of longer processing times compared to other types.

On the other hand, in MOLAP (Multidimensional OLAP), data is automatically managed in multiple dimensions. Currently, it is the most widely used system in companies due to its speed and versatility when fed with data from the Data Mart (Golfarelli & Rizzi, 2006). In this system, the dimensions of the cubes are defined beforehand using a mix of details and aggregations. However, MOLAP requires a large amount of disk space to function (Kimball & Ross, 2016).

Data Mining

Data mining systems are tools used to extract hidden information from transactional databases (Turban et al., 2008). The system kernel is supported by a very complex statistical structure. Data mining systems are sometimes mistakenly confused with OLAP, even though they are completely different. In OLAP, in order to get an answer, the operator must perform a whole series of queries on the data present in the DWH. This operation implies that the user knows all the variables to be considered beforehand. In contrast, in data mining, the organizational actor will have to receive the answer without knowing the variables and processes to consider in order to make the best decision. It is an automatic process useful for identifying the structures present within the data, where structure refers to patterns, predictive models, rules, and relationships (Nemati & Barko, 2001). Data mining tools can be referred to as predictive analysis systems and contain various functions within them, the main ones being.

1. Basket analysis: an analysis process for finding affinities, usually analyzing consumer's purchasing habits (joint purchases).
2. Fraud detection: a tool used by the postal police and government associations to identify potential fraud or terrorist actions, highlighting the importance of data mining in maintaining security and preventing illegal activities.
3. Clustering: used within marketing to identify homogeneous customer groupings in terms of purchasing behavior and socio-demographic characteristics.
4. Text mining: a function that allows recognition of sequences of words, defined as patterns, and to categorize documents with common and/or similar topics. It can be understood as the extension of data mining or knowledge discovery in databases (Simoudis,

1996). The highlight of this function is the ability to find and extract information from unstructured data (Tan, 1999). This feature allows cataloging invoices, emails, and information present on the Web (company portal, web pages, forums, etc.).

The development of these technologies has significantly strengthened and improved the functioning of Document Management systems and, more generally, of corporate content management platforms (Enterprise Content Management). To enhance, improve, and speed up the information acquisition process, ontological engines for advanced recognition of natural languages have been introduced into text mining systems.

Apart from the mentioned systems, the broader category of Knowledge Management Systems (KMS) may encompass Decision Support Systems (DSS), structured data management platforms also known as Document Management Systems (DMS), and overall systems for managing corporate content Enterprise Content Management (ECM).

2.4 The New Decision-Making Paradigm

When discussing decision support systems, the focus is often on the technical aspects, overlooking other crucial factors (Courtney, 2001). However, a notable study by Gorry and Scott Morton delved into the decision-making process within Anthony's model (Anthony, 1965), using Simon's definition of the process (Simon, 1961). This definition divides the process into four phases: intelligence, design, choice, and implementation, providing a comprehensive understanding (Gorry & Scott Morton, 1971).

The intelligence phase, a cornerstone of the decision-making process, entails meticulous problem identification, comprehensive information and variable analysis, and a deep understanding of motivations and consequences (Courtney, 2001). In the design phase, potential solutions are identified, along with models and actions for each scenario. The third phase involves selecting the best solution and outlining future effects, including evaluation errors and uncertainties.

Simon's approach to describing reality was deemed simplistic and linear. In response, Mintzberg conducted a study on 25 companies (Mintzberg et al., 1976) and transformed Simon's linear model into an incremental one (Simon, 1961). This evolution is significant as it introduces a more realistic and practical approach to decision-making. The new model involves generating the overall decision step-by-step through small attempts, which are then combined to form the final decision (Martinez, 2004). If the decision is complex, unexpected, or new, the decision-maker proceeds with caution and in small steps, comparing themselves with other decision-makers in the company. In some cases, partial solutions are accepted.

The decision-making process culminates with the implementation of the choice and control of the results. This phase is crucial as it underscores the role of the decision-maker in adapting to the actual results and initiating a new decision-making process if they differ from the expected ones. The output is often a "sub-optimal" solution due to limited rationality and subjective variables. Mintzberg identifies three macro phases within the decision-making process: identification, development, and selection (Mintzberg et al., 1976).

The process of problem-solving involves several key phases. The first phase, recognition, is essential for identifying the problem, critical issues, variables, and necessary information for its resolution. This phase requires sense-making processes based on beliefs, where workers evaluate different perspectives and reach a mutually agreed solution. The recognition phase also incorporates sense-making processes based on conventions, particularly through comparison.

Following recognition is the diagnosis phase, where additional information is collected and reprocessed to better understand the problem. The complexity of the procedures in this phase depends on the severity and urgency of the problem. Past experience and knowledge play a crucial role in this phase, contributing to a better understanding of the problem.

In the development phase, potential alternatives to address the problem are proposed. Information related to the problem is drawn from organizational memory, and if necessary information is not available, solutions must be created from scratch. This phase involves an iterative process, with the final solution emerging from trial and error. The analysis is used to eliminate less probable solutions, and evaluation leads to the identification of a sub-optimal solution. It's important to note that the final solution, a product of continuous learning and improvement, must be approved by the competent corporate body before implementation, highlighting the dynamic nature of the problem-solving process.

While the decision-making process, as described in Mintzberg's model, is a complex interplay of internal and external factors (Martinez, 2004), it's important to note the potential inefficiencies that can arise. Mintzberg identified internal factors as the primary cause of decision-making slowdown (Mintzberg, 1979; Mintzberg et al., 1976). These inefficiencies, such as management's low interest in the problem, the time required to gather all the necessary information, the poor feasibility of the solution due to costs and time, and the ineffectiveness of the solution, can significantly impact our decision-making outcomes. Recognizing and addressing these inefficiencies is crucial for improving our decision-making processes and organizational effectiveness.

The decision-making process and the activities involved in it can be structured, unstructured, or partially structured (Gorry & Scott Morton, 1971). Decision support systems (DSS) were originally designed to help manage decision-making processes that are unstructured or semi-structured (Courtney, 2001; Gorry & Scott Morton, 1971). Human–machine interaction enables the conversion of unstructured actions into structured ones that are objective and measurable. The input sources used by DSS are critical to their successful operation and can be either internal or external. Internal sources, which come from a company's information system, must be accurate and up-to-date, while external sources typically involve future estimates or trends. External variables are usually the most frequently used sources in the decision-making process, as DSS is designed to support strategic actions.

Conventional DSS automate the decision-making process proposed by Simon and Mintzberg (Mintzberg et al., 1976; Simon, 1961). In summary, the decision-maker will enter general information into the DSS after clearly understanding the problem to be solved. The system will then automatically search for relevant variables (internal and external), generate possible scenarios, identify risks, alternatives, and critical issues.

Having at his disposal the statistically most probable model and the possible alternatives, the organizational actor will be able to make his own choice, which in a subsequent phase will have to be evaluated and possibly corrected if it turns out to be ineffective or inefficient. In Mintzberg's model, the decision support system is mainly used to automate and speed up the identification, development and selection phases (Mintzberg et al., 1976).

Over the years, decision support systems' features have been integrated into executive applications in Information Systems. This has expanded the use of the tool from just staff to entire corporations. Knowledge management systems have evolved from using artificial intelligence and expert systems for top management to supporting decision-makers (Bonczek et al., 1981; DeSanctis & Gallupe, 1987; Holsapple, 2002). The concept of decision support systems has developed into a service that facilitates knowledge-sharing and collaboration between different organizational actors. Such a decision support system supports decision-makers in both the information collection and decision-making phases and allows for the sharing of solutions (Courtney & Paradice, 1993; Holsapple, 2002).

However, there is one critical issue in the decision-making process, the "unconscious" choice, which can be potentially dangerous for the organization. After objectively analyzing the situation, the decision-maker may unconsciously try to circumvent the obstacle by relying on a mix of solutions already present in the organizational memory and known personal experiences. The incorrect interpretation of the situation, validated through the "distorted" use of a mental model, could lead to anomalies in the decision-making process. The decision-maker may convince themselves of the solution and undertake incorrect actions that are potentially dangerous for the organization. Bechara's model (Bechara et al., 1997) shows the mental models present in the organizational memory, also defined as a "library", and the past personal experiences of the decision-maker.

Decision-making is intricately linked to the effective use of personal and collective mental models. To reduce the potential risks of making the wrong choices, it is essential to use feedback mechanisms to validate or challenge beliefs, expectations, and mental models. In organizational settings, individuals often rely on mental models to bring order to situations where information is limited. By organizing information, all pertinent details regarding the situation, issue, and steps taken to address it can be integrated, establishing a correspondence between mental and actual models (Hofstadter, 1984; Zardini et al., 2016).

Historically, decision support systems (DSS) mainly addressed structured or semi-structured problems stored in the organizational memory, neglecting unstructured problems, which pose a distinct challenge. Solutions developed using semi-structured information were utilized for resolving or planning present and future strategic actions (Courtney, 2001).

According to Courtney's UST (Unbounded Systems Thinking) or multiple perspective paradigm, the focal point of the decision-making process and DSS systems should be the "mental model," not the technology in use (Courtney, 2001). The mental model and the information it encompasses, vital for decision-making, are closely intertwined (Churchman, 1971; Linstone & Mitroff, 1994). This is because they stem from the personal experience of the organizational actor or the collective experience contained in the organizational memory, underscoring the significance of individual perspectives (refer to Fig. 2.5).

The decision-makers, through their mental model, influence and are influenced by every activity in the decision-making process. The decision-maker's experience shapes the problem and the actions taken to solve it. As a result, the decision support system (DSS) tailors the decision-making process by selecting useful information from the company's Information System that can be saved, shared, and reused. This streamlines decision-making and fosters the development of new tacit knowledge for future use.

In advanced DSS, the actor plays a critical role in defining the problem and the necessary information for the process. The system then adapts to these needs by researching and reworking information, checking for existing solutions within the organizational memory, and providing the decision-maker with pre-existing resolutions or new models tailored to their decision-making needs.

For the UST (or multi-perspective) model to be used within a DSS, it must meet specific requirements:

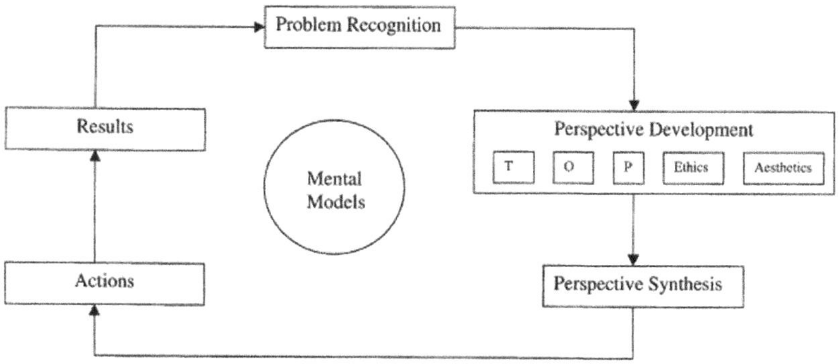

Fig. 2.5 The new paradigm for DSS systems (Courtney, 2001)

- The DSS, through the FSO, should help resolve conflicts between the organizational, technological, and human resources perspectives by modeling the system to coordinate them. During system implementation, all three perspectives must be analyzed, and useful elements extracted to resolve critical issues and ensure coordination.
- During the information research and identification phase, the DSS should consider the methodologies and techniques used by human resources and the structural characteristics of the organization.
- The system should integrate the three components and favor their interdependencies. There are no applications or formulas in the DSS that guarantee system integration. Therefore, an organizational study must be conducted beforehand to identify the role of each person, their needs, the organizational structure, and all the processes present therein.

The decision support system is designed to support the decision-maker, not replace them. The worker maintains a dominant and invaluable position in the decision-making process as the "source" and "consumer" of knowledge.

To create an efficient knowledge management environment, organizations need to change their organizational structure. The mechanistic idea of organization should be replaced with a community-based structure where actors enhance organizational memory and knowledge through mutual interactions.

The volume of information and the need for faster response times to external requests are driving changes in Knowledge Management and Business Intelligence systems within organizations. To address this, Data Warehouse and Data Mart systems are being transformed, and real-time data warehouse systems (RDW or Active Data Warehouse, ADW) are being introduced.

The implementation of RDW has paved the way for the advancement and adoption of decision support systems in various functional and operational domains. Active Data Warehouses are a viable option for providing real-time access to tactical and strategic information.

Transitioning from the traditional Data Warehouse (DWH) to the more advanced Real-time Data Warehouse (RDW) is not just a technological upgrade (Burdett & Singh, 2004). It's a strategic move that can enhance your company's processes, user experience, and organizational coordination.

Transitioning from the traditional Data Warehouse (DWH) to the more advanced Real-time Data Warehouse (RDW) is not just a technological upgrade (Burdett & Singh, 2004). It's a strategic move that can enhance your company's processes, user experience, and organizational coordination.

Automated Decision Support (ADS) or Enterprise Decision Management (EDM) systems automate all repetitive operations at a managerial level, enabling real-time updating of information and significantly reducing the latency present in the decision-making process. This reduction in latency, which refers to the time gap between the moment an event or change is perceived and the moment a decision is implemented (Hackathorn, 2004), can lead to substantial improvements in Business Intelligence and value creation.

There are three types of latency: data latency, analysis latency, and decision/action latency. While research on Business Intelligence focuses on reducing data latency, improving the decision-making process, and creating value, the other two components should also be acted upon (Panian, 2009). Specifically, the analysis process is critical, and the analysis latency—the time between receiving the information and making the decision—must be reduced. Finally, there is the latency between the decision and its implementation. Automated Decision Support (ADS) or Enterprise Decision Management (EDM) systems automate all repetitive operations at a managerial level, enabling real-time updating of information and significantly reducing the latency present in the decision-making process. This reduction in latency, which refers to the time gap between the moment an event or change is perceived and the moment a decision is implemented (Hackathorn, 2004), can lead to substantial improvements in Business Intelligence and value creation. There are three types of latency: data latency, analysis latency, and decision/action latency. While research on Business Intelligence focuses on reducing data latency, improving the decision-making process, and creating value, the other two components should also be acted upon (Panian, 2009). Specifically, the analysis process is critical, and the analysis latency, the time between receiving the information and making the decision, must be reduced. Finally, there is the latency between the decision and its implementation.

The duration of the decision-making process depends on the combination of three latencies. Any increase in latency prolongs the decision-making cycle, impacting the efficiency and overall value of the organization (as shown in Fig. 2.6).

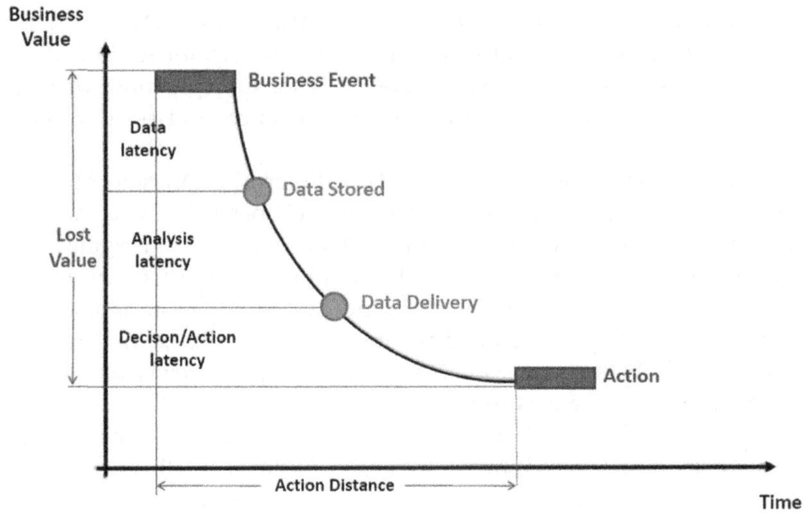

Fig. 2.6 The types of Latency (Panian, 2009)

Integrating decision support systems (DSS) tools with other Knowledge Management (KM) and Business Intelligence (BI) applications is crucial for streamlining processes, reducing latency, and automating routine decisions within the organization.

The decision support system (DSS) is instrumental in minimizing data and analysis latency, as depicted in (Fig. 2.7). By streamlining the decision-making process, the system enables operators to execute operational and tactical actions precisely when needed, contributing to the organization's overall value (Panian, 2009).

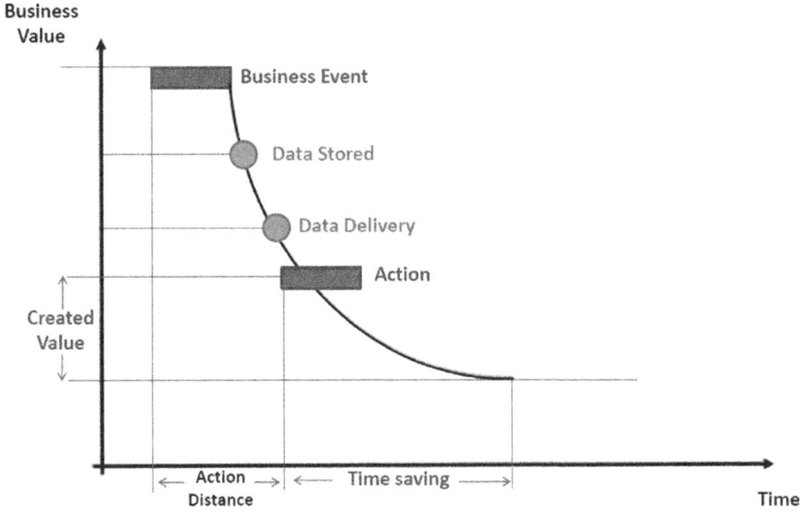

Fig. 2.7 la riduzione della latenza totale (Panian, 2009)

References

Abecker, A., Bernardi, A., Hinkelmann, K., Kühn, O., & Sintek, M. (1997, March). Towards a well-founded technology for organizational memories. In *Proceedings AAAI spring symposium on artificial intelligence in knowledge management*. Stanford University.

Ackoff, R. L. (1989). From data to wisdom. *Journal of Applied Systems Analysis, 16*(1), 3–9.

Aguilar, F. J. (1967). *Scanning the Business Environment*. Macmillan.

Anthony, R. N. (1965). Planning and control systems: A framework for analysis. (No Title).

Bechara, A., Damasio, H., Tranel, D., & Damasio, A. R. (1997). Deciding advantageously before knowing the advantageous strategy. *Science, 275*(5304), 1293–1295.

Bellandi, G. (2009). *La conoscenza partecipata*.

Bellinger, G., Castro, D., & Mills, A. (2004). Data, information, knowledge, and wisdom.

Beretta, S. (2002). Unleashing the integration potential of ERP systems: The role of process-based performance measurement systems. *Business Process Management Journal, 8*(3), 254–277.

Berthon, P., Pitt, L. F., & Ewing, M. T. (2001). Corollaries of the collective: The influence of organizational culture and memory development on perceived decision-making context. *Journal of the Academy of Marketing Science, 29*(2), 135–150.

Bonczek, R. H., Holsapple, C. W., & Whinston, A. B. (1981). A generalized decision support system using predicate calculus and network data base management. *Operations Research, 29*(2), 263–281.

Bordin, P., & Selva, A. (2002). Investire nell'innovazione tecnologica. *Mondo digitale*, 4.

Burdett, J., & Singh, S. (2004). Challenges and lessons learned from real-time data warehousing. *Business Intelligence Journal, 9*(4), 31–39.

Chiucchi, M. S. (2004). *Sistemi di misurazione e di reporting del capitale intellettuale: criticità e prospettive* (Vol. 19, pp. 1–221). Giappichelli.

Churchman, C. W. (1971). *The design of inquiring system*. Basic Books.

Cleveland, H. (1987). The twilight of hierarchy: Speculations on the global information society. *International Journal of Technology Management, 2*(1), 45–66.

Conner, K. R., & Prahalad, C. K. (1996). A resource-based theory of the firm: Knowledge versus opportunism. *Organization Science, 7*(5), 477–501.

Cooley, M. (1987). *Architect or Bee? The Price of a New Technology*.

Courtney, J. F., & Paradice, D. B. (1993). Studies in managerial problem formulation systems. *Decision Support Systems, 9*(4), 413–423.

Courtney, J. F. (2001). Decision making and knowledge management in inquiring organizations: toward a new decision-making paradigm for DSS. *Decision support systems, 31*(1), 17–38.

Davenport, T. H., & Prusak, L. (1998). *Working knowledge: How organizations manage what they know*. Harvard Business Press.

Demsetz, H. (1997). The firm in economic theory: A quiet revolution. *The American Economic Review, 87*(2), 426–429.

DeSanctis, G., & Gallupe, R. B. (1987). A foundation for the study of group decision support systems. *Management Science, 33*(5), 589–609.

Dieng, R. (2000). Guest editor's introduction: Knowledge management and the internet. *IEEE Intelligent Systems, 15*(03), 14–17.

Dieng, R., Corby, O., Giboin, A., & Ribiere, M. (1999). Methods and tools for corporate knowledge management. *International Journal of Human-Computer Studies, 51*(3), 567–598.

Dosi, G. (2009). The contribution of economic theory to the understanding of a knowledge-based economy. In *The economic impact of knowledge* (pp. 123–129). Routledge.

El Sawy, O. A., & Pauchant, T. C. (1988). Triggers, templates and twitches in the tracking of emerging strategic issues. *Strategic Management Journal, 9*(5), 455–473.

Foray, D. (2000). *Characterising the knowledge base: Available and missing indicators. Organização para a cooperação e o desenvolvimento econômico. Knowledge management in the learning society.*

Foss, N. J. (1996). Knowledge-based approaches to the theory of the firm: Some critical comments. *Organization Science, 7*(5), 470–476.

Gabrielli, G. (Ed.). (2006). *Conoscenza, apprendimento, cambiamento. La gestione dei programmi di knowledge e change management* (Vol. 1). FrancoAngeli.

Gallupe, B. (2001). Knowledge management systems: Surveying the landscape. *International Journal of Management Reviews, 3*(1), 61–77.

Gilad, B., & Gilad, T. (1985). A systems approach to business intelligence. *Business Horizons, 28*(5), 65–70.

Gnoato, F., & Roveda, L. (2008). Una visione strategica del knowledge management. *Harvard Business Review Italia, 7*(8), 56–65.

Golfarelli, M., Lechtenbörger, J., Rizzi, S., & Vossen, G. (2006). Schema versioning in data warehouses: Enabling cross-version querying via schema augmentation. *Data & Knowledge Engineering, 59*(2), 435–459.

Gorry, G. A., & Scott Morton, M. S. (1971). *A framework for management information systems.*

Hackathorn, R. (2004). The BI watch real-time to real-value. *DM Review, 14*, 24–29.

Hammer, M., & Champy, J. (2009). *Reengineering the corporation: Manifesto for business revolution, a. Zondervan.*

Hansen, T., Dirckinck-Holmfeld, L., Lewis, R., & Rugelj, J. (1999). Using telematics to support collaborative knowledge construction. *Collaborative Learning: Cognitive and Computational Approaches, 169*, 196.

Hofstadter, D. (1984). *The copycat project: An experiment in nondeterminism and creative analogies.*

Holsapple, C. W. (2002). Advances in business problem solving: Bridging business and computing disciplines. In *Business modelling: Multidisciplinary approaches economics, operational, and information systems perspectives* (pp. 403–448).

Inmon, W. H. (2000). Creating the data warehouse data model from the corporate data model. *PRISM Tech Topics, 1*(2).

Kakabadse, K., Kouzmin, N., & Kakabadse, A. (2001). From tacit knowledge to knowledge management: Leveraging invisible assets. *Knowledge and Process Management, 8*(3), 137–154.

Kaplan, S., Schenkel, A., von Krogh, G., & Weber, C. (2001). Knowledge-based theories of the firm in strategic management: A review and extension. *International Journal of Project Management, 25*(56), 143–158.

Kimball, R., & Ross, M. (2016). *The kimball group reader: Relentlessly practical tools for data warehousing and business intelligence remastered collection*. Wiley.

Kogut, B., & Zander, U. (1993). Knowledge of the firm and the evolutionary theory of the multinational corporation. *Journal of International Business Studies, 24*, 625–645.

Laudon, K. C., & Laudon, J. P. (2003). *Essentials of management information*. Pearson.

Linstone, H. A., & Mitroff, I. I. (1994). *The challenge of the 21st century: Managing technology and ourselves in a shrinking world*. SUNY Press.

Macintosh, A., Filby, I., & Kingston, J. (1999). Knowledge management techniques: teaching and dissemination concepts. *International journal of human-computer studies, 51*(3), 549–566.

Martinez, M. (2004). *Organizzazione, informazioni, tecnologie* (pp. 1–352). Il mulino.

Mintzberg, H. (1979). An emerging strategy of "direct" research. *Administrative Science Quarterly, 24*(4), 582–589.

Mintzberg, H., Raisinghani, D., & Theoret, A. (1976). The structure of "unstructured" decision processes. *Administrative Science Quarterly, 21*, 246–275.

Mintzberg, H., & Waters, J. (1990). Studying deciding: An exchange of views between Mintzberg and Waters, Pettigrew, and Butler. *Organization Studies, 11*(1), 1–16.

Mokyr, J. (2006). Useful knowledge as an evolving system: The view from economic history. In *The economy as an evolving, complex system III: Current perspectives and future directions* (pp. 309–336). Oxford University Press.

Nemati, H. R., & Barko, C. D. (2001). Issues in organizational data mining: A survey of current practices. *Journal of Data Warehousing, 6*(1), 25–36.

Nonaka, I. (1991). The knowledge creating company. *Harvard Business Review, 69*, 96–104.

Nonaka, I., & Takeuchi, H. (1998). A theory of the firm's knowledge-creation dynamics. In *The dynamic firm, the role of technology, strategy, organization, and regions* (p. 27). Oxford University Press.

Panian, Z. (2009). Just-in-time business intelligence and real-time decisioning. *Recent Advances in Applied Informatics and Communications, Proceedings of AIC, 9*, 106–111.

Papavassiliou, G., & Mentzas, G. (2003). Knowledge modelling in weakly-structured business processes. *Journal of Knowledge Management, 7*(2), 18–33.

Porter, M. E. (1980). Industry structure and competitive strategy: Keys to profitability. *Financial Analysts Journal, 36*(4), 30–41.

Profili, S. (2004). *Il knowledge management. Approcci teorici e strumenti gestionali* (Vol. 97). FrancoAngeli.

Quagini, L. (2004). *Business intelligence e knowledge management. Gestione delle informazioni e delle performances nell'era digitale* (Vol. 26). FrancoAngeli.

Quagli, A. (2001). *Knowledge management: la gestione della conoscenza aziendale: il caso Cap Gemini Ernst & Young*. Egea.

Raisinghani, M. S. (Ed.). (2004). *Business intelligence in the digital economy: Opportunities, limitations and risks*. Igi Global.

Rowley, J. (2007). The wisdom hierarchy: Representations of the DIKW hierarchy. *Journal of Information Science, 33*(2), 163–180.

Rullani, E. (2004). *La fabbrica dell'immateriale*. Produrre valore con la conoscenza.

Sharda, R., Delen, D., Turban, E., Aronson, J., & Liang, T. (2014). Business intelligence and analytics. *System for Decesion Support, 398*, 2014.

Shiffrin, R. M., & Schneider, W. (1977). Controlled and automatic human information processing: II. Perceptual learning, automatic attending and a general theory. *Psychological Review, 84*(2), 127.

Simon, H. A. (1957). Background of decision making. *Naval War College Review, 10*(3), 1–24.

Simon, H. A. (1961, May 9–11). *Modeling human mental processes*. Papers presented at the western joint IRE-AIEE-ACM computer conference (pp. 111–119).

Simoudis, E. (1996). Reality check for data mining. *IEEE Intelligent Systems, 11*(05), 26–33.

Spender, J. C., & Grant, R. M. (1996). Knowledge and the firm: Overview. *Strategic Management Journal, 17*(S2), 5–9.

Stalk, G., Evans, P., & Shulman, L. E. (1992). HBR.

Tan, A. H. (1999, April). Text mining: The state of the art and the challenges. In *Proceedings of the pakdd 1999 workshop on knowledge disocovery from advanced databases* (Vol. 8, pp. 65–70).

Tardivo, G. (2008). L'evoluzione degli studi sul Knowledge Management. *Sinergie, 76*, 21–42.

Teece, D. J. (1998). Capturing value from knowledge assets: The new economy, markets for know-how, and intangible assets. *California Management Review, 40*(3), 55–79.

Teece, D. J. (2000). Strategies for managing knowledge assets: The role of firm structure and industrial context. *Long Range Planning, 33*(1), 35–54.

Tronti, L. (2015). Economia della conoscenza, innovazione organizzativa e partecipazione cognitiva: Un nuovo modo di lavorare. *Economia & Lavoro, 49*(3), 7–20.

Turban, E., Sharda, R., Aronson, J. E., & King, D. (2008). *Business intelligence: A managerial approach* (pp. 58–59). Pearson Prentice Hall.

Vandenbosch, B., & Higgins, C. (1996). Information acquisition and mental models: An investigation into the relationship between behaviour and learning. *Information Systems Research, 7*(2), 198–214.

Van Heijst, G., Van der Spek, R., & Kruizinga, E. (1997). Corporate memories as a tool for knowledge management. *Expert Systems with Applications, 13*(1), 41–54.

Vicari, S. (2008). Conoscenza e impresa. *Sinergie* (maggio-agosto 2008), 43–66.

Wiig, K. M. (1997). Knowledge management: An introduction and perspective. *Journal of Knowledge Management, 1*(1), 6–14.

Zardini, A., Rossignoli, C., & Ricciardi, F. (2016). A bottom-up path for IT management success: From infrastructure quality to competitive excellence. *Journal of Business Research, 69*(5), 1747–1752.

Zeleny, M. (1987). Management support systems: Towards integrated knowledge management. *Human Systems Management, 7*(1), 59–70.

Zmud, R. W. (1984). An examination of "push-pull" theory applied to process innovation in knowledge work. *Management Science, 30*(6), 727–738.

CHAPTER 3

An Introduction to Artificial Intelligence

Anna Monreale

3.1 Introduction

Artificial intelligence (AI) has gained much attention in the last years due to the recent advancements in computer hardware and network speeds, the availability of vast amount of data and their pervasiveness, the scalability of cloud computing, and the sophistication of the Machine Learning and Deep Learning algorithms. However, analyzing the literature many definitions of Artificial intelligence have been published to eliminate potential ambiguities and misinterpretations that might be caused by the broad and vague definition of AI as "the capacity of computers or other machines to exhibit or simulate intelligent behaviour" (OED Online, 2019).

For understanding the concept of AI, we should first analyze the meaning of terms "*artificial*" and "*intelligence*," separately. *Artificial* refers to something that is made by humans as a replication of something occurring naturally (Mikalef & Gupta, 2021). *Intelligence* refers to cognitive activities such as the ability to learn, reason, understand, comprehend knowledge, and apply knowledge and experience for problem-solving. Therefore, the combination of the two terms leads to the understanding of artificial intelligence as a set of methods and tools and technologies making machines capable to imitate human-like behaviors by replicating cognitive processes to address specific tasks typically complex for humans.

M. Pierotti et al., *Artificial Intelligence in Accounting and Auditing*,
https://doi.org/10.1007/978-3-031-71371-2_3

AI focuses on emulating human learning mechanisms, processing information, extracting knowledge from data, making inferences to achieve predetermined organizational and societal goals (Mikalef & Gupta, 2021).

Considering the different AI-based systems and technologies and their functionalities we can distinguish three main types of AI requiring various levels of human-machine interactions: *Assisted AI, Augmented AI*, and *Autonomous AI*.

Assisted AI refers to technology that can support humans in performing routine and repetitive tasks and in decision-making. It speeds up and makes human activities more accurate, and the machine is a tool used by a human operator. This means that the final decision is made by humans who retain decision-making responsibilities. The systems based on this form of AI require constant human inputs and only work well with well-defined inputs and outputs. Examples of assisted AI include speech recognition tools, transcribing spoken words into written text and driving safety systems, controlling speed, and activating the brakes if necessary.

Augmented AI refers to technology that can help in overcoming the cognitive limitations of humans and integrating AI with human expertise makes it possible to enhance decisions and optimize actions. The main goal is to have an AI with an assistive role, i.e., supporting humans enhancing their intelligence rather than replacing them. Typically, organizations may gain access to enormous amounts of data that if processed adequately could improve the decision-making process. Unfortunately, humans cannot process such amount of data timely and effectively given their growing complexity, thus it becomes fundamental to exploit AI able to apply analytical intelligence to gain useful data-driven insights (Borges et al., 2020). Examples of Augmented AI include machine learning algorithms able to find patterns and make predictions based on the inference of customers' needs and risks.

Autonomous AI refers to technology which does not require human collaboration or input to make decisions and take actions. It may be considered as a fully independent agent capable of adapting its behavior to different situations. Autonomous AI is characterized by intuitive intelligence, enabling the AI to effectively adjust to novel situations, and empathetic intelligence, enabling the AI to adequately interact with humans when necessary (Huang & Rust, 2018). Examples of Autonomous AI include automated trading algorithms in financial markets capable to make buy and sell decisions on the basis of market data and predefined rules, and self-driving cars. However, since Autonomous AI operates without human supervision and collaboration, ethical and social implications should be considered; we will discuss these aspects in Chapter 4. Each of the above AI types may provide solutions in different applications combining different techniques and models including data mining, machine learning, and deep learning.

3.2 Data Mining and Machine Learning

Data mining is the process of analyzing exceptionally large collections of data (often called Big Data) for the extraction of meaningful information and *hidden knowledge*, i.e., unexpected patterns and trends. To guide users of data mining tools in the knowledge discovery some rigorous procedures have defined for determining the so-called knowledge discovery process. Such a process starts with understanding domain knowledge, selecting a dataset, data preprocessing, data reduction, data mining tasks execution for pattern extraction, patterns interpretation, and consolidation of discovered knowledge. Data mining tasks can be divided into two main categories: *descriptive* and *predictive* tasks. Naturally, each category of tasks has different objectives of analysis and describes different types of possible data mining activities. *Descriptive* tasks have the goal of presenting the key features of the data. They essentially derive models that summarize the relationship in data, permitting in this way to study the most important aspects of the data. In contrast, *predictive* tasks have the specific objective of predicting the value of some target attribute of an object on the basis of observed values of other attributes of the object.

Data mining typically uses a combination of data analysis, statistics, and machine learning (i.e., the process of learning through experience described in the data and making predictions) to transform raw data into useful knowledge.

Machine learning (ML) is one of the most important subfields of AI aiming at defining and developing methods for building analytical models capable of learning patterns from data. In other words, these methods train machines how to learn from data and improve their performance without explicitly providing instructions by programming them. They imitate the human learning process to solve some tasks for which we cannot write a simple algorithm. As an example, there exist some tasks, such as recognizing an animal in a photograph or distinguishing among several types of flowers, which as humans we can do without being aware of how we do them. Thus, in ML we try to imitate humans in doing these types of tasks by providing a problem to solve, a lot of examples, representing combinations of problem-solution, and an initial general model with many parameters. The learning process improves the model's performance in terms of accuracy for the specific task by adjusting the initial parameters and exploiting the examples (data) provided in input. Data are used for optimizing the model's parameters. This means that based on this training activity, the initial general model becomes more coherent with the training data and specialized in the specific task; this model becomes the algorithm for that task. ML can be applied in many contexts where often we have many data in different forms, and we want to develop data-driven services always more personalized.

Today, the development of such services is possible given the enormous amount of data we continuously produce with our daily activities. This data can be exploited to understand our needs and interests and for posing the basis for personalized data-driven services for users. In case we need to apply ML methods to large amount of data (often called Big Data) we need to integrate those methods in a data mining process which enables us to extract from a lot of raw data simple, precise, and valuable data models with a better predictive power.

Machine learning algorithms are divided into two types: *supervised* and *unsupervised* machine learning. Supervised learning starts with knowledge of the output values. In contrast, unsupervised learning does not have explicit outputs to predict. Supervised learning aims to find and learn a computational function that best approximates the relationship between attributes and the outcome variable in the data. Unsupervised learning does not have explicit outputs to predict, and its objective is to infer and reveal the hidden structure in data.

Supervised Machine Learning

Supervised machine learning refers to methods for learning models from training data consisting of labeled examples. This means that human experts prepared data and labeled them, and the algorithm exploits the association between data and labels to learn a model accurate in labeling new unlabeled data. For example, given a set of bank transactions described by some characteristics and associated with the label *fraudulent* or *legitimate*, the supervised machine learning algorithm will build a model that will be able to recognize *fraudulent* bank transactions generating an alarm. In case the task requires to predict a label, the task is called *classification*, while in case it is required to predict a quantity (e.g., the risk score of a customer) the task is called *regression*. Another supervised task is *forecasting* aiming at predicting the future trend of an indicator. For example, observing the past behavior/trend of an indicator (e.g., the sales over the year of a product in a store chain) the supervised machine model can learn how to predict future values of sales.

Classification Models

Classification is one of the most important machine learning tasks. The input data of a classification algorithm is a set of records. Each record is composed of a tuple (x, c), where x is the attribute set and c is a special attribute, called *class label* (also known as category or target attribute). Given a set of records the *classification task* learns a target function f that maps each attribute set x to one of the predefined class labels c. Therefore, a classification model is an abstract representation of the relationship between the attribute set and its class label. The model can be represented in many ways, such as a tree, a set of rules, a probability table, etc. The model is said to classify an instance (x, c) correctly if $f(x) = c$.

Classification techniques can be used to distinguish objects of different classes (i.e., as descriptive model) and to predict the class label of unknown records (i.e., as predictive model).

In general, a classification technique requires: (a) building a model that assigns each record in the input data (training set) to a given class label; (b) using the classification model to classify new unknown records belonging to the so-called test set. The process of building a model by exploiting a specific learning algorithm is called "induction" while the process to predict label by the learned model is known as "deduction." The classification model should both fit the input data well and correctly predict the class labels of new unknown records. In literature, there are different models to compute the classification tasks such as decision tree classifiers, neural networks, support vector machines, and so on.

There exist three different types of classification tasks: (i) binary classification; (ii) multiclass classification; and (iii) multilabel classification. Binary classification is the task to classify instances into two mutually exclusive groups or categories (class labels). For example, the problem of churn forecast and spam email detection are two classical problems of binary classification. Multiclass classification requires classifying instances into three or more groups or categories. Therefore, multiclass classifier is trained to predict one from three or more classes for an item. For example, a multiclass classifier could be used to classify some financial operation as high-risk, medium-risk, or low-risk. The model would learn to identify certain features that are associated with each risk level. Multilabel classification is a task that assigns multiple labels to the same instance. This type of task is quite common in medicine where a patient can be associated with a set of symptoms simultaneously, e.g., fever, headache, and cold.

Among the different classification models, **decision tree classifiers** are the most used when dealing with tabula data, given their good trade-off between performance and interpretability. Indeed, decision trees are considered as interpretable models, i.e., machine learning models that do not hide the reasoning behind the final decision on a given instance. This model solves a classification problem by setting a series of carefully crafted questions about the attributes of the instances. Each time an answer is received, a follow-up question is asked until it is possible to decide instances class labels. The questions and answers can be organized into a hierarchical structure called *a decision tree*.

It starts with the root node which describes the first test condition on one of the attributes and assigns each possible outcome to a branch. Each branch may lead to another decision node (internal node with an attribute test condition) or a terminal leaf node which is associated with a class label. A decision tree uses a recursive divide-and-conquer procedure by starting with the whole dataset and repeatedly applying the attribute test conditions to create the *purest* possible subset of records, with respect to the class label, using the available attributes.

An example of a simple decision tree is depicted in Fig. 3.1. This model can classify a financial transaction as fraudulent or legitimate based on various attributes.

The figure reports the following attributes:

- *Transaction amount*: The monetary value of the transaction.
- *Transaction location*: The geographical location where the transaction occurred (e.g., overseas or domestic).
- *Transaction time:* The timestamp indicating the time of the transaction.

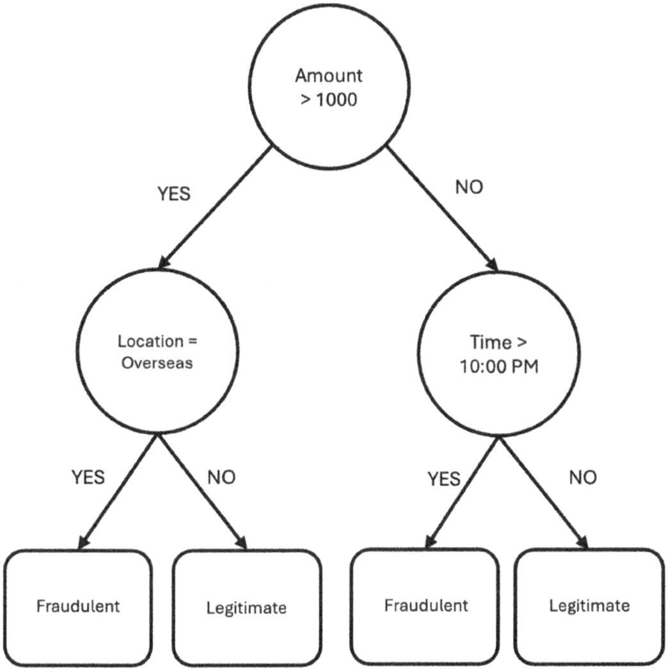

Fig. 3.1 Decision tree classifying financial transactions as fraudulent or legitimate

Analyzing the decision tree we can provide the following interpretation:

- The decision tree begins with a root node asking whether the transaction amount is greater than 1000 euros.
- If the transaction amount exceeds 1000 euros, the tree branches to the left, where it further investigates whether the transaction location is overseas.
- If the transaction is indeed overseas, it is classified as fraudulent.
- If the transaction is domestic, it is labeled as legitimate.
- If the transaction amount is not greater than 1000 euros, the tree branches to the right, where transaction time is tested.
- If the transaction occurs after 10:00 PM, it is classified as fraudulent.
- If the transaction occurs before 10:00 PM, it is deemed legitimate.

We highlight that this is a simplified example for illustrative purposes. In practice, decision trees for fraud detection may involve more complex attribute tests and multiple decision nodes to capture interesting patterns indicative of fraudulent activity.

Another interpretable classifier is the **Naive Bayes classifier**, rooted in Bayesian inference. It is a probabilistic method used for classification tasks across various domains. It is based on the Bayes' theorem, a fundamental concept in statistics that enables us to update our beliefs about the probability of a hypothesis given observed evidence. This theorem provides a mathematical framework for reasoning about uncertainty and making predictions based on available data.

Bayesian inference begins with a prior belief about the likelihood of a hypothesis, which is then updated based on observed evidence to compute the posterior probability of the hypothesis given the data. In the context of classification, the hypothesis represents the class label, and the evidence corresponds to the features associated with each instance. By computing the posterior probabilities for each class label, we can make informed decisions about the most likely class label for a given instance.

The Naive Bayes classifier introduces a simplifying assumption that the features are conditionally independent given the class label. While this assumption may not hold true for all datasets, it allows for efficient computation and often yields surprisingly good results, particularly in text classification tasks. This assumption simplifies the computation of class-conditional probabilities and enables the classifier to scale well to high-dimensional feature spaces.

There are several variants of the Naive Bayes classifier, each making different distributional assumptions about the data. Gaussian Naive Bayes assumes that continuous features follow a Gaussian distribution, making it suitable for datasets with continuous-valued features. Multinomial Naive Bayes, on the other hand, is designed for discrete features, such as word counts in text data. Bernoulli Naive Bayes works with binary feature vectors, assuming a Bernoulli distribution, which is commonly used in binary text classification tasks.

Training a Naive Bayes classifier involves estimating the prior probabilities of each class and the class-conditional probabilities of each feature given the class labels from the training data. Once trained, the classifier can make predictions by computing the posterior probabilities for each class and selecting the class with the highest probability. Despite its simplicity, Naive Bayes classifiers can be surprisingly effective, particularly in scenarios where the independence assumption holds reasonably well.

Naive Bayes classifiers offer several advantages, including simplicity, efficiency, and robustness to irrelevant features. They are easy to implement, require minimal computational resources, and often perform well in practice, especially in text classification tasks. However, they also have limitations, such as the naive assumption of feature independence, which may not hold true for all datasets. Additionally, Naive Bayes classifiers require a relatively large amount of training data to estimate reliable probabilities and may struggle with capturing complex relationships between features.

In conclusion, the Naive Bayes classifier serves as a powerful and versatile tool for classification tasks, offering a balance between simplicity and performance. While it may not be suitable for all scenarios, its effectiveness in various applications, coupled with its ease of implementation and interpretability, makes it a valuable addition to the toolkit of machine learning practitioners.

Another very simple method addressing the classification problem is the **k-Nearest Neighbor classifier** (Cover & Hart, 1967). This approach, differently from the decision tree, does not learn a model but uses directly the training instances when it is necessary to classify the new instance. These types of classifiers are known as *lazy learners*. The basic idea of the k-Nearest Neighbor classifier is to assign the class label to a new instance by looking for the *k training* records which are the most similar to the record to be classified (called *nearest neighbors*) and determining the label as the most frequent label among the nearest neighbors. The drawback of this method is the need to determine the correct value of *k* neighbors to be considered and the computational cost due to the large amount of memory required to store the training data.

Ensemble Models

To improve classification accuracy, alternative classification techniques exploit the opportunity of aggregating prediction of multiple classifiers. These techniques produce models called *ensemble models*. These techniques build a set of base classifiers from training data and classify a new instance considering the vote of each base classifier for the prediction. The general process for constructing an ensemble classifier given a set of data is depicted in Fig. 3.2.

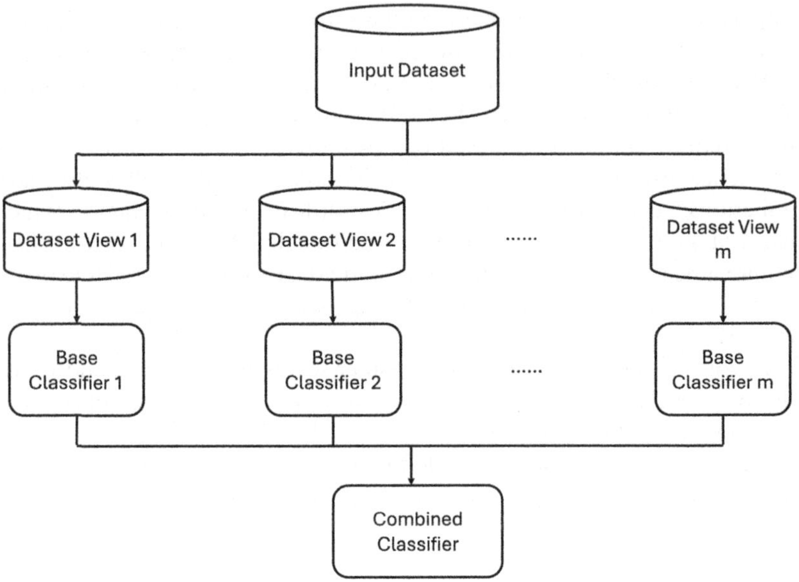

Fig. 3.2 Schema describing the process for learning an ensemble classifier

The basic idea is to create multiple data views starting from the same input data, use each data view for learning a base classifier and then aggregating their prediction when classifying new unlabeled instances. The ensemble of classifiers can be obtained by different approaches. Some methods like bagging and boosting base their process on the manipulation of the training set. They create multiple training sets resampling the original data according to some sampling distribution which determines the probability of an instance to be selected during the sampling. Then, each dataset is used by a learning algorithm for generating a base classifier.

Other techniques like random forest create different datasets by randomly selecting a subset of features from the original dataset. Each dataset then is used for learning a base classifier that in the case of random forest is a decision tree.

In case the number of classes is high it is possible to apply a method that is based on class label manipulation. The basic idea is to transform a multiclass dataset into a binary classification dataset. The class labels are randomly partitioned in two disjoint subsets A and B. The relabeled records are used to train a base classifier. The process of class relabeling and model training is repeated many times with the aim of obtaining different base classifiers. To predict the label of a new instance each base classifier is applied. In case the prediction is A then all the classes belonging to A will receive a vote; while if the prediction is B, all the classes belonging to B will receive a vote. The class with the highest vote will be assigned to the new instance. Ensemble models are often stabler with respect to base classifiers. The aggregation of different base classifiers built on top of various training sets may help the errors due to the variability of training data.

Bagging, also known as *bootstrap aggregating*, is a machine learning ensemble technique that repeatedly samples records with replacement from a dataset according to a uniform probability distribution. Thus, given a training set *D* of size *n*, it generates *m* training sets D_1, D_2, …, D_m. Since the sampling is performed with replacement each training dataset may have duplicated records. Each training dataset is called *bootstrap sample*. Then, the models learned from the *m bootstrap* sample are combined by majority vote on the predictions. Although it is usually applied to decision tree models, it can be used with any type of method.

Bagging improves generalization error by diminishing the variance of the underlying classifiers. The efficacy of bagging is contingent on the stability of the base classifiers. If some base classifier exhibits instability, bagging mitigates errors due to fluctuations in the training data. Conversely, if some base classifier is stable, resilient to minor perturbations in the training set, the ensemble's error strongly depends on the bias in the base classifier. In such cases, bagging might not substantially enhance the performance of the base classifiers and could potentially degrade it. Moreover, since each record has an equal probability of selection, bagging avoids focusing on any specific instance of the training data. This characteristic renders bagging less susceptible to model overfitting, particularly when applied to noisy data.

Boosting is a machine learning ensemble technique able to transform weak learners to strong ones. It is based on the question posed: "Can a set of weak learners create a single strong learner?" A weak learner is a classifier that exhibits only marginal correlation with the true classification, capable of labeling examples slightly better than random guessing. Conversely, a strong learner denotes a classifier that demonstrates arbitrary and substantial correlation with the true classification.

Most of the boosting algorithms rely on an iterative process aimed at learning weak classifiers, incorporating them into the ultimate strong classifier, and dynamically adjusting the distribution of training examples. This adaptation ensures that the base classifiers focus on instances that pose challenges for accurate classification.

In contrast to bagging, where each training example holds equal weight throughout, boosting assigns different weights to individual examples. These weights may be adaptively modified at the conclusion of each boosting round. Misclassified input instances gain a higher weight and instances that are classified correctly lose weight. Thus, future weak learners focus more on the examples that previously weak learners misclassified.

Over the years, numerous implementations of the boosting algorithm have developed, showing differences in two key aspects: (1) the methodology employed for updating the weights of training examples at the end of each boosting round, and (2) the approach used to combine predictions from base classifiers. One of the most popular boosting algorithms is AdaBoost introduced in (Freund & Schapire, 1997). AdaBoost's strength lies in its ability to adaptively prioritize difficult-to-classify instances, progressively improving the model's accuracy by assigning more influence to misclassified examples. This adaptability often leads to superior generalization performance compared to individual weak classifiers.

One limitation of AdaBoost is its sensitivity to noisy data and outliers, as it may assign too much emphasis to these instances. Additionally, it can be prone to overfitting if the weak classifiers are too complex.

Random forest is a category of ensemble methods specifically tailored for decision tree classifiers. It aggregates the predictions of multiple decision trees, generated based on the values of an independent set of random vectors (Breiman, 2001). Unlike the adaptive approach in AdaBoost, random forest employs fixed probability distributions to generate random vectors, introducing randomness into the model-building process. Bagging is a special case of random forest when applied to decision trees. Each decision tree uses a random vector that is generated from some fixed probability distribution. One method involves the random selection of F input features at each node of the decision tree for splitting. Rather than considering all available features, the decision to split a node is made based on this subset of the whole set of features. The tree is then expanded without any pruning, potentially alleviating bias in the resulting tree.

This approach, referred to as Forest-RI (with RI denoting random input selection), results in trees grown based on a selected subset of features, introducing diversity among the trees in the ensemble. After constructing these trees, their predictions are aggregated using a majority voting scheme. To further enhance randomness, bagging can be employed to generate bootstrap samples for Forest-RI, introducing additional diversity during the training process.

Random forest is effective in handling high-dimensional data, capturing complex relationships in the data, and providing robust predictions. Its versatility and performance have made it a popular choice in machine learning.

Neural Network Models

The study of Artificial Neural Networks (ANNs) draws inspiration from the structure and functioning of biological neural systems, particularly the human brain. The basic building blocks of the human brain are neurons, which are interconnected through axons and dendrites. Axons transmit nerve impulses, while dendrites receive these impulses, and the contact points between them, known as synapses, play a crucial role in learning by adjusting the strength of connections.

ANNs mimic this structure in a simplified manner. They consist of interconnected nodes and direct links, with nodes representing artificial neurons and links representing the connections between them. One of the simplest types of ANNs is the *perceptron*.

A perceptron is a binary classifier that takes multiple binary inputs and produces a single binary output. Each input is associated with a weight, which represents the strength or significance of that input. The weights are parameters that the perceptron learns during the training process. This model computes a weighted sum of its input values and applies a threshold to determine the output. The model can be trained to solve classification problems by adjusting the weights of the input connections based on the observed errors in its predictions.

The training process often involves the use of a learning algorithm, such as the perceptron learning rule, to update the weights iteratively. By repeatedly presenting input instances and adjusting the weights based on the errors, the perceptron can learn to classify new, unseen instances. It is important to note that a single-layer perceptron has limitations and can only learn linearly separable instances. To handle more complex tasks, multi-layer perceptron and deeper neural network architectures are often employed. Deeper neural networks will be presented and discussed in Sect. 3.3.

Regression Models

Regression models belong to methods of supervised learning and are used for capturing the relationships between independent and dependent variables, with the main purpose of predicting an outcome which is typically a numerical target. The main goal of a regression model is to reveal patterns that characterize the distribution of data points and exploit them to make accurate predictions for new data points or input values. The most common regression models are the **simple linear regression** model and the **multiple linear regression** model. The first one assumes a linear relationship between a target and a predictor variable. Thus, the model aims at fitting a straight line representing the data points. For example, one might relate the sales and the advertising expenditure and thus, use a linear regression model for predicting the sales based on the amount of advertising expenditure. Before attempting to fit a linear model to observed data, one should first verify the relationship between the observed variables. This does not necessarily imply that one variable *causes* the other, but that there is some significant association between the two variables confirmed by a reasonable measure of correlation. The most common approach for fitting a regression line is the method of *least-squares* which computes the best-fitting line for the observed data point by minimizing the sum of the squares of the vertical deviations from each data point to the line. Note that, in case a data point lies on the fitted line exactly, then its vertical deviation is equal to zero. Since the deviations are squared, then by summing them there are no cancelations between positive and negative values.

Simple linear regression considers that the target, i.e., the dependent variable is explained by only one independent variable. However, sometimes this is not sufficient and to explain a dependent variable becomes fundamental using more than one independent variable. In this case multiple regression models are more suitable for this task. The basic assumption of these models, however, is that there are no very high correlations between the independent variables. They can be seen as an extension of simple linear models.

Unsupervised Machine Learning

Unsupervised machine learning constitutes a crucial branch of machine learning, dedicated to extracting patterns, structures, and knowledge from unlabeled data. Unlike supervised learning, which relies on labeled datasets to train predictive models, unsupervised learning operates in scenarios, in which data lacks predefined categories or target variables. Therefore, the methods belonging to that category can only rely on data characteristics and their relationships for discovering uncovered valuable insights and facilitating data-driven decision-making. Unsupervised learning encompasses a diverse array of techniques and algorithms, each tailored to address specific data analysis tasks. Clustering, association rule mining, and anomaly detection are among the most prominent unsupervised learning methods.

Clustering

Clustering algorithms aim at grouping similar data points together based on predefined similarity metrics, such as distance measures or density-based criteria. Popular clustering approaches include centroid-based clustering, density-based clustering, and hierarchical clustering.

Centroid-based clustering is a class of clustering algorithms that partition data into clusters based on the proximity of data points to cluster centers or centroids. These methods aim to identify representative points (centroids) within the data space and assign data points to the nearest centroid, thereby forming clusters. Among centroid-based clustering algorithms, K-means is one of the most popular and widely used due to its simplicity and efficiency. The essence of K-means clustering lies in its iterative optimization process, aiming at extracting K clusters by minimizing the within-cluster sum of squared distances with an iterative procedure that adjusts cluster centroids. The methodology can be summarized by the following steps:

- Initial centroids: The algorithm randomly selects K points among the points to be grouped and uses them as an initial set of cluster centroids.
- Iterative assignment: Each data point is assigned to the nearest centroid, forming clusters.
- Centroids update: For each cluster the centroid is recomputed averaging the data point within the cluster.

- Convergence: Repeating the assignment and update steps until convergence criteria are met, i.e., when no longer significantly change between iterations exists or when a specified number of iterations is reached.

This algorithm presents some drawbacks. First of all, it is sensitive to the initialization of the centroids indeed, K-means results may vary based on initial centroid positions, thus its application typically requires multiple runs. Also determining the optimal number of K clusters is not trivial and often requires domain expertise or application of heuristic methods. Finally, K-means assumes clusters are spherical and equally sized, which may not hold for complex data distributions.

Density-based clustering is a class of clustering algorithms that partition data into clusters based on the density distribution of data points. These methods operate by identifying dense regions of data points separated by regions with lower density. They are suitable for datasets with irregular or non-convex clusters and, thus typically they enable the discovery of clusters with different sizes and shapes. One of the most popular algorithms of this category is Density-Based Spatial Clustering of Applications with Noise (DBSCAN). It does not require the specification of the number of clusters to be extracted, but it is able to automatically determine it based on the density distribution of the data. DBSCAN, instead, requires some input information for defining the density threshold to be considered and identify for each point its neighbors (close data points). The methodology is based on the following key notions:

- *Core* points: Data points with a sufficient number of neighbors within a specified radius.
- *Border* points: Data points that are reachable from a core point but do not have enough neighbors to be considered core points themselves.
- Noise points: Data points that are not reachable from any core point and do not have enough neighbors to form a cluster.

The algorithm proceeds as follows: for each data point, DBSCAN calculates the number of neighboring points within a radius (required input of the algorithm). If the number of neighbors is greater than or equal to a given threshold, the point is labeled as a core point. Then, for each core point, it recursively expands the cluster by including all reachable points, i.e., points that are not cores but are neighbors of core points. Finally, DBSCAN assigns each point to a cluster based on its core point or connectivity to a core point. Points that are neither core nor border points are labeled as noise.

One of the most important advantages of this method is its robustness to noise and outliers, however, determining input information for defining a good neighborhood and density threshold can be not an easy task for some datasets.

Hierarchical clustering is a category of clustering algorithms which group similar data points into clusters based on their pairwise distances or similarities. These methods construct a hierarchical structure of clusters, allowing for a more complete exploration of the data's underlying structure. Given the hierarchical structure found the resulting clustering is not a partition of the data space but we can have a cluster inside another one. The key idea behind hierarchical clustering is to iteratively merge or split clusters based on their similarity, creating a hierarchical tree-like structure known as a dendrogram (see Fig. 3.3).

This dendrogram provides insights into the relationships between data points and the formation of clusters at different levels of granularity. In the literature, there are two main approaches to hierarchical clustering:

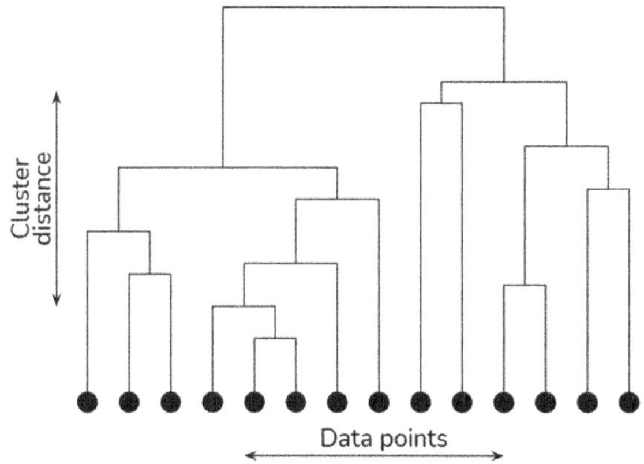

Fig. 3.3 Dendrogram generated by hierarchical clustering

- Agglomerative hierarchical clustering, which is a bottom-up approach, starting with each data point as a separate cluster and iteratively merges the most similar pairs of clusters until all data points belong to a single cluster.
- Divisive hierarchical clustering which applies a top-down approach. It starts with all data points belonging to a single cluster and recursively divides clusters into smaller clusters until each data point is in its own cluster.

In general, divisive clustering is less commonly used in practice due to its computational complexity.

Hierarchical clustering offers several advantages, including its ability to produce a hierarchical representation of the data's structure, its flexibility in handling various types of data and distances/similarities, and its intuitive visualization through dendrograms. Additionally, hierarchical clustering does not require the number of clusters to be predefined, making it suitable for exploratory data analysis.

However, hierarchical clustering also has some limitations, such as its computational complexity, particularly for large datasets, and its sensitivity to the choice of distance metric and linking/merging criteria. Moreover, the interpretation of dendrograms can be subjective, requiring careful consideration of the clustering results.

Clustering analysis has various applications in accounting and auditing. For example, it can be used to assess financial risks by grouping similar transactions, accounts, or entities based on their risk profiles. By clustering financial data, auditors can identify clusters of transactions or accounts that pose a higher risk of financial loss, non-compliance, or fraud, allowing them to prioritize audit procedures and allocate resources more effectively (Chapter 9).

Association Rule Mining

Association rule mining is a well-known technique in data mining and machine learning used to discover interesting patterns, relationships, and associations within large datasets. It is particularly used for discovering hidden relationships between items, events, or variables that occur together frequently.

The primary objective of association rule mining is to identify rules of the form "if X then Y," where X and Y are itemsets, events, or variables. These rules represent strong relationships or associations between different elements in the dataset, providing valuable insights into the underlying patterns and behaviors represented in the data.

The process enabling the association rule mining typically involves two main steps, i.e., first extracting frequent itemsets and then, deriving interesting association rules from frequent itemsets. One of the widely used algorithms for association rule mining is Apriori. The key idea behind the Apriori algorithm is the Apriori principle, which states that if an itemset is frequent, then all its subsets must also be frequent. This principle allows for the efficient pruning of candidate itemsets reducing the computational complexity of finding frequent itemsets.

For extracting frequent itemsets, this algorithm starts by identifying all frequent individual items (singletons) in the data. These items are considered frequent if their occurrence satisfies a minimum frequency threshold. Based on the frequent items generate the candidates of size two and so on. In general, given the frequent itemsets of size k-1 compose them applying a specific strategy for generating itemsets of size k. After generating candidate itemsets, Apriori prunes any candidate itemsets that contain subsets that are not frequent. This pruning step ensures that only potentially frequent itemsets are retained for further evaluation, reducing the search space and computational overhead. Finally, it scans the data to count the frequency of each candidate itemset and discards infrequent ones. This process of itemsets generation and frequency-based filtering is applied until no new frequent itemsets can be generated.

Once all frequent itemsets have been identified, apriori derives association rules from them based on predefined confidence thresholds. Given an association rule "if X then Y," its confidence is the proportion of transactions containing X that also contain Y.

The extracted association rules are evaluated based on metrics such as frequency, confidence, and interestingness to assess their significance and relevance. The most interesting and actionable rules are selected for further analysis and interpretation.

This unsupervised approach finds various applications in accounting and auditing, offering insights into patterns, relationships, and anomalies within financial data. For example, it can provide insights into the relationships between different financial variables and metrics, helping auditors analyze financial statements more effectively. By identifying correlations between financial indicators, auditors can assess the financial health and performance of an organization, identify trends or anomalies, and make informed decisions based on the analysis (Chapter 9).

Anomaly Detection

Anomaly detection, also known as outlier detection, is a critical task in data analysis that focuses on identifying patterns or instances that deviate significantly from the norm within a dataset. Anomalies, or outliers, can represent unusual events, rare occurrences, errors, or potential threats that warrant further investigation. The goal of anomaly detection is to distinguish between normal behavior and abnormal behavior within the data, allowing for timely identification and mitigation of potential risks or issues. These algorithms typically operate under the assumption that anomalies are rare occurrences that differ significantly from the majority of the data points. By leveraging statistical measures, clustering algorithms, or density estimation methods, these techniques can uncover anomalies based solely on the characteristics of the data.

One of the fundamental challenges in unsupervised anomaly detection is distinguishing between normal variation and truly anomalous behavior within the data. This requires techniques capable of capturing the complex and often subtle patterns that may indicate anomalous instances. Furthermore, unsupervised methods must be robust to variations in data distribution, noise, and the presence of multiple types of anomalies.

Three main approaches can be used for addressing the problem of detecting anomalies. Some methods exploit the assessment of statistical properties of the data to identify instances that fall outside expected ranges or exhibit unusual patterns. These methods called statistical methods, involve Z-score normalization, Gaussian distribution modeling, or quantile-based methods.

Other methods exploit clustering algorithms, as the ones presented above, to group similar data points together based on their proximity in the data space. Anomalies are then identified as data points that do not belong to any cluster or belong to small, sparse clusters.

Other interesting methods are those based on density estimation: density-based methods, such as kernel density estimation or local outlier factor (LOF) which estimate the underlying density distribution of the data and identify regions of low density as potential anomalies. Data points located in sparse or isolated regions are flagged as outliers.

Anomaly detection techniques in accounting may help to identify irregularities, errors, or fraudulent activities within financial data. For example, a company can enhance its ability to detect and prevent fraudulent or erroneous expenses, ensuring compliance with company policies and regulatory requirements.

3.3 Deep Learning

Deep learning models represent a class of artificial neural networks that are capable of learning complex patterns and representations from data. These models have gained significant attention and popularity in recent years due to their remarkable ability to automatically discover complex structures and relationships in large-scale datasets.

The core of deep learning is artificial neural networks, presented above, inspired by the structure and function of the human brain's interconnected neurons. Deep learning models leverage deep neural networks, which are neural networks with multiple hidden layers between the input and output layers. These hidden layers enable deep neural networks to learn increasingly abstract and complex representations of the input data as information propagates through the network. By hierarchically composing simple, nonlinear functions learned by each layer, deep neural networks can capture complex patterns and relationships in high-dimensional data.

Deep learning models can be supervised and unsupervised; among the unsupervised we have a new generation of deep learning models called generative models which are able to generate new synthetic but realistic instances.

Before providing more details on the different categories of deep networks, we highlight that their remarkable ability in addressing different tasks is not without challenges and limitations. First, deep networks typically require large amounts of (labeled) training data to learn meaningful representations of the input-output mapping. In case of labeled data are required their acquisition can be expensive, time-consuming, or impractical for certain tasks, especially in certain domains. Moreover, learning deep networks involve numerous hyperparameters, such as learning rate, batch size, network architecture, and regularization parameters, which need to be carefully tuned to achieve optimal performance. Finding the right set of hyperparameters can be challenging and often requires extensive experimentation and computational resources. Last but not the least important issue, deep networks are often referred to as "black-box" models due to their complex and opaque nature, making it difficult to interpret how the model arrives at its predictions or decisions. Lack of interpretability can hinder trust, accountability, and regulatory compliance, particularly in domains where transparency and explanation are important. We will address such issues in Chapter 4.

Supervised Deep Learning Models

Deep networks are primarily used for supervised learning tasks, which involve training a model to learn a mapping (i.e., discriminative function) from input data to output labels based on labeled training examples. In supervised learning, the model is provided with input-output pairs, and the goal is to learn a function that can accurately predict the output labels for new, unseen inputs.

The training process of discriminative deep learning models typically involves two main steps: forward propagation and backpropagation. During forward propagation, input data is fed into the neural network, and information is sequentially processed through each layer to generate predictions or decisions. After forward propagation, the output of the model is compared to the data ground truth using a loss function, which quantifies the difference between the predicted and actual values. Backpropagation involves computing the gradients of the loss function with respect to the model's parameters and using these gradients to update the parameters iteratively via optimization algorithms such as stochastic gradient descent.

There are different architectures of discriminative deep learning models, each tailored to specific types of data and tasks:

- Convolutional Neural Networks are widely used for image analysis and classification.
- Recurrent Neural Networks are well-suited for sequential data processing tasks, such as natural language processing and time series analysis.
- Long Short-Term Memory Networks and Gated Recurrent Units (GRUs) are variants of Recurrent Neural Network designed to capture long-range dependencies in sequential data.

Unsupervised Deep Learning Models and Generative Models

While deep networks are most commonly associated with supervised learning tasks, they are also widely used in unsupervised learning settings, where the goal is to extract meaningful patterns or representations from unlabeled data. Unsupervised learning with deep networks encompasses a variety of techniques and architectures tailored to tasks such as clustering, dimensionality reduction, and generative modeling.

Autoencoders are architectures where the model is trained to reconstruct the input data from a compressed representation called the latent space. They consist of an *encoder* network that maps the input data to the latent space and a *decoder* network that reconstructs the input from the latent representation. By learning to encode and decode the input data, autoencoders effectively capture the underlying structure and features of the data without requiring explicit labels. The learning objective is to minimize the reconstruction error between the input data and the reconstructed output. Therefore, the training process involves feeding the input data into the autoencoder, encoding it into the latent space, decoding it back to the original space, and computing the reconstruction error. This error is then used to update the parameters of the encoder and decoder networks through backpropagation and gradient descent algorithms.

A variant of autoencoders are **Variational Autoencoders (VAEs)** that introduce probabilistic principles to the latent space. Unlike traditional autoencoders, which learn deterministic representations, VAEs learn a probabilistic distribution over the latent space. This enables them to generate new data samples by sampling from the learned distribution, effectively capturing the uncertainty and variability inherent in the data.

In VAEs the encoder network maps the input data to the parameters of a probability distribution in the latent space, typically a Gaussian distribution with a mean and variance. The decoder network, instead, takes samples from the latent space distribution and reconstructs the input data. Unlike traditional autoencoders, which output deterministic reconstructions, VAEs output probabilistic reconstructions that capture the uncertainty in the data.

VAEs are trained using a variational inference approach, where the objective is to maximize the evidence lower bound (ELBO) on the log-likelihood of the data. This involves jointly optimizing two objectives:

- Reconstruction Loss which measures the discrepancy between the input data and the reconstructed output, encouraging the model to generate accurate reconstructions.
- KL Divergence Loss which measures the discrepancy between the learned latent space distribution and a prior distribution, typically a standard Gaussian. This encourages the latent space to follow a simple distribution, facilitating efficient sampling and generation.

In the category of generative models, we can find **Generative Adversarial Networks (GANs)**, where two neural networks, a generator and a discriminator, are trained adversarially. The generator learns to generate synthetic data samples that are indistinguishable from real data, while the discriminator learns to distinguish between real and fake samples. GANs have demonstrated remarkable success in generating realistic images, text, and other types of data. The training process of GANs involves a competitive interplay between the generator and the discriminator. Initially, the discriminator is trained using real data samples from the training set, correctly labeled as *real*, and *fake* data samples generated by the generator, correctly labeled as *fake*. The discriminator improves its ability to distinguish between real and fake data. The generator then takes random noise as input and generates fake data. The discriminator is used to evaluate this fake data. The generator's objective is to generate data that is realistic enough to fool the discriminator into classifying it as real. The training process continues iteratively, with the generator and discriminator improving their abilities over time. Ideally, this process converges to a point where the generator produces realistic data samples that are indistinguishable from real data, and the discriminator cannot reliably differentiate between real and fake data.

Generative models can assist and support many tasks in accounting and auditing. For example, given their ability of generating new synthetic instances these models can be also used for addressing the task of fraud detection or risk management. These because starting from real data they can generate additional data for producing more detailed and complete analyses involving more examples of fraudulent transactions and risk profiles.

Generative Large Language Models

Various generative models have emerged across diverse domains. Textual generative models, for instance, have the ability to generate textual data based on textual or visual inputs (OpenAI, 2023; Google Gemini Team, 2023), while others, known as visual generative models, can produce images or videos using textual and visual inputs (Betker et al., 2023).

Among the textual generative models, we can find a class of language models called "Generative Pre-trained Transformer" (GPT). The category of GPT refers to generative Large Language Models (LLMs) that use deep learning techniques for extensive training with an enormous quantity of data. An example of GPT model is ChatGPT, specifically designed and fine-tuned for conversational usage to produce human-like text response to human requests.

GPT and similar models rely on a transformer architecture enabling the learning of complex patterns and dependencies in text data. During training, they learn from large amounts of text how to predict the next word or sequence of words given the preceding context. Once trained, these models can generate text by sampling from the probability distribution of words conditioned on the input context. Their ability in producing textual data makes them valuable for various natural language processing tasks, including text generation, language translation, summarization, and question answering.

Generative Large Language Models (generative LLMs) like GPT have been widely used in a range of applications, from chatbots and virtual assistants to content generation, code completion, and even creative writing assistance. However, it is essential to note that while LLMs like GPT are powerful generative models, they are primarily based on predictive learning and do not generate entirely new data samples like GANs or VAEs. Generative LLMs are built on the transformer architecture, a deep neural network able to handle sequential data efficiently. The transformer architecture employs self-attention mechanisms to weigh the importance of different words in a sentence by computing attention scores. These scores indicate how much focus the model should give to each word when processing the input sequence. The self-attention mechanism calculates attention scores for each word in the input sequence based on its relationship with every other word in the sequence. This allows the model to capture both local and long-range dependencies between words in a sentence. Words that are semantically or syntactically related are assigned higher attention scores, indicating their importance in understanding the overall meaning of the sentence. Unlike traditional sequential models like RNNs or LSTMs, which have limitations in capturing long-range dependencies due to their sequential nature, the transformer architecture can capture long-range dependencies more effectively through self-attention. This enables the model to understand and process sentences or documents more comprehensively, leading to better performance in tasks such as language understanding, translation, and text generation.

Generative LLMs are typically pre-trained on large corpora of text data using unsupervised learning techniques. During pre-training, the model learns to predict the next word or sequence of words in a sentence based on the preceding context. This process allows the model to capture complex patterns and relationships in language. While pre-training provides a strong foundation, generative LLMs can also be fine-tuned on specific tasks or domains using supervised learning techniques. Fine-tuning allows the model to adapt to the specific characteristics of a given task or dataset, leading to improved performance and better text generation quality.

Generative LLMs have been applied in various fields and industries, including chatbots, virtual assistants, language translation, summarization, question answering, and creative writing. These models have demonstrated impressive capabilities in generating high-quality and contextually relevant text across different domains and languages.

In the field of auditing and accounting generative LLMs can be used in different ways. As an example, they can be very useful for assisting developing effective chatbots working as virtual assistant for auditors providing real-time guidance or answering complex accounting questions.

3.4 Conclusion

This chapter presented an introduction to the different types of artificial intelligence and provides an overview on techniques and models typically exploited by AI-based systems. We discussed the most used supervised and unsupervised machine learning models presenting some examples to show the power of their application in real-world applications. We also discussed deep learning models with a particular focus on generative AI models such as generative large language models. The potential power of AI technologies could improve the quality and efficacy of accounting and auditing processes. Clearly, the application of such AI systems in real-world contexts, where their use could have a significative impact on both human and industrial life, requires guarantees of reliability and the enhancement of user trust on their abilities and their effectiveness.

References

Betker, J., Goh, G., Jing, L., Brooks, T., Wang, J., Li, L., Ouyang, L., Zhuang, J., Lee J., & Guo Y., et al. (2023). Improving image generation with better captions. *Computer Science, 2*(3), 8. https://cdn.openai.com/papers/dall-e-3.pdf

Borges, A. F., Laurindo, F. J., Spínola, M. M., Gonçalves, R. F., & Mattos, C. A. (2020). The strategic use of artificial intelligence in the digital era: Systematic literature review and future research directions. *International Journal of Information Management, 57*(17), 102225

Breiman, L. (2001). Statistical modeling: The two cultures (with comments and a rejoinder by the author). *Statistical Science, 16*(3), 199–231.

Cover, T. M., & Hart, P. E. (1967). Nearest neighbor pattern classifications. *IEEE Transaction on Information Theory, 13*(1), 21–27.

Freund, Y., & Schapire, R. E. (1997). A decision-theoretic generalization of on-line learning and an application to boosting. *Journal of Computer and System Sciences, 55*(1), 119–139.

Google Gemini Team. (2023). *Gemini: A Family of Highly Capable Multimodal Models.*

Huang, M. H., & Rust, R. T. (2018). Artificial intelligence in service. *Journal of Service Research, 21*(2), 155–172.

Mikalef, P., & Gupta, M. (2021). Artificial Intelligence Capability: Conceptualization, measurement calibration, and empirical study on its impact on organizational creativity and firm performance. *Information & Management*, Online. https://doi.org/10.1016/j.im.2021.103434

OED Online. (2019). Oxford University Press. Retrieved from August 15, 2019, from https://www.oed.com/view/Entry/271625?redirectedFrom=artificial+intelligence

OpenAI. (2023). Gpt-4 Technical Report.

OpenAI. (2024). *Sora*. https://openai.com/sora. Accessed 14 March 2024.

REFERENCES

CHAPTER 4

The Need of Trustworthy Artificial Intelligence

Anna Monreale

Although artificial intelligence may positively contribute to the well-being and advancement of our society under different perspectives, the application of AI may arise different ethical and legal challenges. Unfortunately, in a variety of high-stake domains these challenges can jeopardize the trust in the AI systems and thus, they can limit their adoption. Consequently, it becomes fundamental to develop Trustworthy AI. This chapter will discuss ethical and legal requirements such as privacy, fairness, and transparency of AI systems and will overview technological solutions to guarantee those requirements.

4.1 Introduction

The opportunity of learning from big volumes of data has brought several new benefits to different domains and the field of financial and economic accounting and auditing is not an exception. The effectiveness of Deep Learning and Machine Learning has been proven valuable in multiple applications, and their capability to process vast amounts of data, identify patterns, and make predictions presents unprecedented opportunities to enhance the efficiency, accuracy, and reliability of financial and industrial practices.

However, the pervasive use of AI systems based on deep learning and machine learning algorithms that exploit and combine sensitive and

M. Pierotti et al., *Artificial Intelligence in Accounting and Auditing*,
https://doi.org/10.1007/978-3-031-71371-2_4

confidential data raises several concerns. Therefore, opportunities for improvements due to the AI technologies are accompanied by concerns regarding its trustworthiness and ethical implementation.

Trustworthy AI is not merely a technical challenge but a fundamental necessity, because elements such as integrity of financial reporting or reliability of audits cannot be an option. Therefore, it is crucial to ensure that AI systems employed in these fields are transparent, accountable, secure, unbiased, and lawful, i.e., complying with regulations.

Data used for learning such AI systems may contain biases which sometimes are difficult to track or discover when fed into opaque and complex DL models, which raises issues of transparency and explainability. Furthermore, several liability issues arise if the AI system is defective, including mal-practice and thus, liability of users (e.g., auditors and managers), exploiting such AI systems, due to their negligent reliance. The importance of considering the ethical and legal implications of the development and use of AI systems is made evident by the many national and international organizations' recommendations. Some examples are the OECD's recommendations[1] on the *main five values-based principles for the responsible stewardship of trustworthy Artificial Intelligence* signed up by the OECD's 36 member countries, along with Argentina, Brazil, Colombia, Costa Rica, Peru, and Romania, and adopted later in 2019, by G20 Trade Ministers and Digital Economy Ministers; the ethics guidelines for the development trustworthy AI published in 2019 by the High-Level Expert Group on Artificial Intelligence (AI HLEG),[2] the guidelines on regulation of AI released by US administration[3] and the European AI Act[4] regulation, which is the first of its kind in the world.

In this chapter, we first provide an overview on the main aspects related to the very recent AI Act, then we discuss some ethical and legal aspects related to the development of AI technologies with a focus on fairness, privacy, and explainability discussing how to address such aspects from the technical viewpoint.

[1] OECD. Recommendation of the council on artificial intelligence, oecd/legal/0449 (2019).

[2] High-Level Expert Group on AI. The Ethics Guidelines for Trustworthy Artificial Intelligence (AI). https://ec.europa.eu/futurium/en/ai-alliance-consultation (04, 2019).

[3] White House's Office of Science and Technology Policy. Guidance for regulation of artificial intelligence applications. https://www.whitehouse.gov/wp-content/uploads/2020/01/Draft-OMB-Memo-on-Regulation-of-AI-1-7-19.pdf (2019).

[4] https://eur-lex.europa.eu/legal-content/EN/TXT/?uri=CELEX:52021PC0206.

4.2 AI Regulation

Until recently, the field of artificial intelligence (AI) was governed by only a few norms and guidelines. Although numerous documents existed that outlined ethical principles to guide the use of AI systems (Fjeld, 2020; Floridi et al., 2018), there were very few binding and enforceable regulatory acts in place. Moreover, the binding legal acts that did exist were far from comprehensive, primarily addressing privacy issues without covering the broader implications and applications of AI technology.

This regulatory gap has increasingly attracted the attention of experts from various fields, including jurists, computer scientists, and policymakers. Many have criticized the lack of robust legal frameworks, emphasizing the urgent need for more thorough and enforceable regulations to ensure that AI technologies are developed and deployed responsibly. Even representatives from major tech companies have joined the call for more stringent AI regulation, recognizing the potential risks and ethical dilemmas posed by unregulated AI.

Despite a strong consensus on the necessity for regulation, there has been significant debate over the specific characteristics and content of such regulatory measures. The challenge lies in balancing innovation with safety, privacy, and ethical considerations.

In the European Union, this division has been addressed through a lengthy process of consensus-building. The three main bodies involved in the legislative process are the Commission, the Council, and Parliament, which have collaboratively reached an agreement on a specific and wide-ranging text called "AI Act." Their main scope was to establish a comprehensive legal framework that not only addresses privacy concerns but also covers the broader ethical and societal implications of AI, setting a precedent for AI regulation worldwide.

The main characteristic of the AI Act is its risk-based approach, distinguishing between AI systems posing unacceptable, high, limited, and low or minimal risk. Therefore, AI technology can be adopted in case risks are eliminated and mitigated as much as possible.

As evident from the risk categories, the Act explicitly prohibits harmful AI applications and classifies them as AI with "unacceptable risk". Examples of this category are: (i) social scoring systems evaluating or classifying individuals or groups based on social behavior or personal traits, causing detrimental or unfavorable treatment of those people (see the scoring system adopted in China); (ii) manipulative AI distorting behaviors and impairing informed decision-making, causing significant harm, (iii) systems exploiting vulnerabilities related to age, disability, or socio-economic circumstances to distort behavior, causing significant harm.

Some AI systems are considered "High risk" under the AI Act. Examples are AI systems intended to be used: (i) for the recruitment or selection of natural persons; and (ii) in the field of education and vocational training for assessing leaning outcome or determining access or admission or to assign natural persons to educational and vocational training institutions. Since these AI technologies can potentially impact safety and fundamental rights, they must adhere to specific legal requirements before entering the EU market. Providers of such systems must ensure transparency, implement human oversight, and establish a risk assessment system. Additionally, AI technologies are subject to a conformity assessment to verify compliance with these standards. The Act also imposes obligations on general-purpose AI models, such as generative AI, which may be incorporated into various AI systems.

Certain AI systems are considered with low or minimal risk by the Act (e.g., AI-enabled video games and spam filters). These systems must comply with light transparency requirements and are encouraged to adopt voluntary codes of conduct.

4.3 Fairness, Explainability, and Privacy in AI Lifecycle

Each stage of the AI system lifecycle from prototype to real-world application of the AI system requires to pay attention to different ethical and legal issues. The AI HLEG in the guidelines for trustworthy AI identified three stakeholders that should play a role in the AI implementation: developers, deployers (i.e., any organization that uses AI in their products), and end-users. The main four stages for an AI system implementation are described in the following along with practical considerations on the ethical aspects.

Design: In this stage the goals of the application are identified, data is acquired, the architecture of the DL model is chosen. Machine learning engineers should put in place proper safeguards to prevent potential ethical and legal risks. In case of financial and economical accounting data, special attention should be paid to potential risks of direct and indirect confidential and private data disclosure. We address this issue in section "Privacy". In such cases, ML developers should apply the privacy-by-design and security-by-design approach for AI applications considering both the system's functional requirements and its ethical and legal requirements. Moreover, data might contain all sorts of biases (see section "Biases and Fairness"). To prevent discriminatory or unintended adverse outcomes, the following requirements for data collection should be satisfied: (i) training the model on a sufficiently representative dataset; (ii) performing a privacy risk assessment on the data and ensuring data protection; (iii) recording of how and why the data was selected.

Development: In this stage, the AI system is developed validated and tested. Developers need to implement the strategies defined in the previous step to develop an *ethical* model. First, *transparency* must be guaranteed during the whole process. This is crucial to ensure traceability and the correct allocation of liability. In this step, it is important to produce a technical documentation and make data and source code available. This is a good practice also for guaranteeing *reliability* and *reproducibility* of results.

In case machine learning or deep learning models exploited by the AI systems are opaque, complex, and incomprehensible to humans, it becomes mandatory to take into consideration the *explainability* requirement by implementing techniques that help in providing tools for explaining the model behavior or the reason of the model decision as described in section "Explainability".

In this phase, developers should implement protection techniques to mitigate privacy and unfairness risks. As we discuss in sections "Biases and Fairness" and "Privacy", some of them transform data to eliminate risks from training data while others mitigate the risks operating on the learning process of the model. The mitigation strategy is a process that should be focused only on cases where it is necessary to reduce its potential negative impact on the model performance. For identifying the area of intervention, a good practice is performing the mitigation only after assessing the corresponding privacy or unfairness risk.

Deployment and maintenance: In this phase, the AI model is typically embedded in an application and becomes a product placed on the market. The product needs to be monitored and updated if needed. The monitoring activity has to verify that such application is working without degradation of the system performance over time. At the same time, the monitoring activity should also evaluate the system's compliance with the ethical requirements. Indeed, some features of the dataset describing a certain population might undergo a significant data distribution drift over time. Such kind of drift might affect both model performance (e.g., accuracy degradation) and ethical aspects, such as privacy protection degradation or fairness degradation. This monitoring is fundamental because, based on the result of this assessment, the deployers might need to retrain the model.

Usage: In this stage, the final product reaches the end-user who should be aware that it is not an interaction with a human being. Users should also be informed and aware about possible ethical and legal risks derived from the use of that application. Moreover, in this phase, the users need explanations of the model prediction results. Explanations provided to final users can be completely different from explanations provided to developers. In this last case, explanations should help in improving the model and highlight technical issues of the model while in the usage phase explanations need to provide insights to end-users that typically make decision based on the AI assistance.

In the following, we provide a focus on the technical aspects of fairness, explainability, and privacy.

Biases and Fairness

Analyzing the entire process for learning a data-driven AI model, we can identify different types of bias sources. Given a learning process we can distinguish the phase that we call *data collection and preparation* and the phase we call *model construction*.

In the first phase we can identify three types of biases that can produce a biased training dataset and thus, unfair learned model: (i) historical bias, (ii) representation bias, and (iii) measurement bias.

Historical bias exists in the real-world and often reflects human bias and prejudices. It occurs even if data are perfectly sampled because it is derived from past behaviors. Some studies demonstrate that some natural language processing applications (e.g., chatbots, machine translation, speech recognition) are affected by real-world biases, for example about women and ethnic minorities, which are incorporated in the large corpora of text used for the learning process (Garg et al., 2018).

Representation bias occurs when the training data is constructed by sampling data from real world and the samples are under-representing some part of the population. Therefore, the learning process derives a model which fails to generalize well for a subset of the population. In other words, this means that if some types of categories are not represented in the training of the data the model performance for such category will not perform accurately. As an example, consider a model for predicting fraudulent transactions. If the model is learned on top of a training dataset which does not contain fraudulent transactions with low amount or related to specific subjects the model will not have elements for identifying such type of fraudulent operations.

Measurement bias can be introduced in the data preprocessing phase when developers by feature engineering or feature selection define the features and labels to be used in a prediction model. Typically, features are proxies of concepts and behaviors we want to capture which is not directly observable and measured. As an example, "creditworthiness" is an abstract concept that can be measured by a proxy like a credit score. Unfortunately, such proxies can become problematic in case they are poor reflections or generate discrimination among different groups.

In the second phase of *model construction*, we can identify the aggregation bias, the learning bias, and the deployment bias.

Aggregation bias is derived from the wrong assumption that some aggregated measures or data are valid proxies for all the different groups of subjects present in the data, or some trends seen in aggregated data also apply to individual data points.

Unfortunately, aggregation bias can lead to a model that is not optimal for any group, or a model that is fit to the dominant population.

Learning bias occurs when the learning process tries to optimize a specific objective function and amplifies the performance disparities across different subjects represented in the data. As an example, the optimization of the overall model performance (e.g., accuracy) may lead to scarifying the performance on specific sub-groups of instances categories which are underrepresented.

Deployment bias occurs when the model is applied in a context where the assumptions, for example on the data distribution, are not valid anymore or in case model output must be interpreted by human decision-makers, thus despite the good performance of the model, the biased interpretation will lead to generation of new biases that will be injected in the real world.

In order to mitigate the potential biases developers can apply the fairness-by-design approach. Approaches for inscribing fairness requirements in AI models can be categorized into methods reaching fairness by transforming training data (preprocessing-based approaches), and methods reaching fairness by acting on the learning algorithms (in-process-based approaches).

The first type of approach is based on the idea of modifying the training data distribution changing the class labels of selected instances close to the decision boundary by assigning different weights to instances based on their group membership or by carefully sampling from each group. The main goal is to balance the underrepresented and well-represented groups (Kamiran et al., 2011).

This second type of approach modifies the learning task incorporating fairness requirements and constraints by-design into the model. Typically, the fairness requirement is taken into consideration in the model objective function with the goal to find an acceptable balance between model performance and fairness guarantee (Du et al., 2019).

Explainability

The need to understand the reasoning behind AI decision support systems, i.e., explicability, is listed as one of the ethical requirements of the EU guidelines for trustworthy AI[5] and is established by the Article 22 of the GDPR[6] introducing a right to explanation. Moreover, this principle is strongly linked to the transparency requirement mentioned in the AI Act. Most state-of-the-art AI models lack transparency and are often referred to as black boxes. An AI system is considered a black box in case it is based on a complex machine learning or deep learning model, whose outcomes cannot be understood or interpreted simply by examining its internal parameters. This lack of transparency stems from a limited human understanding of the model's internal knowledge representation. Indeed, the increasing complexity of their hierarchical layer structure is not straightforwardly interpretable to human beings. Providing a layer of transparency besides being a legal and ethical requirement, it is also fundamental for increasing human trust in such systems and ensuring their adoption in real-world applications, such as financial accounting and auditing, where domain experts can accept AI assistance only in case,

[5] https://digital-strategy.ec.europa.eu/en/library/ethics-guidelines-trustworthy-ai.

[6] https://eur-lex.europa.eu/legal-content/IT/TXT/?uri=CELEX%3A32016R0679.

they can understand the reasoning leading to the final decision. Only knowing the reasons of a decision humans can provide informed and aware decisions.

There are two ways of reaching the level of transparency: avoiding the use of black boxes and to use inherently interpretable model or applying techniques for explaining black-box AI models (see Fig. 4.1).

In the literature, it is recognized a categorization of explanation methods (Adabi et al., 2018; Bodria et al., 2023; Guidotti et al., 2018, 2021) distinguishing: (i) black-box explanation vs. explanation by design, (ii) global vs. local explanations, and (iii) model-specific vs. model-agnostic explainers. Figure 4.1 illustrates an ontology of the taxonomy categorizing XAI methods.

Explainable by design methods: A model is interpretable if it has the ability to explain or to present in understandable terms to a human the reason of its outcome. For example, a prediction model which classifies a transaction as fraudulent is interpretable if it also explains that the classification is because it is related to an amount of money greater that 1000 euros and the time of the transaction is after 10 PM.

In the literature, there is a small number of models that are recognized as inherently interpretable: linear regression models (section "Ensemble Models"), decision trees, and rules (section "Classification Models") (Freitas, 2014).

The explanation by design consists of designing a comprehensible model over the training data which is *interpretable by design* and returns an explanation besides its prediction. Thus, the basic idea is to use this interpretable model directly into the AI system (Rudin, 2019).

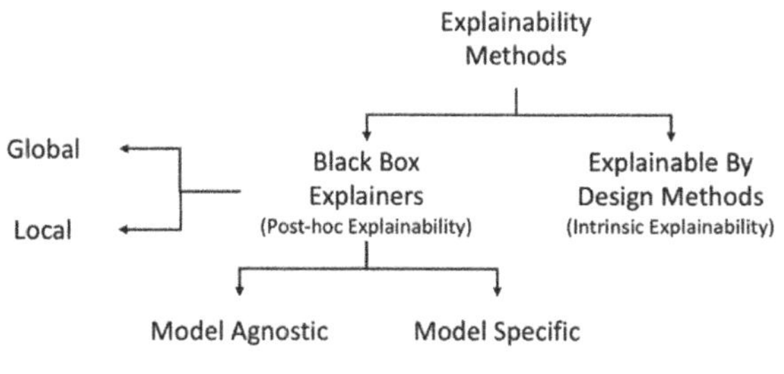

Fig. 4.1 Ontology of the taxonomy of XAI methods (Guidotti et al., 2021)

Deep Learning models are usually preferred to inherently interpretable ones because they capture highly nonlinear relationships between the variables without requiring a feature engineering process and therefore yield higher accuracy with less effort.

Black-Box explanation methods: In case an AI with a black-box model is used, explanation methods are based on the idea to couple the AI model with an explanation model able to interpret the black-box decisions. Thus, starting from a training dataset, the black-box explanation idea is to maintain the high performance of the black-box model used by the AI and to use an explanation method to derive an explanation by reasoning over the black-box model and training data. This kind of approach is the one more addressed nowadays in the XAI research field (Guidotti et al., 2022; Ribeiro et al., 2016, 2018).

In case of black-box explanation methods, we distinguish between *global* and *local* explanations depending on scope of the explanation. **Global explanations** aim to provide an understanding of the entire logic of a model used by an AI system. This involves creating an interpretable model that approximates the behavior of the black-box model, providing a comprehensive interpretation of any possible decision it might make. Achieving global explanations is challenging and is usually feasible only for AI systems working with relational data.

Local explanations, on the other hand, focus on interpreting the decision for a specific instance. Instead of explaining the entire logic underlying the AI model, a local explanation aims to clarify the reasons for the prediction related to a particular input instance. This is typically done by approximating the black-box behavior within the "neighborhood" of the instance being analyzed, meaning it focuses only on similar instances. In such a neighborhood, it is easier to approximate the AI with a simple and understandable model, making the local explanation more accessible and specific to the instance in question (Guidotti et al., 2022; Ribeiro et al., 2016).

Both local and global explanations can be provided by an explanation method which can be m*odel-specific* or *model-agnostic*. *Model-specific* methods are tailored to a particular AI model while model-agnostic explanation methods can explain any black-box AI model. In other words, an explanation method is considered model-specific or not generalizable (Martens et al., 2007) if it can only be used to interpret certain types of black-box models. For instance, if an explanation approach is designed to interpret a random forest and relies on the concept of distance between trees, it cannot be used to explain the predictions of a neural network. Conversely, an explanation method is model-agnostic when it can be applied regardless of the black-box model being explained. In this case, the internal characteristics of the AI are not utilized to build the interpretable model that approximates the black-box behavior.

Privacy

Financial and economical accounting data can be exploited by firm's managers for predictive analysis or by auditors to "digitize" their analytical capabilities exploiting AI models introduced in Chapter 3. The AI models clearly can offer the ability to learn specialized models from data of multiple clients. However, regulations require auditors and managers to adhere to strict data confidentiality and data protection measures.

Learning machine learning and deep learning models from this kind of data while being compliant with data protection regulations poses some challenges. In such a sensitive context, it becomes mandatory to apply the privacy by design principle introduced by Ann Cavoukian in the 1990s (Cavoukian, 2000) and successively elaborated in (Monreale et al., 2014). The main idea is to inscribe the privacy and confidentiality requirements in the design of the knowledge discovery process to balance privacy protection and data utility. This aspect is fundamental because data and model quality, often reduced by mitigation techniques, should be preserved as much as possible to avoid a negative impact on the financial/economic analyses leading to inaccurate and wrong decisions. In DL, the privacy confidentiality risks can arise in two different phases: during the development stage of the AI model, since the training phase of the model requires access to the data which have to be anonymized to avoid client's re-identification (Sweeney, 2002) and during deployment stage when the model is applied to classify new unknown instances.

During the deployment stage a privacy breach occurs in case the adversary can infer sensitive and competitive information about specific clients represented in the training data of the AI model. Some learning algorithms presented in Chapter 3 generate models that explicitly store feature vectors representing data used during the learning phase. Therefore, this type of model (e.g., SVM, neural networks) should be avoided without considering a protection strategy against the reconstruction attacks. Such attacks aim at reconstructing the raw private and confidential data by using apriori knowledge of the feature vectors and accessing the model. However, this kind of privacy issues may arise even if no explicit feature vector is stored in the learned model (e.g., neural networks). In this case, we can have two different attack settings: the adversary can access the ML/DL model and its parameters, or the adversary can only query the model without having access to it. Two attack models can act in these settings: model inversion attacks and membership attacks. In the former the goal of the adversary is to infer some sensitive features used in the learning phase by knowing a set of features and observing the output of the queried model. This attack however does not necessarily entail a privacy breach of a specific client represented in the training data, but allows the adversary the inference of information, about a specific category of clients. This collective breach derives from the use of statistics about a specific population during the learning of the AI model (McSherry, 2016). The problem is due to the fact that given a record and a model, a model inversion attack provides the same result in case the record was used to train the model and when it was not used. In the literature, advanced version of model inversion attacks have been deeply studied to recover training data from deep neural networks in both centralized learning setting (Fredrikson et al., 2015) and collaborative learning setting (Hitaj et al., 2017).

Advanced model inversion attacks have been proposed to recover images from deep neural networks in various learning environments. These attacks have demonstrated effectiveness in both centralized learning settings, where a single entity has complete control over the training data and model, and collaborative learning settings, where multiple entities share control and contribute data and computational resources to the training process. In centralized learning, the attacks exploit the model's access to the comprehensive dataset, while in collaborative learning, they leverage the distributed nature of the data and computations to reconstruct private images.

An attack that infers the presence or not of a specific record in the training data of a ML model is the membership inference attack (Shokri et al., 2017). This attack can directly lead to a privacy breach because, for example, knowing that a certain client is represented in the training data of a ML model associated with a specific confidential information can reveal that the client under analysis has a particular sensitive information. The typical assumptions of this attack are that the adversary's knowledge is the record, and the adversary can only query the ML model and receive the model's output. The membership inference attack exploits ML to attack a ML model. It is based on the learning of a ML model that distinguishes the target model's behavior on the training inputs from its behavior on the inputs that it did not contain in the training data. The method creates multiple shadow models, i.e., ML models that imitate the target model's behavior on known training datasets (typically synthetically generated). By using these models, it is possible to construct a set of data labeled as "in" or "out" of the training dataset. The "in" value derives from the high confidence of the prediction of the target model for an instance. On the labeled dataset it is possible to train the attack model. Recent variants of the membership attack relax the assumption of accessing the prediction confidence and define specific mechanisms for approximate such information with well-defined scores (Monreale et al., 2023).

Most of privacy-preserving techniques for DL are focused on differentially private approaches, sometimes combined with a collaborative training of a model allowing multiple parties to contribute to the learning process without releasing their private data in its original form. Differential privacy is especially effective in preventing membership inference attacks and limiting the effect of model inversion attacks.

Differential privacy (Dwork, 2006) requires that the presence or not of a record in the data does not significantly affect the outcome of any analysis. It ensures a client in the data that any privacy breach will not be due to its participation in the dataset because anything that is learnable from the data with its record is also learnable from the one without its record. For any two datasets D and D' differing in a single record and any output O of function f, $Prob\{f(D) \in O\} \leq e^{\varepsilon} \times Prob\{f(D') \in O\}$. The parameter ε is the privacy budget and controls the trade-off between the accuracy of the differentially private f and the privacy loss. A smaller ε means more noise and stronger privacy level. A fundamental concept of differential privacy is the global sensitivity of the function f that helps in determining the utility of the function f. Techniques for achieving differential privacy are based on randomization of their input. Some approaches first learn a model on original data, and then use either the exponential or Laplacian mechanism to generate a noisy model.

4.4 Conclusion

In this chapter, we discussed the importance to consider ethical and legal compliance of AI systems. We first provided an overview on the European AI Act and then we focused our analysis on the ethical and legal requirements of fairness, explainability, and privacy. The idea of this chapter is also describing in which moment of the AI cycle fairness, privacy, and explainability issues should be assessed and eventually mitigated. We highlighted that from the technical viewpoint in the computer science literature there are well-studied technical solutions for providing trustworthy predictive AI while the study of such aspects for generative AI is almost unexplored. Considering privacy, fairness, and explainability in Generative AI is challenging. Traditional predictive models are easier to audit for fairness, but the same is not valid for Large Language Models. Some researchers recently have highlighted that the state-of-the-art frameworks on fairness either does not logically extend to LLMs or presents a notion of fairness that is intractable for LLMs (Anthis et al., 2024). As a consequence, it is necessary to develop targeted definitions of fairness and employ training algorithms that can enforce these definitions.

Concerning privacy, the capabilities of generative AI raise concerns beyond the traditional data leaks. As an example, sensitive and confidential information in LLMs may be revealed publicly through disclosure in queries or responses of an LLM. Some recent work attempted to address the problem of privacy in LLM (Yan et al., 2024) but we think a deeper analysis and study is necessary to reach solid results in the context of traditional predictive models. Finally, concerning explainability recent works highlight explainability techniques for predictive AI are not directly applicable to generative AI. This because for these particular models it is necessary to take into consideration new dimensions and properties such as the wide diversity of users that potentially can use such systems, interactivity in the explanation phase, and other important aspects (Schneider, 2024).

References

Anthis, J., Lum, K., Ekstrand, M., Feller, A., D'Amour, A., & Tan, C. (2024). The Impossibility of Fair LLMs. arXiv preprint arXiv:2406.03198.

Bodria, F., Giannotti, F., Guidotti, R., et al. (2023). Benchmarking and survey of explanation methods for black box models. *Data Mining and Knowledge Discovery, 37*, 1719–1778. https://doi.org/10.1007/s10618-023-00933-9

Cavoukian, A. (2000). *Privacy design principles for an integrated justice system.* Working Paper. www.ipc.on.ca/index.asp?layid=86%26;fid1=318

Du, M., Liu, N., Yang, F., & Hu, X. (2019). Learning credible deep neural networks with rationale regularization. In J. Wang, K. Shim, & X. Wu (Eds.), *IEEE International Conference on Data Mining, ICDM* (pp. 150–159).

Dwork, C. (2006). Differential privacy. In M. Bugliesi, B. Preneel, V. Sassone, & I. Wegener (Eds.), *Automata, languages and programming, 33rd international colloquium, ICALP 2006, Proceedings, Part II* (Vol. 4052, pp. 1–12). Lecture Notes in Computer Science. Springer.

Fredrikson, M., Jha, S., & Ristenpart, T. (2015). Model inversion attacks that exploit confidence information and basic countermeasures. In *ACM Conference on Computer and Communications Security* (pp. 1322–1333). ACM.

Fjeld, J., et al. (2020). *Principled artificial intelligence: Mapping consensus in ethical and rights-based approaches to principles for AI Berkman klein center research publication, No. 2020–2021.* https://doi.org/10.2139/ssrn.3518482

Floridi, L., et al. (2018). AI4People—An ethical framework for a good Ai society: Opportunities, risks, principles, and recommendations. *Minds & Machines, 28*, 689–707. https://doi.org/10.1007/s11023-018-9482-5

Freitas, A. A. (2014). Comprehensible classification models: A position paper. *ACM SIGKDD Explorations Newsletter, 15*(1), 1–10.

Garg, N., Schiebinger, L., Jurafsky, D., & Zou, J. (2018). Word embeddings quantify 100 years of gender and ethnic stereotypes. *Proceedings of the National Academy of Sciences, 115*(16), E3635–E3644.

Guidotti, R., Monreale, A., Pedreschi, D., & Giannotti, F. (2021). Principles of explainable artificial intelligence. In M. Sayed-Mouchaweh (Eds.), *Explainable AI within the digital transformation and cyber physical systems.* Springer. https://doi.org/10.1007/978-3-030-76409-8_2

Guidotti, R., Monreale, A., Ruggieri, S., et al. (2022). Stable and actionable explanations of black-box models through factual and counterfactual rules. *Data Mining Knowledge Discovery.* https://doi.org/10.1007/s10618-022-00878-5

Guidotti, R., Monreale, A., Ruggieri, S., Turini, F., Giannotti, F., & Pedreschi, D. (2018). A survey of methods for explaining black box models. *ACM Computing Surveys (CSUR), 51*(5), 1–42.

Hitaj, B., Ateniese, G., & Perez-Cruz, F. (2017). Deep models under the gan: Information leakage from collaborative deep learning. In *ACM SIGSAC Conference on computer and communications security* (pp. 603–618).

Kamiran, F., & Calders, T. (2011). Data preprocessing techniques for classification without discrimination. *Knowledge and Information Systems, 33*(1), 1–33.

Martens, D., Baesens, B., Van Gestel, T., & Vanthienen, J. (2007). Comprehensible credit scoring models using rule extraction from support vector machines. *European Journal of Operational Research, 183*(3), 1466–1476.

McSherry, F. (2016). *Statistical inference considered harmful*. https://github.com/frankmcsherry/blog/blob/master/posts/2016-06-14

Monreale, A., Naretto, F., & Rizzo, S. (2023). Agnostic label-only membership inference attack. In S. Li, M. Manulis, & A. Miyaji (Eds.), *Network and system security. NSS 2023*. Lecture Notes in Computer Science, Vol. 13983. Springer. https://doi.org/10.1007/978-3-031-39828-5_14

Monreale, A., Rinzivillo, S., Pratesi, F., Giannotti, F., & Pedreschi, D. (2014). Privacy-by-design in big data analytics and social mining. *EPJ DATA Science, 3*(1), 10.

Ribeiro, M. T., Singh, S., & Guestrin, C. (2016). Why should I trust you? Explaining the predictions of any classifier. In *Proceedings of the 22nd ACM SIGKDD international conference on knowledge discovery and data mining* (pp. 1135–1144). ACM.

Ribeiro, M. T., Singh, S., & Guestrin, C. (2018). Anchors: High-precision model-agnostic explanations. In *Thirty-second AAAI conference on artificial intelligence*.

Rudin, C. (2019). Stop explaining black box machine learning models for high stakes decisions and use interpretable models instead. *Nature Machine Intelligence, 1*(5), 206–215.

Schneider, J. (2024). *Explainable generative AI (GenXAI): A survey, conceptualization, and research agenda*. arXiv preprint arXiv:2404.09554

Shokri, R., Stronati, M., Song, C., & Shmatikov, V. (2017). Membership inference attacks against machine learning models. In *IEEE Symposium on Security and Privacy* (pp. 3–18).

Sweeney, L. (2002). K-anonymity: A model for protecting privacy. *International Journal of Uncertainty, Fuzziness and Knowledge-Based Systems, 10*(5), 557–570.

Yan, B., Li, K., Xu, M., Dong, Y., Zhang, Y., Ren, Z., & Cheng, X. (2024). *On protecting the data privacy of large language models (llms): A survey*. arXiv preprint arXiv:2403.05156

CHAPTER 5

Artificial Intelligence to Support Business Decisions

Federica De Santis

5.1 Introduction

In the digital age, companies are increasingly required to speed-up their decision-making processes and to exhibit flexibility and innovative capabilities in order for them to adequately respond to the growing dynamism of competitive environments, as well as to meet rapidly evolving customers' demand (Baabdullah, 2024; Cao et al., 2021).[1] The so-called digital age started more than a decade ago from the convergence of two intertwined phenomena. On the one hand, huge volumes of data being generated faster than ever from a variety of internal and external sources, in both structured and unstructured forms, became available (McAfee et al., 2012). On the other, the substantive advancements in computer science led to an unprecedented increase in computer power and processing capacity, resulting in an acceleration of technological progresses, which includes the development of new AI techniques[2] (Borges et al., 2021; Reinsel et al., 2018).

[1] See Chapter 1 for further analysis of the changes in the companies' competitive landscape and in their data ecosystem.

[2] See Chapter 3 for a more in-depth examination of technologies related to artificial intelligence.

M. Pierotti et al., *Artificial Intelligence in Accounting and Auditing*,
https://doi.org/10.1007/978-3-031-71371-2_5

In this background, a growing number of companies from almost every industry are motivated to adopt new technologies, and particularly AI-related technologies, mainly because of their disruptive potential and their ability to stimulate transformative thinking (Agrawal & Kirkland, 2018; Borges et al., 2021; Davenport & Ronanki, 2018). As several academics and practitioners underline, AI complements business data analytics with advanced techniques, such as machine learning, neural network and deep learning to collect, process, interpret, and learn from data to provide companies with diagnostic, descriptive, predictive, and prescriptive outcomes (Davenport & Ronanki, 2018; Kaplan & Haenlein, 2019; Rana et al., 2022). Furthermore, recent developments of AI technologies lead to the emergence of so-called generative AI (GenAI) tools such as ChatGPT from OpenAI or CoPilot from Microsoft that have the potential to "take over certain roles traditionally held by humans, such as copywriting, answering customer service inquiries, writing news reports, and creating legal documents" (Agrawal et al., 2022).

Stemming from these considerations, this chapter delves into the transformative impact of AI on data-driven decision-making processes within organizations. It begins by presenting the history and evolution of the application of AI in business contexts, then highlights the resulting opportunities and challenges. The chapter then explores the technical, operational, and ethical hurdles companies face in managing vast amounts of data, while also discussing the benefits of real-time analytics. Finally, we present a summary of key points and future directions for leveraging AI in gaining a competitive edge.

5.2 History and Evolution of Artificial Intelligence in Business Contexts

The history and evolution of AI in business contexts can be traced by means of significant milestones, starting from early theoretical works to the modern application of sophisticated AI algorithms in various business processes (Collins et al., 2021).

The concept of AI dates back to ancient myths and stories about artificial beings endowed with human intelligence (Turner, 2018). However, the term "Artificial Intelligence" was formally coined in 1956 by John McCarthy during the Dartmouth Conference, which is considered the founding event of AI as a field, as "the science and engineering of making intelligent machines" (Collins et al., 2021, p. 2). Early AI research focused on symbolic reasoning and problem-solving, with pioneers like Alan Turing and Marvin Minsky contributing foundational theories and models, and was labeled as strong AI. These knowledge-based AI systems were effective in solving narrow-domain problems, by examining parameters identified in advance by human experts and reaching a solution about the appropriate action to take in each specific situation in the form of "if–then-else." Such systems, however, lacked learning capabilities, so that they were not able to generalize the solutions they reached to new situations and domains (Deng, 2018). Despite the early optimism, therefore, initial AI applications such as the natural language-processing computer program ELIZA (Weizenbaum, 1983) and other as rules-based expert systems showed many breaches and misjudgments. These pioneering systems proved difficult to scale and were limited by the computational power available at the time. Businesses saw limited practical applications, primarily confined to academic and governmental research. This resulted in recurring periods of reduced funding and interest on AI, known as "AI winters," mainly due to unmet expectations (Russell & Norvig, 2016).

During the 1980s a new "AI spring" begun, with a resurgence in the interest on AI and the emergence of expert systems, aimed at mimic human experts' decision-making capabilities. These systems found applications in several domains, such as medical diagnosis, financial analysis, and process control. Companies like IBM and Digital Equipment Corporation began to commercialize AI technologies, leading to a new wave of investments and applications in business contexts (Nilsson, 2009). Notwithstanding the success of expert systems, another "AI winter" occurred in the late 1980s and early 1990s, mainly attributable to the high cost of deployment and maintenance of such systems, and to their inability to handle uncertain or incomplete situations. Therefore, businesses again grew skeptical about AI's potential, and investments in such technology dropped (Crevier, 1993).

With the emergence of machine learning techniques during the 1990s, the field of AI experienced a paradigm shift. During this rising wave of AI, engineers focused on statistical models or simple neural networks as underlying engines that automatically learned or tuned its parameters using the training data so that these algorithms became capable of handling uncertainty and of generalizing well from one condition to another, and from one domain to another (Murphy, 2012; Nilsson, 2009). We now call such algorithms as shallow machine learning, as they lack the abstractions that nowadays data scientists construct by means of "deep" or multiple-layer representations of data in artificial neural networks or cognitive learning algorithms (Deng, 2018). The increase in computational power and the availability of larger datasets enabled business to adopt AI in areas such as customer relationship management (CRM) and fraud detection (Fawcett & Provost, 1997; Peppard, 2000).

Even though the shallow machine learning models performed much better than the pioneering expert systems, they were far from human-level performance, mainly because they do not have the sufficiently large capacity to absorb the huge amount of training data. Further, the learning algorithms, methods, and computing infrastructures were not powerful enough (Deng, 2018, p. 174). As mentioned in the Introduction section, the convergence of the Big Data revolution and the advancements in computing power during the 2010s gave rise to a new era for AI in business. AI technologies like deep learning, neural networks, and natural language processing (NLP) became mainstream, allowing businesses to harness vast amounts of data for actionable insights. Companies like Google, Amazon, and IBM began to offer AI-as-a-Service (AIaaS), making sophisticated AI tools accessible to businesses of all sizes. Applications expanded to include customer service automation (chatbots), predictive analytics, and personalized recommendations (Davenport & Ronanki, 2018).

Despite we are now witnessing the most durable "AI spring," there remain significant challenges (Deng, 2018), and the focus of engineers and data scientists is shifting toward making AI more interpretable (Corbucci et al., 2023; Zhang et al., 2022), ethical (Lehner et al., 2022; Trotta et al., 2023), and aligned with business strategy (Keding, 2021). AI technologies are now crucial to digital transformation initiatives, enhancing efficiency, and competitive advantage (McKinsey, 2024), since they have not only improved organizations' ability to make predictions, but have also substantially reduced the cost of making predictions (Agrawal & Kirkland, 2018; Duan et al., 2019). This means that AI can enhance decision-making, stimulate business model innovation, reinvent business ecosystems, and remake customer experience (Duan et al., 2019).

The ongoing advancements in AI, such as reinforcement learning, autonomous systems, and GenAI, continue to push the boundaries of what is possible in business applications. According to McKinsey's survey on the state of AI adoption in early 2024 (McKinsey, 2024), 72% of organizations adopts AI in at least one function, up from 55% in 2023, and 65% of companies uses GenAI, up from 33% in the previous year (McKinsey, 2024). Similarly, Gartner's 2024 technology trend survey points out that, by 2026, more than 80% of enterprises will have used GenAI-enabled applications in production environments, up from less than 5% in 2023 (Gartner, 2023). As Agrawal et al. (2022) state, "the genie is not going back into the bottle. The forward march of technology will continue, and we must harness the new capabilities to benefit society." It becomes essential to provide a better understanding on what new systems can be built with these new tools and how humans and machines can work together (Miller, 2018).

5.3 Artificial Intelligence Applications in Decision-Making Processes

Classic literature on organizational decision-making posits that every decision is based on the availability of data and information that organizations, managers, and professionals can turn into actionable knowledge (Galbraith, 1968; Simon, 1944). In a dynamic and competitive environment, rationality, rather than intuition, becomes the critical driver of decision-making aimed at achieving business success (Bertini, 1990). In such a scenario, information production should be a systematic and ongoing process that necessarily precedes decision-making and is integrally embedded within the management system. This represents the intelligence of the company, as management oversees, supervises, controls, and corrects all its activities. The management system is the unique source of ideas, choices, and decisions that form the very foundation of the business's existence (Bertini, 1990). These statements maintain their validity also in the so-called digital era. Despite the data deluge we are witnessing (Reinsel et al., 2018), Big Data is "worthless in a vacuum" (De Santis, 2018). To enable such evidence-based decision-making, organizations need efficient processes to turn high volumes of fast-moving and diverse data into meaningful insights (Gandomi & Haider, 2015, p. 140), basing on the assumption that "data is a record, information is a message and knowledge is a model (of how something works)" (Bhimani & Willcocks, 2014, p. 471).

The use of cutting-edge digital technologies significantly transforms the manner in which businesses are run to become more agile, customer-oriented, and effective in an attempt to improve innovativeness and promote economic growth (Ardito et al., 2021; De Santis & D'Onza,

2021). By examining AI's history we observed that this technology and its application in business contexts has experienced "success cycles and periods of mistaken optimism" (Borges et al., 2021, p. 1). While AI-based solutions have long been utilized to automate routine tasks in operations and logistics, the enthusiasm academics and practitioners are showing for AI reached its peak during the last decade, and particularly with the advent of GenAI (Constantiou et al., 2024). The opportunity to exploit extensive computing power combined with the availability of unprecedented volumes of structured and mostly unstructured data flowing in real-time makes AI algorithms able to accomplish more complex and non-routine tasks that require cognitive capabilities, such as making judgments, sensing emotions, and driving processes (Al-Surmi et al., 2022; Benbya et al., 2020; Brynjolfsson & Mcafee, 2017; Cao et al., 2021; McAfee et al., 2012). Consequently, it is anticipated that future managerial decision-making processes will involve a combined effort of humans and machines (Haesevoets et al., 2021; Jarrahi, 2018).

Organizations have now access to hidden insights from data to improve decision-making and knowledge management and to help employees boost their analytic and creative thinking (Brock & von Wangenheim, 2019; Wilson & Daugherty, 2018). However, the potential benefits of using AI in organizational decision-making "can only be realized if human decision-makers accept the use of AI" (Cao et al., 2021, p. 1).

Theoretical Foundations on AI's Adoption in Business Contexts

Since the development of the earliest AI applications, academics have proposed numerous conceptual and research models to explain factors and motivation that can foster or hinder the adoption of AI technologies in organizations (see Table 5.1 for a summary of these theories).

During the first "AI spring," Rogers (1962) developed the *Theory of diffusion of innovations* (DOI) to explain how, why, and at what rate new ideas and technologies spread. This theory posits that five key factors mostly influence technology adoption, namely: Relative advantage, compatibility, complexity, trialability, and observability. Consequently, innovations that are perceived as advantageous, compatible with existing values, simple to use, trialable, and observable are more likely to be adopted. Moreover, DOI theory also categorizes technology adopters into five segments: innovators, early adopters, early majority, late majority, and laggards. This theory has been applied to various fields, and mostly

Table 5.1 Main theories on technology adoption

Theory *Proponent(s)*	*Key concepts*	*Focus on technology adoption*
Diffusion of Innovations (DOI) Rogers (1962)	Relative advantage, compatibility, complexity, trialability, observability, adopter categories	Spread of innovations and factors influencing adoption
Theory of Planned Behavior (TPB) Ajzen (1985)	Attitudes, subjective norms, perceived behavioral control, behavioral intentions	Predicting and understanding behaviors, including technology adoption
Social Cognitive Theory (SCT) Bandura and Cervone (1986)	Observational learning, self-efficacy, outcome expectations, reciprocal determinism	Social influence and personal factors in technology adoption
Technology Acceptance Model (TAM) Davis (1989)	Perceived usefulness, perceived ease of use, behavioral intention, system use	Determinants of technology acceptance and usage
Technology-Organization-Environment (TOE) Framework Tornatzky and Fleischer (1990)	Technological context, organizational context, environmental context	Factors from three contexts influencing technology adoption
Resource-Based View (RBV) Wernerfelt (1984)	Valuable, rare, inimitable, non-substitutable resources, organizational capabilities	Internal resources and capabilities as determinants of technology adoption
Institutional Theory Dimaggio and Powell (1983)	Mimetic, coercive, normative pressures, legitimacy	Influence of institutions and regulatory systems on organizational behavior and technology adoption
Unified Theory of Acceptance and Use of Technology (UTAUT) Venkatesh et al. (2003)	Performance expectancy, effort expectancy, social influence, facilitating conditions, moderators	Integrating elements from multiple models to explain user intentions and behaviors regarding technology use

Source Author's own elaboration

by marketing practitioners, to understand how technologies, including AI, diffuse through organizations and societies.

The *Theory of Planned Behavior* (TPB) (Ajzen, 1991) was first proposed in 1985 as an adaptation of the earlier Theory of Reasoned

Action (TRA) proposed by Fishbein and Ajzen (1975). This posits that attitudes toward behavior, subjective norms, and perceived behavioral control influence behavioral intentions, which in turn predict actual behavior. Perceived behavioral control, in fact, relates to people's perception of how easy or difficult is to carry out a desired behavior. TPB has been used over time to predict a wide range of behaviors, including technology adoption (e.g., Kumari & Devi, 2023; White Baker et al., 2007). In the context of AI, factors such as self-efficacy and perceived control over AI usage can represent significant predictors of adoption intentions.

Bandura and Cervone (1986) also contributed to this stream of research by proposing the *Social Cognitive Theory* (SCT), which posits that behavior is influenced by personal factors, behavioral patterns, and environmental influences through reciprocal determinism. According to SCT, therefore, self-efficacy and outcome expectations are the most influential factors in technology adoption. Specifically, users' expectations in terms of both performance-related and personally beneficial outcomes influence their behavior, and self-efficacy, i.e., "the assessment of one's ability to carry out the curses of action necessary to deal with potential scenarios" (Bandura & Cervone, 1986) influences the expectations for both kind of outcomes (Gupta et al., 2024).

In 1989 Davis introduced the Technology Acceptance Model (TAM) as an extension of Fishbein and Ajzen's TRA. According to the TAM, perceived usefulness and perceived ease of use are the primary determinants of technology acceptance, where the former represents extent to which someone thinks that utilizing a specific technology would be beneficial, while perceived ease of use is regarded to as the degree to which a person believes that using a specific technology is effortless (Davis, 1989). Over time, scholars proposed potential extension of the original TAM by adding other constructs capable of influencing users' attitudes toward technology. By considering also job relevance, subjective norm, image, output quality, and result demonstrability, Venkatesh and Davis (2000) developed the so-called TAM2. Later on Venkatesh and Bala (2008) also developed the TAM3, which also considers the impact of perceived enjoyment and computer anxiety on the adoption of a new technology. Overall, TAM and its extensions has been widely validated across various contexts, including Internet banking and mobile commerce (Gupta et al., 2024).

During the 1980s and the 1990s, other theories were developed to explain the factors that stimulate organizational change, though not strictly limited to changes due to technological innovation. Specifically, we can trace back to this line of research the *Resource-Based View* of the firm (RBV) (Wernerfelt, 1984) and the Institutional Theory (Dimaggio & Powell, 1983). The RBV posits that organizations gain competitive advantage by utilizing a set of valuable, rare, imperfectly imitable, and non-substitutable organizational resources. More in detail, an organization's resources comprise tangible and intangible assets, such as managerial skills, organizational procedures and routines, and information and knowledge (Barney, 1991). In its subsequent developments, the RBV has been a relevant theoretical perspective in understanding how investments in information technology generate value and enable firms to attain performance gains (Mikalef & Gupta, 2021). Accordingly, RBV theorists point out that the adoption of digital technologies, such as data analytics and AI, can constitute a new source of competitive advantage due to its potential to maximize the use of key resources, including data and knowledge derived from open innovation (Arias-Pérez et al., 2023). In the context of AI, indeed, RBV emphasizes the importance of organizational capabilities, such as data infrastructure, skilled personnel, and innovation culture. Studies have shown that firms with stronger resources and capabilities are more likely to adopt and benefit from AI technologies (Bharadwaj, 2000).

Institutional Theory (Dimaggio & Powell, 1983) can be applied as reference theory to understand technology adoption. According to its proponents, Institutional Theory explores how institutions (e.g., cultural norms, regulatory systems, and competitive environments) influence the behavior of individuals and organizations. In fact, a firm gains legitimacy by conforming to three external forces: mimetic, which refers to copying successful firms; normative, which relates to actions deemed desirable and appropriate by professionals or stakeholders in a particular business context; and coercive, which refers to regulation (Arias-Pérez et al., 2023, p. 1793). With specific regards to technology adoption, Institutional Theory posits that also this process is driven by the need to conform to institutional pressures, including mimetic, coercive, and normative pressures. Thus, these theoretical foundations can be applied to understand how regulatory requirements, industry standards, and competitive pressures influence (i.e., foster or inhibit) firms' AI adoption (Currie, 2012; Lai et al., 2006).

One of the most widespread theories on the adoption of new technologies in business contexts in the *Technological, organizational, and environmental* (TOE) *framework* developed by Tornatzky and Fleischer

(1990). The TOE framework posits that technological, organizational, and environmental contexts influence technology adoption, where technological context includes the characteristics of the technology itself in terms of its superiority over alternative options, the organizational context encompasses the resources, processes, and structure of the organization, and the environmental context involves the external environment, including industry characteristics, market structure, and regulatory environment (Tornatzky et al., 1990). This way, the TOE framework provides a comprehensive view of the factors affecting businesses' technology adoption decisions (Gupta et al., 2024).

More recently, Venkatesh et al. (2003) developed the *Unified Theory of Acceptance and Use of Technology* (UTAUT) by integrating eight earlier models, including TAM, TRA, and the TPB. The proponents of UTAUT identify four key factors to explain the probability of technology adoption: Performance expectancy (i.e., a technology's ability to improve job performance), effort expectancy (i.e., level of ease associated with the using technology), social influence (i.e., the influence other people's beliefs exert on technology adoption), and facilitating conditions (i.e., the ability of firms' organizational and technological infrastructure in supporting the use of technology). These key factors are then moderated by four further elements: Gender, age, experience, and voluntariness of use. The UTAUT has been used to study the adoption of various technologies, including AI, highlighting the importance of contextual factors as it allowed to recognize a significant variance in user intentions and behavior under the voluntary condition (Venkatesh et al., 2003).

All the theoretical frameworks presented above provide academics and practitioners with interpretive lenses through which it is possible to explain technology adoption and diffusion. Academics, however, highlight that there is still a scant of research on developing theoretical models aimed at understanding the factors that can influence an individual's technology avoidance intention (Cao et al., 2021). In recent times, therefore, some scholars entered this field of research by offering promising theories. Specifically, we refer to the Technology Threat Avoidance Theory (TTAT) developed by Liang and Xue (2009) and to the Integrated AI Acceptance-Avoidance Model (IAAAM) proposed by Cao et al. (2021). Within the TTAT model, the core constructs that directly influence IT users' avoidance motivation are perceived technology threats and effectiveness, as well as the costs and self-efficacy associated with safeguarding measures. This motivation subsequently affects their avoidance behavior.

According to TTAT, users' threat perceptions are shaped by the perceived likelihood of the threat occurring, the perceived severity of its negative consequences, and the interaction between these factors (Liang & Xue, 2009).

Finally, the IAAAM draws from UTAUT and TTAT to "understand the factors that influence managers' attitudes and behavioral intentions" toward the use of AI in decision-making processes (Cao et al., 2021, p. 11). In so doing, the authors proposed and tested three distinct group of factors as capable of: technology acceptance (facilitating conditions, peer influence, performance expectancy, effort expectancy, attitude, and intention to use), technology threat avoidance (perceived threat in terms of perceived severity and perceived susceptibility), and concerns of personal development and wellbeing.

Artificial Intelligence for Operational, Tactical, and Strategic Decisions

According to classical literature on organizational decision-making (Anthony, 1965), business decisions can be classified into three distinct categories: Operational, tactical, and strategic decisions in relation to the different levels of managerial responsibility. Business decisions have been also classified by Simon (1979) basing on their structure as: Structured, semi-structured, and unstructured decisions.

Strategic decisions are mainly designed to answer for the long-term integrity of the organization, as they are assumed to define the goals and nature of the organization. The assumption of these decisions is the truly entrepreneurial aspect of management (Bertini, 1990) where, for example, the decision to move to a related area of activity is made. The variety of possible actions, the need for information from external sources, and the application of criteria based on general business goals rather than specific organizational concerns have resulted in these decisions commonly being labeled as unstructured (Simon, 1979). When dealing with tactical decisions, we are in the management control domain, where strategic goals are interpreted and translated into targets and operating criteria, thus making decision-making processes quite clearly bounded by the decisions assumed at the strategic level (Edwards et al., 2000). Therefore, tactical decisions are usually referred to as more structured that strategic ones. At the operational control level, the decisions involved are even more precise and limited in range, being concerned with managing the firm's day-to-day activities according to the criteria already established at the strategic and (mostly) at the management control level. These decisions tend to be still more structured, relying mainly on information that come from the inside of the organization, and specifically from the transactions processing systems (Anthony, 1965; Simon, 1979) (Fig. 5.1).

Edwards et al. (2000) conducted on-field experiments to analyze the roles of expert systems, one of the earliest forms of AI, in organizations and their effectiveness in relation to the different decision-making levels and decisions' structure. The results of their study revealed that expert systems were highly effective in replacing decision-makers to automate operational decisions, and particularly they allowed significant improvements in decision-making efficiency. Contrastively, these systems showed limitations when used to substitute humans in assuming unstructured, strategic decisions. When used to assist managers in taking decisions, thus following an augmentation approach, instead, expert systems proved their effectiveness as they allowed better decision at all three decision-making levels. However, such effectiveness manifested itself only through their users and not necessarily in terms of time reductions. Further, the users

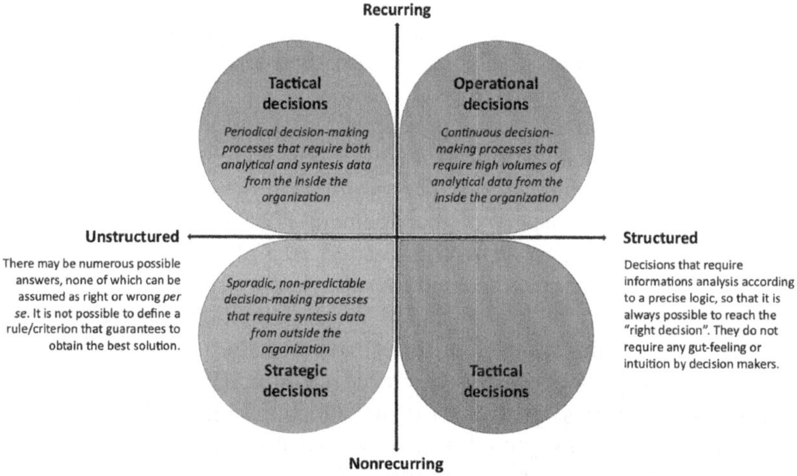

Fig. 5.1 Types of decisions in business contexts (*Source* Author's own elaboration)

of expert systems used with a supporting role did not believe that they had learned from using the system.

Over the last twenty years, AI technology's progresses made it possible for algorithms to perform more complex tasks that require cognitive capabilities (Duan et al., 2019), thus opening new opportunities for improving decision-making efficiency and effectiveness. In this respect, Davenport and Ronaki (2018) distinguished among three categories:

- *Cognitive Process Automation*, that exploit Robotic Process Automation to automate back-office administrative and financial activities.
- *Cognitive Insights*, that consist in using machine learning algorithms to detect patterns in data and interpret their meaning.
- *Cognitive engagement*, that refers to the use of machine learning and GenAI tools such as natural language processing chatbots or intelligent agents to involve customers, employees, and other stakeholders.

The vast abundance of AI-based tools and algorithms, combined with the ever-increasing growth in data availability, opens new opportunities to enhance business decisions. With reference to strategic planning, which we know is mostly characterized by unstructured and nonrecurring decisions, AI provides managers with the possibility to analyze large datasets to predict market trends, customer behavior, and potential risks (Agrawal & Kirkland, 2018). Further, AI provides data-driven insights that support strategic decisions, improving the accuracy and reliability of forecasts (Brynjolfsson & Mcafee, 2017). However, these opportunities come with distinctive challenges, mainly attributable to the costs of investing in AI, in terms of technological infrastructure, talent, and maintenance (Fountaine et al., 2019).

Regarding management control or tactical decisions, AI can optimize resource allocation, helping managers to improve efficiency and reduce costs (Davenport & Ronanki, 2018). Moreover, AI systems can continuously monitor and analyze performance metrics, providing real-time feedback to managers (Ransbotham et al., 2017). However, integrating AI with legacy systems can be complex and time-consuming (Barton & Court, 2012). Moreover, there is often a shortage of skilled personnel who can manage and interpret AI systems (Bughin et al., 2018).

From an operational perspective, it is well known that AI technologies are highly effective in automating repetitive, low-judgmental, and structured tasks with high precision and efficiency, thus reducing human error and freeing up employees for higher-value work (Chui et al., 2016; Manyika et al., 2017). Nevertheless, the use of AI also presents some risks and challenges for operational decision-making. Specifically, over-reliance on AI can lead to operational disruptions if the technology fails (Makridakis, 2017). Further, academic and practitioners have expressed concerns about the risk of job displacement and algorithmic bias (Dwivedi et al., 2021; Frey & Osborne, 2017; Varsha, 2023).

The Automation-Augmentation Debate

The use of AI to make decisions has been one of the most important applications in AI history (Duan et al., 2019). We know that AI applications are now able to perform tasks that require cognition and that were typically associated with human intelligence (Lichtenthaler, 2018; Wilson & Daugherty, 2018). This implies that extracting value from AI investments should not be taken for granted, since employees may show negative or positive mindset toward AI, depending on the specific situation at hand (Borges et al., 2021; Lichtenthaler, 2019). Since its first wave, practitioners and academics used to contest and dispute AI's use by individuals as well as in business contexts (Cao et al., 2021; Duan et al., 2019). Several commentators are still concerned about AI's "dark side," in terms of its potentially disastrous implications and impact on humans and society (Dwivedi et al., 2021; Jarrahi, 2018; Shrestha et al., 2019). Over time, scholars have proposed different classifications and interpretive frameworks intended to explain what roles AI plays in decision-making process, as well as what posture human employees adopt when confronted with the opportunity to use AI algorithms (Cao et al., 2021; Dwivedi et al., 2021; Lichtenthaler, 2019).

Since the beginning of this debate, there was always the unresolved question of whether AI were supposed to completely substitute human decision-makers, or to replace them for just a part of their job, or rather to augment decision-makers (Cao et al., 2021). Bader and his colleagues were pioneers in proposing a framework suggesting that AI, in the form of knowledge-based systems, can act in six different roles in its relationship to humans: assistant, critic, second opinion, expert consultant, tutor, and automaton (Bader et al., 1988, p. 271). Following a similar vein, Davenport and Kirby (2016), Raisch and Krakowski (2021), and Krakowski et al. (2023) propose an approach to integrate humans and AI that distinguishes between an automation approach and an augmentation approach to algorithmic decision-making. When decision processes are automated through AI, humans do note exert any control on algorithm's outcomes, so that they remain "out-of-the-loop." When AI augment decision-making processes, humans remain "in-the-loop" and algorithms are used to support human decisions (Langer & Landers, 2021).

Daugherty and Wilson (2018) contribute to this stream of literature by proposing a further distinction between three types of AI augmentation capabilities, namely amplification, interaction, and embodiment. With *amplification* tools, AI analyzes huge volumes of data, often in real-time, to provide companies with unprecedented data-driven insights, thus significantly overcoming human brain's analytics capabilities. Some examples of how AI can amplify humans' job can be found in product development. So, Kartell, an Italian design company established in 1949, launched in 2018 its first chair model entirely developed by the cooperation between an AI algorithm and a famous designer, Philippe Stark (Bellizzi, 2019). As Stark pointed out,[3] "*everything started from a question posed to the AI: would you know how to rest our body using the least amount of material? And Artificial Intelligence, without any culture and memories, without influence, responded only with intelligence, its artificial intelligence allowing us to design the first chair outside of our brain, our habits and how we are used to thinking. A new, unlimited world therefore opens up before us.*" A similar experience was that of the Elbo chair, developed in 2016 by the designers Arthur Harsuvanakit and Brittany Presten who collaborated with Dreamcatcher, Autodesk's generative design CAD system to spin out potential design solutions they might not think of. Also in this case, the use of AI resulted in a product with 18 percent less material than the model the designers started with, and that shows fewer signs of stress in its joints (Rhodes, 2016).

In the case of *interaction*, AI tools employ advanced interfaces such as natural language processing to facilitate interactions between people or on behalf of people (Daugherty & Wilson, 2018). An example of AI as an interaction agent is the case study reported by Presti et al. (2023). The authors presented the case of an Italian manufacturing company that,

[3] https://makerfairerome.eu/it/da-kartell-la-prima-sedia-creata-con-lintelligenza-artificiale/.

through the application of a sensor system on the machinery sold to customers, developed a software enabling its customers to dynamically interact with the machinery. This interaction allows for scheduled maintenance based on the operating parameters of the machines, constant performance monitoring to prevent downtime, and access to a variety of predictive and diagnostic tools useful for finding effective real-time solutions to potential machinery's malfunctions.

The third category of human–machine collaboration is *embodiment*. As compared to amplification and interaction where AI interfaces seem almost invisible, embodiment usually occurs in tangible, physical spaces. Embodiment deals with physical augmentation and consists in combining AI with sensors, motors, and actuators that allow robots to share workspace with humans and engage in physically collaborative work, like package-carrying autonomous carts, and drones that deliver medicine. The robots Amazon uses in its warehouses are a good example of this type of collaboration. These robots carry shelves full of merchandise to the human workers, who plucks the items off the shelves and puts them in a box to ship without needing to walk miles a day to retrieve them for packaging (Daugherty & Wilson, 2018).

Despite various attempts to clearly distinguish among different approaches to innovate decision-making process with AI, scholars seem to unanimously reach the conclusion that when humans and machines work together, organizations can reach significant performance improvements (Wilson & Daugherty, 2018), thus suggesting that establishing a synergy between humans and machines constitutes the best way of introducing AI in business decision-making processes (Haesevoets et al., 2021; Jarrahi, 2018). This view is also consistent with Davenport and Harris' (2007) and Davenport and Kirby's (2016) suggestion of a symbiotic enhancement approach to the use of AI in organizations. All these contributions seem to suggest the need for companies to prefer an augmentation approach to AI over an automation one (Miller, 2018).

More recently, some authors proposed a different perspective trying to solve the automation vs. augmentation debate, according to which "automation and augmentation are not only separable and conflicting but in fact fundamentally interdependent" (Raisch & Krakowski, 2021, p. 203). Consistently with this view, Agrawal et al. (2017) posit that "AI will substantially raise the value of human judgment." Despite the greater efficiency and effectiveness of machines in making predictions will lead AI to substitute for human prediction in decision-making, machines' predictions are simultaneously complement to human judgment. As a consequence, the more the use of AI will make predictions faster and cheaper, the more the need to exercise human judgment. To summarize, these recent points of view stress out that "automation and augmentation are not good or evil per se" (Raisch & Krakowski, 2021, p. 203), as more often augmentation constitutes both the driver and outcome of automation and the two approaches to AI's use develop and fold into one another across space and time. Following a temporal perspective, augmentation often results from a co-evolutionary process during which managers use an augmentation approach to further explore complex tasks that are difficult to automate. In so doing, managers learn from machines and machines learn from humans through an iterative process, where humans and machines interact to learn new rules or create models and improve them over time. According to a spatial perspective, in fact, managerial processes represent a sequence of tasks in which automation and augmentation can co-exists. When organizations automate a task that was formerly reserved for humans, this change could affect the adjacent human tasks and lead managers to start interacting with AI, thus implying the augmentation of such adjacent tasks (Raisch & Krakowski, 2021).

To summarize, research demonstrated that "the technology's greater power is in complementing and augmenting human capabilities" (Daugherty & Wilson, 2018, p. 13). Firms adopting AI technologies achieve the most significant improvements "when humans and machines work together," since this collaborative intelligence is able to enhance both AI and humans' complementary strengths (Wilson & Daugherty, 2018, p. 5). This is what Daugherty and Wilson (2018) called "the missing middle," where humans and machines do not fight each other for a job but act as symbiotic partners that push each other to better performance. Therefore, as Agrawal et al. (2022) underline, "the question is not whether AI will be good enough to take on more cognitive tasks but rather how we'll adapt," and the key to answer this question is "figuring out how to redesign our economic systems to fully engage the working population. That will require system solutions that don't just shift the same tasks between people and machines [...] but disrupting old ways of doing things and generating new ones." In the so-called missing-middle indeed, "companies can reimagine their business processes to take advantage of collaborative teams of humans working alongside machines" (Daugherty & Wilson, 2018, p. 15).

Challenges and Future Trends of Using AI for Business Decisions

As we look toward the future, several emerging trends and innovations in AI are poised to revolutionize decision-making processes within organizations. These advancements promise to enhance the capabilities of AI systems, making them more integrated, intelligent, and indispensable in business contexts (Bughin et al., 2018; Dwivedi et al., 2021). Simultaneously, the use of AI to enhance business decisions still brings distinctive challenges (Duan et al., 2019; Trotta et al., 2023). These can range from data management risks such as data privacy, bias, or intellectual property infringement to model management risks, which tend to focus on inaccurate output or lack of explainability. A third big risk category is security and incorrect use (McKinsey, 2024).

Data Quality and Issues in Data Management

The use of every technology solution in business contexts, including AI, should always start from a thorough consideration of data quality and availability. In fact, the accuracy and reliability of AI's suggestions depend heavily on the quality of input data (Davenport, 2018; Sayyadi, 2024). Managers must recognize their crucial role in ensuring data quality (Rana et al., 2022; Xu et al., 2002), since many businesses still struggle with incomplete datasets, data silos, and issues like consistency, deduplication, and completeness, which make developing accurate predictive models challenging (Fan & Geerts, 2022; Sayyadi, 2024).

Since the earliest applications of Big Data analytics to enhance decision-making processes at all levels (i.e., strategic, tactical, and operational), the "quality vs. quantity" dilemma has represented one of the most relevant and pervasive threats for organizations aiming at transforming their business according to a data-driven perspective (Bhimani & Willcocks, 2014; De Santis, 2018). The use of poor quality or inappropriate data can be harmful for the firm, as results of data processing fail in assisting managers to assume reasonable and successful decisions, thus causing a waste of organizational resources (De Santis & Presti, 2018).

Over time, several commentators have underlined that to ensure the quality of input data through efficient data management and sound procedures for data extraction, transformation, and loading constitute one of the most influential critical success factors for AI projects (Merhi, 2023).

AI Integration with Legacy Systems

Integration refers to the AI systems' capability to interact with existing systems and databases "to collect, aggregate, store, and use accurate data" (Merhi, 2023, p. 4). The quality of the input data directly impacts the final output of AI systems, making integration a crucial factor for successful AI implementation. Davenport (2018, pp. 34–35) reports the results of a survey conducted with "cognitive aware" executives, 47% of whom affirmed that they found extremely difficult to integrate cognitive projects with existing processes and systems. The survey also revealed that it is often easier to design a model than to exploit it, precisely because of the complexity of embedding it in an existing system. Organizations must effectively manage the integration between AI systems, as well as their integration with other currently implemented information systems, through the use of enterprise information integration and/or enterprise application integration systems (Merhi, 2023).

Transparency and Interpretability. Looking for Explainable AI (XAI)

As AI systems become more complex, the need for transparency and interpretability in AI-driven decisions is growing, since the opacity that surrounds AI design is causing increasing concerns for stakeholders (Balasubramanian et al., 2022; Fosso Wamba & Queiroz, 2023). Transparency of AI models refers to their ability or inability to explain how they reach decisions (Davenport, 2018; Van Lent et al., 2004). To address transparency issues, the concept of Explainable AI (XAI) has recently emerged, with reference to AI models aimed at making algorithmic decisions more understandable to humans by providing clear explanations of how conclusions are reached (Adadi & Berrada, 2018). This is crucial for building trust in AI systems, particularly in high-stakes domains such as healthcare, finance, and legal services. In this respect, Davenport (2018) underlines that, due to a certain degree of variability in the need for transparency, companies can classify AI projects accordingly and focus much on ensuring transparency for those that involve regulators' or customers' needs. For example, the General Data Protection Regulation (GDPR) issued by the European Union in 2018 states that individuals affected by computer-based decisions have "right to an explanation," i.e., they have a right to know why and how the decision was made. That could significantly hinder the use of less transparent technologies such as deep learning, and could favor other techniques, though considerable effort will be required in the future to tackle the challenges and open issues with XAI (Adadi & Berrada, 2018).

AI Hallucination and Biases

Several scholars discuss about the risk of AI biases, such as the gender bias experienced by Apple,[4] the African American defendant bias by COMPAS (Varsha, 2023), or flawed hiring algorithms (Davenport, 2018). When dealing with possible AI biases, the risk is twofold. First, the algorithm may have hidden biases due to poor data quality in the training dataset, thus regardless of the intent of the designer. This is the case, for example, of an algorithm that learns which job applicants to accept for an interview that perpetrates gender, racial, or other prejudices that affected human recruiting decisions in the past, as these decisions constitute the historical dataset used to train the system (Brynjolfsson & Mcafee, 2017). The second risk relates to the characteristics of AI systems, that work according to statistical truth rather than to literal truth. This means that the learning capabilities of algorithms manifest themselves as the ability of computing "more correct" solutions as additional data become available (Lindebaum et al., 2020). The "correctness" of the solutions proposed by AI is defined basing on their predictive accuracy, i.e., in relation to historical data. This means that it becomes challenging, if not impossible, to ensure that a AI system will work in all cases—especially in situations that weren't represented in the training data (Brynjolfsson & Mcafee, 2017). Balasubramanian et al. (2022) describe this phenomenon as "algorithmic myopia" or reduction in routine diversity.

It would be harmful for AI initiatives' success to ignore such possibilities of algorithmic biases, as this would prevent organizations from experiencing the benefits of more objective and data-driven approaches to decision-making. To avoid such problems, possible while not exhaustive solutions relates to: increasing algorithms' transparency, thus reducing the "black-boxing" effect, preventing the introduction of variables or features susceptible of creating biases, and trying not to focus the system on a single business metric or outcome (Davenport, 2018).

[4] https://www.bbc.com/news/business-50365609.

Ethical and Legal Concerns

Ananny (2016) identifies three approaches to understand the ethics of technologies: The first one related to policy and regulations, the second one referred to anticipating ethical concerns, and the third one focuses on the values and beliefs of technologists themselves. According to a regulatory approach, technologies' development and use should be constrained by standards and ethical rules aimed at "punishing errors, teaching best practices, and preventing future failures" (Ananny, 2016, p. 95).

The anticipatory approach starts from assuming the value neutrality of AI (Du & Xie, 2021), according to which "AI has no cultural or ethical background" (Khogali & Mekid, 2023, p. 9). By adopting this view, the users of technology, through their decision processes, are the only responsible for any ethical or unethical actions and outcomes without any potential influence of technological tools, which cannot be considered as morally good or bad per se (Du & Xie, 2021).

Following the third approach, commentators recognize that technologies actually embed ethical values and are able to significantly influence human beings' ethical decision-making (Gaggioli et al., 2017; Wallach & Allen, 2010). Products embedding AI technologies cam thus actively affect their users, by changing how they perceive and act in the world, and also the way they interact with each other (Du & Xie, 2021).

Overall, dealing with AI ethics mainly relates to ensuring that organizations using data-driven decision-making processes avoid doing any harm to the societies and economies in which they operate. This implies that "there are a variety of ethical gray areas when it comes to technology deployment generally and AI in particular" (Daugherty & Wilson, 2018) and that companies should ask themselves whether the AI systems they use are free from biases, and whether they treat all groups equally, with specific reference to more vulnerable ones (Davenport, 2018; Varsha, 2023). Actually, ethical issues arise even before any action is recommended or performed by the AI system, with privacy being reported as one of the main ethical considerations behind AI implementation (Benbya et al., 2020). Moreover, the ever-increasing ubiquity of AI in business and social contexts, with data collection expanding from explicit interactions between the firm and the customer, to include the customers' social and home life, via personal wearables and other Internet-enabled devices, can make AI's use going unchecked and unchallenged, thus rising ethical and reputational threats (Canhoto & Clear, 2020).

In such scenario, scholars underline the need to design and develop an ethical reference framework to regulate the scientific use of AI applications in decision-making, so that it would be possible to consider and address what can negatively affect the level of justice among individuals or increase the threats for individuals and their future (Baabdullah, 2024). The ongoing initiatives to create a cutting-edge technological environment must take carefully into account these issues to fully reap the benefits of AI applications. In this respect, AI technologies must follow several ethical principles, such as transparency, reliability, and fairness and their responsible development must move from the introduction of human values into AI, the promotion of openness, and the commitment of humans and machines working together (Du & Xie, 2021; Khogali & Mekid, 2023).

This position calls governments into action in the first place. Governments' role is considered crucial for tackling the ethical concerns and legal challenges, particularly those related to the responsibility for and the explainability of decisions made by autonomous AI system (Duan et al., 2019).

5.4 Conclusions

This chapter provided an in-depth overview of the potentialities and challenges of integrating AI technologies into businesses' decision-making processes. The analysis of academic and professional contributions on this topic highlighted that to successfully reap the benefits of such integration, companies must first invest in robust AI infrastructure, that includes not only advanced hardware and software solutions but mostly the development of skilled and confident employees capable of implementing and managing AI technologies (Daugherty & Wilson, 2018). In this regard, the analysis of the automation vs. augmentation debate underlined that fostering collaboration between humans and AI would lead to enhanced decision-making processes and better performance. This entails designing AI systems that complement human skills rather than replace them, so that both AI and humans' complementary strengths can be enhanced (Davenport & Kirby, 2016; Wilson & Daugherty, 2018). This is what Daugherty and Wilson (2018) called "the missing middle," where humans and machines do not fight each other for a job but act as symbiotic partners that push each other to better performance.

Moreover, organizations should focus on developing comprehensive data governance frameworks. These frameworks must address data quality, security, privacy, and ethical considerations. The European Union's General Data Protection Regulation (GDPR) and similar regulations worldwide underscore the importance of adhering to stringent data protection standards. Implementing strong governance practices not only ensures compliance but also builds trust with stakeholders both within and outside the organization and outside (Abraham et al., 2019). Finally, businesses must stay vigilant about emerging AI trends and innovations to maintain a competitive edge in the current environmental turbulence (Chatterjee et al., 2021; Mikalef & Gupta, 2021).

Summarizing, by investing in AI infrastructure, fostering a data-driven culture, implementing robust governance frameworks, stimulating human-AI collaboration, and staying attuned to emerging trends, organizations can effectively harness the potential of AI. These strategies will not only enhance decision-making processes but also drive innovation and sustain competitive advantage in the evolving business landscape.

References

Abraham, R., Schneider, J., & Vom Brocke, J. (2019). Data governance: A conceptual framework, structured review, and research agenda. *International Journal of Information Management, 49*, 424–438. https://doi.org/10.1016/j.ijinfomgt.2019.07.008

Adadi, A., & Berrada, M. (2018). Peeking inside the black-box: A survey on explainable artificial intelligence (XAI). *IEEE Access, 6*, 52138–52160. https://doi.org/10.1109/ACCESS.2018.2870052

Agrawal, A., Gans, J., & Goldfarb, A. (2017, luglio 26). How AI will change the way we make decisions. *Harvard Business Review*. https://hbr.org/2017/07/how-ai-will-change-the-way-we-make-decisions

Agrawal, A., Gans, J., & Goldfarb, A. (2022, dicembre 12). ChatGPT and how AI disrupts Industries. *Harvard Business Review*. https://hbr.org/2022/12/chatgpt-and-how-ai-disrupts-industries

Agrawal, A., & Kirkland, R. (2018). The economics of artificial intelligence. *McKinsey Quarterly, 3*, 102–108.

Ajzen, I. (1991). The theory of planned behavior. *Organizational Behavior and Human Decision Processes, 50*(2), 179–211. https://doi.org/10.1016/0749-5978(91)90020-T

Al-Surmi, A., Bashiri, M., & Koliousis, I. (2022). AI based decision making: Combining strategies to improve operational performance. *International*

Journal of Production Research, 60(14), 4464–4486. https://doi.org/10.1080/00207543.2021.1966540

Ananny, M. (2016). Toward an ethics of algorithms: Convening, observation, probability, and timeliness. *Science, Technology, & Human Values, 41*(1), 93–117. https://doi.org/10.1177/0162243915606523

Anthony, R. N. (1965). *Planning and control systems: A framework for analysis*. Harvard University Press.

Ardito, L., Cerchione, R., Mazzola, E., & Raguseo, E. (2021). Industry 4.0 transition: A systematic literature review combining the absorptive capacity theory and the data–information–knowledge hierarchy. *Journal of Knowledge Management, 26*(9), 2222–2254. https://doi.org/10.1108/JKM-04-2021-0325

Arias-Pérez, J., Chacón-Henao, J., & López-Zapata, E. (2023). Unlocking agility: Trapped in the antagonism between co-innovation in digital platforms, business analytics capability and external pressure for AI adoption? *Business Process Management Journal, 29*(6), 1791–1809. https://doi.org/10.1108/BPMJ-10-2022-0484

Baabdullah, A. M. (2024). The precursors of AI adoption in business: Towards an efficient decision-making and functional performance. *International Journal of Information Management, 75*, 102745. https://doi.org/10.1016/j.ijinfomgt.2023.102745

Bader, J., Edwards, J., Harris-Jones, C., & Hannaford, D. (1988). Practical engineering of knowledge-based systems. *Information and Software Technology, 30*(5), 266–277. https://doi.org/10.1016/0950-5849(88)90019-5

Balasubramanian, N., Ye, Y., & Xu, M. (2022). Substituting human decision-making with machine learning: Implications for organizational learning. *Academy of Management Review, 47*(3), 448–465. https://doi.org/10.5465/amr.2019.0470

Bandura, A., & Cervone, D. (1986). Differential engagement of self-reactive influences in cognitive motivation. *Organizational Behavior and Human Decision Processes, 38*(1), 92–113. https://doi.org/10.1016/0749-5978(86)90028-2

Barney, J. (1991). Firm resources and sustained competitive advantage. *Journal of Management, 17*(1), 99–120. https://doi.org/10.1177/014920639101700108

Barton, D., & Court, D. (2012). Making advanced analytics work for you. *Harvard Business Review, 90*(10), 78–83.

Bellizzi, F. (2019, aprile 9). Kartell presenta la prima sedia progettata dall'intelligenza artificiale. *La Repubblica*. https://design.repubblica.it/2019/04/09/kartell-presenta-la-prima-sedia-progettata-dallintelligenza-artificiale/

Benbya, H., Davenport, T. H., & Pachidi, S. (2020). Artificial intelligence in organizations: Current state and future opportunities. *MIS Quarterly*

Executive, 19(4). https://papers.ssrn.com/sol3/papers.cfm?abstract_id=3741983

Bertini, U. (1990). *Il sistema d'azienda*. Giappichelli Editore.

Bharadwaj, A. S. (2000). A resource-based perspective on information technology capability and firm performance: An empirical investigation. *MIS Quarterly, 24*(1), 169. https://doi.org/10.2307/3250983

Bhimani, A., & Willcocks, L. (2014). Digitisation, big data and the transformation of accounting information. *Accounting and Business Research, 44*(4), 469–490. https://doi.org/10.1080/00014788.2014.910051

Borges, A. F., Laurindo, F. J., Spínola, M. M., Gonçalves, R. F., & Mattos, C. A. (2021). The strategic use of artificial intelligence in the digital era: Systematic literature review and future research directions. *International Journal of Information Management, 57*, 102225.

Brock, J. K.-U., & von Wangenheim, F. (2019). Demystifying AI: What digital transformation leaders can teach you about realistic artificial intelligence. *California Management Review, 61*(4), 110–134. https://doi.org/10.1177/1536504219865226

Brynjolfsson, E., & Mcafee, A. (2017). Artificial intelligence, for real. *Harvard Business Review, 1*, 1–31.

Bughin, J., Hazan, E., Lund, S., Dahlström, P., Wiesinger, A., & Subramaniam, A. (2018). Skill shift: Automation and the future of the workforce. *McKinsey Global Institute, 1*(2018), 3–84.

Canhoto, A. I., & Clear, F. (2020). Artificial intelligence and machine learning as business tools: A framework for diagnosing value destruction potential. *Business Horizons, 63*(2), 183–193. https://doi.org/10.1016/J.BUSHOR.2019.11.003

Cao, G., Duan, Y., Edwards, J. S., & Dwivedi, Y. K. (2021). Understanding managers' attitudes and behavioral intentions towards using artificial intelligence for organizational decision-making. *Technovation, 106*, 102312.

Chatterjee, S., Rana, N. P., Dwivedi, Y. K., & Baabdullah, A. M. (2021). Understanding AI adoption in manufacturing and production firms using an integrated TAM-TOE model. *Technological Forecasting and Social Change, 170*, 120880. https://doi.org/10.1016/J.TECHFORE.2021.120880

Chui, M., Manyika, J., & Miremadi, M. (2016). Where machines could replace humans-and where they can't (yet). *The McKinsey Quarterly*, 1–12.

Collins, C., Dennehy, D., Conboy, K., & Mikalef, P. (2021). Artificial intelligence in information systems research: A systematic literature review and research agenda. *International Journal of Information Management, 60*, 102383. https://doi.org/10.1016/j.ijinfomgt.2021.102383

Constantiou, I., Joshi, M. P., & Stelmaszak, M. (2024). Introduction to research handbook on artificial intelligence and decision making in organizations. In *Research handbook on artificial intelligence and decision making in organizations* (pp. 1–15). Edward Elgar Publishing.

Corbucci, L., Guidotti, R., & Monreale, A. (2023). Explaining black-boxes in federated learning. In L. Longo (A c. Di), *Explainable Artificial Intelligence* (pp. 151–163). Springer Nature. https://doi.org/10.1007/978-3-031-44067-0_8

Crevier, D. (1993). *AI: The tumultuous history of the search for artificial intelligence*. Basic Books, Inc.

Currie, W. L. (2012). Institutional isomorphism and change: The national programme for IT–10 years on. *Journal of Information Technology, 27*(3), 236–248. https://doi.org/10.1057/jit.2012.18

Daugherty, P. R., & Wilson, H. J. (2018). *Human+ machine: Reimagining work in the age of AI*. Harvard Business Press.

Davenport, T. H. (2018). *The AI advantage: How to put the artificial intelligence revolution to work*. The MIT Press.

Davenport, T. H., & Harris, J. G. (2007). *Competing on analytics: The new science of winning*. Harvard Business School Press.

Davenport, T. H., & Kirby, J. (2016). *Only humans need apply: Winners and losers in the age of smart machines*. Harper Business Press.

Davenport, T. H., & Ronanki, R. (2018). Artificial intelligence for the real world. *Harvard Business Review, 96*(1), 108–116.

Davis, F. D. (1989). Perceived usefulness, perceived ease of use, and user acceptance of information technology. *MIS Quarterly*, 319–340.

Deng, L. (2018). Artificial intelligence in the rising wave of deep learning: The historical path and future outlook [perspectives]. *IEEE Signal Processing Magazine, 35*(1), 180–177. https://doi.org/10.1109/MSP.2017.2762725

De Santis, F. (2018). *Auditing and management control systems in the age of big data*. Franco Angeli.

De Santis, F., & D'Onza, G. (2021). Big data and data analytics in auditing: In search of legitimacy. *Meditari Accountancy Research, 29*(5), 1088–1112. https://doi.org/10.1108/MEDAR-03-2020-0838

De Santis, F., & Presti, C. (2018). The relationship between intellectual capital and big data: A review. *Meditari Accountancy Research, 26*(3), 361–380. https://doi.org/10.1108/MEDAR-10-2017-0222

Dimaggio, P. J., & Powell, W. W. (1983). The iron cage revisited: Institutional isomorphism and collective rationality in organizational fields. *American Sociological Review, 48*(2), 147–160.

Duan, Y., Edwards, J. S., & Dwivedi, Y. K. (2019). Artificial intelligence for decision making in the era of Big data—Evolution, challenges and research agenda. *International Journal of Information Management, 48*, 63–71. https://doi.org/10.1016/j.ijinfomgt.2019.01.021

Du, S., & Xie, C. (2021). Paradoxes of artificial intelligence in consumer markets: Ethical challenges and opportunities. *Journal of Business Research, 129*, 961–974. https://doi.org/10.1016/j.jbusres.2020.08.024

Dwivedi, Y. K., Hughes, L., Ismagilova, E., Aarts, G., Coombs, C., Crick, T., Duan, Y., Dwivedi, R., Edwards, J., & Eirug, A. (2021). Artificial intelligence (AI): Multidisciplinary perspectives on emerging challenges, opportunities, and agenda for research, practice and policy. *International Journal of Information Management, 57*, 101994.

Edwards, J. S., Duan, Y., & Robins, P. C. (2000). An analysis of expert systems for business decision making at different levels and in different roles. *European Journal of Information Systems, 9*(1), 36–46. https://doi.org/10.1057/palgrave.ejis.3000344

Fan, W., & Geerts, F. (2022). *Foundations of data quality management*. Springer Nature.

Fawcett, T., & Provost, F. (1997). Adaptive fraud detection. *Data Mining and Knowledge Discovery, 1*(3), 291–316. https://doi.org/10.1023/A:1009700419189

Fishbein, M., & Ajzen, I. (1975). *Belief, attitude, intention, and behavior: An introduction to theory and research*. Addison-Wesley.

Fosso Wamba, S., & Queiroz, M. M. (2023). Responsible artificial intelligence as a secret ingredient for digital health: Bibliometric analysis, insights, and research directions. *Information Systems Frontiers, 25*(6), 2123–2138. https://doi.org/10.1007/s10796-021-10142-8

Fountaine, T., McCarthy, B., & Saleh, T. (2019). Building the AI-powered organization. *Harvard Business Review, 97*(4), 62–73.

Frey, C. B., & Osborne, M. A. (2017). The future of employment: How susceptible are jobs to computerisation? *Technological Forecasting and Social Change, 114*, 254–280. https://doi.org/10.1016/j.techfore.2016.08.019

Gaggioli, A., Riva, G., Peters, D., & Calvo, R. A. (2017). Positive technology, computing, and design: Shaping a future in which technology promotes psychological well-being. In *Emotions and affect in human factors and human-computer interaction* (pp. 477–502). Elsevier. https://doi.org/10.1016/B978-0-12-801851-4.00018-5

Galbraith, J. K. (1968). The new industrial state. *Science and Society, 32*(2).

Gandomi, A., & Haider, M. (2015). Beyond the hype: Big data concepts, methods, and analytics. *International Journal of Information Management, 35*(2), 137–144. https://doi.org/10.1016/j.ijinfomgt.2014.10.007

Gartner, Inc. (2023). *Top 10 strategic technology trends for 2024* [Survey]. https://www.gartner.com/en/articles/gartner-top-10-strategic-technology-trends-for-2024

Gupta, R., Nair, K., Mishra, M., Ibrahim, B., & Bhardwaj, S. (2024). Adoption and impacts of generative artificial intelligence: Theoretical underpinnings and research agenda. *International Journal of Information Management Data Insights, 4*(1), 100232. https://doi.org/10.1016/j.jjimei.2024.100232

Haesevoets, T., De Cremer, D., Dierckx, K., & Van Hiel, A. (2021). Human-machine collaboration in managerial decision making. *Computers in Human Behavior, 119*, 106730. https://doi.org/10.1016/j.chb.2021.106730

Jarrahi, M. H. (2018). Artificial intelligence and the future of work: Human-AI symbiosis in organizational decision making. *Business Horizons, 61*(4), 577–586. https://doi.org/10.1016/J.BUSHOR.2018.03.007

Kaplan, A., & Haenlein, M. (2019). Siri, Siri, in my hand: Who's the fairest in the land? On the interpretations, illustrations, and implications of artificial intelligence. *Business Horizons, 62*(1), 15–25. https://doi.org/10.1016/j.bushor.2018.08.004

Keding, C. (2021). Understanding the interplay of artificial intelligence and strategic management: Four decades of research in review. *Management Review Quarterly, 71*(1), 91–134. https://doi.org/10.1007/s11301-020-00181-x

Khogali, H. O., & Mekid, S. (2023). The blended future of automation and AI: Examining some long-term societal and ethical impact features. *Technology in Society, 73*, 102232. https://doi.org/10.1016/j.techsoc.2023.102232

Krakowski, S., Luger, J., & Raisch, S. (2023). Artificial intelligence and the changing sources of competitive advantage. *Strategic Management Journal, 44*(6), 1425–1452. https://doi.org/10.1002/smj.3387

Kumari, A., & Devi, N. C. (2023). Blockchain technology acceptance by investment professionals: A decomposed TPB model. *Journal of Financial Reporting and Accounting, 21*(1), 45–59. https://doi.org/10.1108/JFRA-12-2021-0466

Lai, K., Wong, C. W. Y., & Cheng, T. C. E. (2006). Institutional isomorphism and the adoption of information technology for supply chain management. *Computers in Industry, 57*(1), 93–98. https://doi.org/10.1016/j.compind.2005.05.002

Langer, M., & Landers, R. N. (2021). The future of artificial intelligence at work: A review on effects of decision automation and augmentation on workers targeted by algorithms and third-party observers. *Computers in Human Behavior, 123*, 106878. https://doi.org/10.1016/j.chb.2021.106878

Lehner, O. M., Ittonen, K., Silvola, H., Ström, E., & Wührleitner, A. (2022). Artificial intelligence based decision-making in accounting and auditing: Ethical challenges and normative thinking. *Accounting, Auditing & Accountability Journal, 35*(9), 109–135. https://doi.org/10.1108/AAAJ-09-2020-4934

Liang, H., & Xue, Y. (2009). Avoidance of information technology threats: A theoretical perspective. *MIS Quarterly, 33*(1), 71. https://doi.org/10.2307/20650279

Lichtenthaler, U. (2018). Beyond artificial intelligence: Why companies need to go the extra step. *Journal of Business Strategy, 41*(1), 19–26. https://doi.org/10.1108/JBS-05-2018-0086

Lichtenthaler, U. (2019). Extremes of acceptance: Employee attitudes toward artificial intelligence. *Journal of Business Strategy, 41*(5), 39–45. https://doi.org/10.1108/JBS-12-2018-0204

Lindebaum, D., Vesa, M., & Den Hond, F. (2020). Insights from "The machine stops <i>"</i> to better understand rational assumptions in algorithmic decision making and its implications for organizations. *Academy of Management Review, 45*(1), 247–263. https://doi.org/10.5465/amr.2018.0181

Makridakis, S. (2017). The forthcoming artificial intelligence (AI) revolution: Its impact on society and firms. *Futures, 90*, 46–60.

Manyika, J., Chui, M., Miremadi, M., Bughin, J., George, K., Willmott, P., & Dewhurst, M. (2017). A future that works: AI, automation, employment, and productivity. McKinsey Global Institute Research. *Technical Report, 60*, 1–135.

McAfee, A., Brynjolfsson, E., & Dearstyne, B. W. (2012). Big data's management revolution. *Harvard Business Review, 90*(12), 16–17.

McKinsey. (2024). *The state of AI in early 2024: Gen AI adoption spikes and starts to generate value* [Survey]. https://www.mckinsey.com/capabilities/quantumblack/our-insights/the-state-of-ai/

Merhi, M. I. (2023). An evaluation of the critical success factors impacting artificial intelligence implementation. *International Journal of Information Management, 69*, 102545. https://doi.org/10.1016/j.ijinfomgt.2022.102545

Mikalef, P., & Gupta, M. (2021). Artificial intelligence capability: Conceptualization, measurement calibration, and empirical study on its impact on organizational creativity and firm performance. *Information & Management, 58*(3), 103434. https://doi.org/10.1016/j.im.2021.103434

Miller, S. M. (2018). AI: Augmentation, more so than automation. *Asian Management Insights (Singapore Management University), 5*(1), 1–20.

Murphy, K. P. (2012). *Machine learning: A probabilistic perspective.*

Nilsson, N. J. (2009). *The quest for artificial intelligence.* Cambridge University Press.

Peppard, J. (2000). Customer relationship management (CRM) in financial services. *European Management Journal, 18*(3), 312–327. https://doi.org/10.1016/S0263-2373(00)00013-X

Presti, C., De Santis, F., & Bernini, F. (2023). Value co-creation via machine learning from a configuration theory perspective. *European Journal of Innovation Management, 26*(7), 449–477. https://doi.org/10.1108/EJIM-01-2023-0104

Raisch, S., & Krakowski, S. (2021). Artificial intelligence and management: The automation–augmentation paradox. *Academy of Management Review, 46*(1), 192–210. https://doi.org/10.5465/AMR.2018.0072

Rana, N. P., Chatterjee, S., Dwivedi, Y. K., & Akter, S. (2022). Understanding dark side of artificial intelligence (AI) integrated business analytics: Assessing firm's operational inefficiency and competitiveness. *European Journal of Information Systems, 31*(3), 364–387. https://doi.org/10.1080/0960085X.2021.1955628

Ransbotham, S., Kiron, D., Gerbert, P., & Reeves, M. (2017). Reshaping business with artificial intelligence: Closing the gap between ambition and action. *MIT Sloan Management Review, 59*(1). https://search.proquest.com/openview/83d554491afeb2435c6c2e386821c60c/1?pq-origsite=gscholar&cbl=26142

Reinsel, D., Gantz, J., & Rydning, J. (2018). The digitization of the world—From edge to core. In *International Data Corporation (IDC) White Paper* (Fascicolo November). https://www.seagate.com/files/www-content/our-story/trends/files/idc-seagate-dataage-whitepaper.pdf

Rhodes, M. (2016, October 3). So. Algorithms are designing chairs now. *Wired*. https://www.wired.com/2016/10/elbo-chair-autodesk-algorithm/

Rogers, E. M. (1962). *Diffusion of innovations*. Free Press of Glencoe.

Russell, S. J., & Norvig, P. (2016). *Artificial intelligence: A modern approach*. Pearson.

Sayyadi, M. (2024). How to improve data quality to empower business decision-making process and business strategy agility in the AI age. *Business Information Review*. https://doi.org/10.1177/02663821241264705

Shrestha, Y. R., Ben-Menahem, S. M., & von Krogh, G. (2019). Organizational decision-making structures in the age of artificial intelligence. *California Management Review, 61*(4), 66–83. https://doi.org/10.1177/0008125619862257

Simon, H. A. (1944). Decision-making and administrative organization. *Public Administration Review, 4*(1), 16. https://doi.org/10.2307/972435

Simon, H. A. (1979). Rational decision making in business organizations. *The American Economic Review, 69*(4), 493–513.

Tornatzky, L. G., Fleischer, M., & Chakrabarti, A. K. (1990). *The processes of technological innovation*. Lexington Books.

Trotta, A., Ziosi, M., & Lomonaco, V. (2023). The future of ethics in AI: Challenges and opportunities. *AI & Society, 38*(2), 439–441. https://doi.org/10.1007/s00146-023-01644-x

Turner, J. (2018). *Robot rules: Regulating artificial intelligence*. Springer.

Van Lent, M., Fisher, W., & Mancuso, M. (2004). An explainable artificial intelligence system for small-unit tactical behavior. *Proceedings of the National Conference on Artificial Intelligence*, 900–907. https://cdn.aaai.org/IAAI/2004/IAAI04-019.pdf

Varsha, P. S. (2023). How can we manage biases in artificial intelligence systems—A systematic literature review. *International Journal of Information Management Data Insights, 3*(1), 100165. https://doi.org/10.1016/j.jjimei.2023.100165

Venkatesh, M., & Davis, G. B., & Davis, F. D. (2003). User acceptance of information technology: Toward a unified view. *MIS Quarterly, 27*(3), 425. https://doi.org/10.2307/30036540

Venkatesh, V., & Bala, H. (2008). Technology acceptance model 3 and a research agenda on interventions. *Decision Sciences, 39*(2), 273–315. https://doi.org/10.1111/j.1540-5915.2008.00192.x

Venkatesh, V., & Davis, F. D. (2000). A theoretical extension of the technology acceptance model: Four longitudinal field studies. *Management Science, 46*(2), 186–204. https://doi.org/10.1287/mnsc.46.2.186.11926

Wallach, W., & Allen, C. (2010). *Moral machines: Teaching robots right from wrong* (First issued as an Oxford University Press paperback). Oxford University Press.

Weizenbaum, J. (1983). ELIZA—A computer program for the study of natural language communication between man and machine. *Communications of the ACM, 26*(1), 23–28. https://doi.org/10.1145/357980.357991

Wernerfelt, B. (1984). A resource-based view of the firm. *Strategic Management Journal, 5*(2), 171–180. https://doi.org/10.1002/smj.4250050207

White Baker, E., Al-Gahtani, S. S., & Hubona, G. S. (2007). The effects of gender and age on new technology implementation in a developing country: Testing the theory of planned behavior (TPB). *Information Technology & People, 20*(4), 352–375. https://doi.org/10.1108/09593840710839798

Wilson, H. J., & Daugherty, P. R. (2018). Collaborative intelligence: Humans and AI are joining forces. *Harvard Business Review, 96*(4), 114–123.

Xu, H., Nord, J. H., Brown, N., & Nord, G. D. (2002). Data quality issues in implementing an ERP. *Industrial Management and Data Systems, 102*(1), 47–58. https://doi.org/10.1108/02635570210414668

Zhang, C. (Abigail), Cho, S., & Vasarhelyi, M. (2022). Explainable artificial intelligence (XAI) in auditing. *International Journal of Accounting Information Systems, 46*. https://doi.org/10.1016/J.ACCINF.2022.100572

CHAPTER 6

Artificial Intelligence for Risk Management

Federica De Santis

6.1 Introduction

Since decades scholars and practitioners devoted attention to the relationship between business performance and risks (Florio & Leoni, 2017). Risk is inherently embedded in business operations (Scott et al., 2022) and arises from changes occurring in variables, both internal and external to the organization, that decision-makers are often unable to capture and foresee (Knight, 1921). Risk is also dynamic, as it changes throughout the company's lifecycle, and characterized by a systematic nature, as it derives from multifaceted cause-and-effect relationships among various events and conditions (Dezzani, 1971; Sassi, 1940).

According to the traditional academic literature, risks stem from the combination of two distinct but intertwined phenomena: the ever-changing dynamics of events affecting the organization, and the humans' inability to predict such events (Bertini, 1969). This creates what Gordon et al. (2009) refer to as environmental uncertainty, that makes it difficult for organizations to identify and adequately respond to the risks affecting its ability to succeed and even survive in the marketplace. Since the need to confront environmental uncertainty is inherent to all business activities, both scholars and practitioners have always underlined the need for companies to adopt risk management practices (Florio & Leoni, 2017; Sassi, 1940).

M. Pierotti et al., *Artificial Intelligence in Accounting and Auditing*,
https://doi.org/10.1007/978-3-031-71371-2_6

At least during the initial phases of its development, risk management was introduced according to a silo-based approach and was mostly focused on confronting financial risks. Such an approach, however, presented significant limitations, since it allowed to manage one risk at a time, thus preventing companies to capture the actual interrelations among different types of risks (Florio & Leoni, 2017; Grace et al., 2015). Over the last two decades, a paradigm shift has occurred in the way to view risk management, leading companies to assume a holistic posture toward risk management, namely an Enterprise Risk Management approach (Beasley et al., 2005; Gordon et al., 2009), which implies that risks assessment, quantification, and management must encompass the entire organization, throughout all functions and levels (Florio & Leoni, 2017). This need has become particularly apparent within the current hypercompetitive and turbulent environment, where companies are increasingly required to confront a multiplicity of risks, ranging from internal disruptions to global catastrophes, that threaten the efficiency and effectiveness of business processes, thus challenging their long-term stability (D'Onza, 2008; Rodríguez-Espíndola et al., 2022; Zhu, 2024).

Risk management (in the form of Enterprise Risk Management), therefore, constitutes a complex system in which a multiplicity of human and technical elements interact with each other to mitigate potential threats to companies' success and survival (Arena & Arnaboldi, 2014; D'Onza, 2008). Such a complex system comprises a processual dimension, where risk identification, assessment, communication, and prevention represent its constituent activities, and a static dimension, that comprises human, physical, and technical resources. Risk management processes occur during the entire organizations' lifecycle and aim at ensuring the safeguard of the value created by the company by appropriately treating risks that have been identified and addressed (Zagaria, 2017). This way, researchers underline that risk management can enhance firms' performance by supporting them to avoid losses, bankruptcy, and reputational damage (Baxter et al., 2013; Hirsch, 2018). Moreover, risk management is believed to improve decision-making and resource allocation processes (Florio & Leoni, 2017; Grace et al., 2015).

In so doing, risk management bases its effectiveness on the firms' ability to obtain and retrieve useful data that can be converted into relevant and timely information. Data thus constitutes the cornerstone of risk management, as it is used to inform risk assessments, monitor risks, and help to detect new types of risks. In recent times, the disruptive challenges occurred in competitive environments, which includes the advent of global financial crises, the proliferation of digital footprints left by businesses and consumers because of the growing digitalization of society, and the Covid-19 pandemic, have forced risk management systems to evolve. It is now essential for companies to harness the potential of accessing a wide array of data sources with powerful data analytics tools to enhance risk management processes with the opportunity to generate timely insights that inform risk-preventative policies, procedures, controls, and early identification, thus reducing the occurrence and gravity of operational loss events (Cornwell et al., 2023; Roberts & Tonna, 2022).

In the current digitalized world, AI and machine learning are pivotal in risk management due to their ability to enhance accuracy beyond traditional models, manage extensive structured and unstructured data, and enable agile responses to market changes. These technologies have proven effective in problem-solving and are expected to advance further with the increasing adoption of Big Data. By automating routine tasks and processing vast amounts of diverse data, AI and machine learning uncover complex relationships and achieve higher risk-model accuracy. However, to ensure long-term, large-scale implementation, it is essential to foster a scientific mindset and innovative culture across enterprises (Araz et al., 2020; Roberts & Tonna, 2022).

Stemming from the above, this chapter aims at exploring how the traditional function of risk management is evolving to confront new and emerging risks, and how AI technologies can enhance risk management practices, as well as what are the main challenges related to the adoption of advanced digital technologies in managing business risks.

6.2 Fundamentals of Risk Management

We know that current risk management practices are designed and implemented according to an Enterprise Risk Management approach, that can be defined as "a process, effected by an entity's board of directors, management, and other personnel, applied in strategy setting and across the enterprise, designed to identify potential events that may affect the entity, and manage risk to be within its risk appetite, to provide reasonable assurance regarding the achievement of entity objectives" (COSO, 2004, p. 2).

Every organization, regardless of their dimension or industry, needs to identify assess and confront risks emerging during their lifecycle (Aven & Thekdi, 2019). To some extent, however, firms' size and industry can affect the types of risks to which they are exposed, or the way companies design their risk management system. Depending on the size of the organization, risk management activities and systems may be more or less formalized, or different techniques and tools may be employed basing on its industry. As a way of example, companies operating in the financial sector usually adopt more sophisticated risk management tools, as they are required to comply with specific norms and regulations (e.g., the Basel Accords issued over time) (Cornwell et al., 2023).

Even though risk management can assume different configurations across the wide variety of business realities, it is possible to identify some distinctive elements that jointly allow us to define a company's risk management system, i.e., actors, processes, and techniques and tools. Actors constitute the subjective dimension of risk management and include all the people that, at the various organizational levels, are involved in identifying, assess, and treat risks. Risk management occurs along the entire organization thus involving a multiplicity of actors from the apex of the company's hierarchy toward the lower, operational levels. Therefore, risk management actors comprise all the people that operate within an organization (Zagaria, 2017).

The risk management process risks implies assuming decisions and taking actions aimed at mitigating potential harm to the company. Both literature and practice in risk management typically identify three main phases: identification, assessment, and treatment (D'Onza, 2008). Risk identification entails the search, identification, and analysis of events that could have adverse consequences for the company. This phase is the most critical in the risk management process because unidentified risks cannot be treated, potentially leaving the company unable to effectively address the consequences of such risks if they materialize (Selleri, 2006).

The most common types of risk companies are required to confront according to classical academic literature on risk management can be summarized as follows (Roberts & Tonna, 2022, p. 9):

- Credit risk, that refers to the possibility of a financial loss occurring because of a borrower's failure to repay loan obligations.
- Interest rate risk, which manifests itself as a loss due to movement in interest rates.

- Market risk, that is the risk of loss to institutions earnings from movement in market prices.
- Operational risks, related to losses deriving from a failed internal process, people, system, or external events.
- Insurance risk, that relates to harmful or unexpected events, threats, or perils for which insurances are provided.
- Liquidity risk, which is the risk arising from a firm's in ability to meet its short term obligations as they become due is the risk arising from a firm's in ability to meet its short-term obligations as they become due.
- Reputation risk, that corresponds to the risk of financial and non-financial loss due to public opinion.
- Strategy risk, which is the risk from adverse business decisions or lack of responsiveness to changes in the industry and operating environment.
- Compliance risk, that arises from violations of laws or regulations, internal policies and procedures, or ethical standards.

More recently, new types of risks are emerging (Holtz et al., 2023; Roberts & Tonna, 2022), such as:

- technological risks (e.g., cyberattacks or data breaches)
- risks related to climate change
- risks connected to the Covid-19 pandemic
- climate change and sustainability risks
- geopolitical uncertainty.

Risk identification usually starts from the recognition of corporate's objectives, because risks can be defined as all the events that can hinder or prevent the achievement of a company's goals. Once risks have been identified, effective risk management requires the identification of the risks' root causes and the understanding of the factors that trigger harmful events. After identifying risks, their magnitude is assessed based on the probability of occurrence and potential impact. The combination of probability and impact determines the company's risk exposure, which increases with the likelihood of the event and the potential negative deviation from the target. Determining risk exposure is highly complex and sometimes requires simplifying assumptions about various factors (D'Onza, 2008; Presti & Greco, 2019; Zagaria, 2017).

The third risk management system's element, that constitutes its objective dimension, consists of the techniques and tools that actors employ to effectively carry out the process. Risk management techniques can be examined concerning the three main phases: risk identification, assessment, and treatment. For example, traditional risk identification tools can be classified into four categories (D'Onza, 2008):

- Techniques aimed at analyzing business activities and external environment, that includes process maps, organizational charts, various types of management and strategic reports, questionnaires, and resource inventories.
- Risk models, such as risk register and risk-resource matrices.
- Reporting tools, including adverse events' databases and key risk indicators.
- Causal analysis techniques, such as cause-and-effect diagrams and fault tree analysis.

The first group of techniques is employed to acquire knowledge of the structural and operational characteristics of the company and the external environment, which, as mentioned, is a necessary prerequisite for identifying risk factors. The business activity analysis techniques that fall into this first category do not originate within the field of risk management but can be utilized to understand the specificities of the operational and environmental context. These techniques enable the analyst to develop knowledge regarding management activities, company resources, organizational and technical structures, the characteristics of production factors, and so forth.

Risk models, on the other hand, are the typical tools used in risk management practices. Risk models apply quantitative methods, analytics, and algorithms to quantify financial and non-financial risks (Roberts & Tonna, 2022). They identify potential risk factors associated with a specific context (such as a business sector, company process, or production factors). The risk register identifies some standard risk factors from which specific events characterizing a particular business context can be identified. One of the most well-known models proposes a schematic representation of risk factors at three levels: environmental risks, process risks, and risks related to decision-making information. In the classical approach followed in risk management practice, the resource-risk matrix is particularly used in exposure analysis. It seeks to identify risks based on material assets and hypothesizes certain typical types of risks to which they might be exposed, such as fraud, embezzlement, environmental disasters. Among the tools used in the phase of identifying hazardous phenomena, the hazard and operability study (HAZOP), preliminary hazard analysis (PHA), and checklists are noteworthy (Misani, 1994; Selleri, 2006).

The tools for reporting critical issues are designed to detect harmful events (this is the case for the database of events) or to monitor the trend of critical factors characterizing business activities (which is typical in the use of key risk indicators—KRIs). The techniques for analyzing the causes of risks are aimed at identifying the causal complex that originates hazardous events and the factors influencing the likelihood of their occurrence. Among the most commonly used techniques in this field are the cause-and-effect diagram and fault tree analysis. These methods enable the identification of specific risks associated with elementary activities, which are then interconnected to highlight the chain relationships between hazardous manifestations (D'Onza, 2008).

Risk assessment techniques can be classified as quantitative and qualitative techniques. Quantitative ones find their roots in probability theory and in statistics and are used to establish causal links between threatening events and their consequences for the organization, in situations where business experts' knowledge was the most reliable source of information (Nateghi & Aven, 2021). Among others, quantitative risk assessment techniques comprise historical series analysis, probabilistic models, simulation techniques, sensitivity analysis, and stress testing. Over time, these techniques have been mostly applied in financial companies (Cornwell et al., 2023).

With qualitative risk assessment techniques, subjective experts' evaluations constitute the basis for determining the probability and impact of risky events. As a way of example, these techniques include the subjective probability assessment and the individual self-assessment. While these techniques are far more easy to apply in business contexts, the reliability of their results may be influenced by the cognitive biases of the actors involved in the evaluation process (D'Onza, 2008).

Within traditional ERM frameworks, risk identification and assessment usually involve manual processes, such as periodic and sample-based audits, assurances, likelihood-severity risk matrices, and controls testing.

However, the reactive and subjective nature of these approaches hampers risk management effectiveness (Cornwell et al., 2023). Moreover, traditional risk assessment techniques are computationally expensive and often provide low fidelity due to the need of set up binding model assumptions. They often rely on experience and intuition, making it difficult to identify potential factors or accurately predict risks, such as with qualitative techniques (Zhu, 2024).

When based on quantitative techniques, traditional risk mode assumes that data is generated by specific processes characterized by known probability distributions, and that the additional precision gained from more data is often negligible and not worth the cost of collecting and processing large-scale data. In contrast, Big Data analysis via AI algorithms allows for non-parametric learning from vast amounts of data without predefined probability distributions or functional dependencies. This approach supports high-dimensional data and can include unstructured data like images, location data, and social network interactions, offering an improved perspective over classical methods (Nateghi & Aven, 2021).

Stemming from the abovementioned pitfalls of traditional risk identification and assessment methods, data analytics is expected to revolutionize the field from three critical perspectives. First, the integration of internal and external data will enable more scientific, population-based risk assessments, reducing the biases inherent in current qualitative and sample-based methods, that are influenced by individuals' experiences and perceptions. Second, data-driven approaches offer the opportunity to facilitate continuous monitoring of the evolving risk landscape, unlike the irregular and static assessments typical of manual methods. Third, the predictive power and capability of advanced analytics to model complex relationships offer a comprehensive approach. These advancements will transform risk management into a key component of decision-making processes, driving revenue rather than merely focusing on defense and compliance (Araz et al., 2020; Cornwell et al., 2023; Roberts & Tonna, 2022).

Traditional risk assessment techniques, which rely on probability theory to draw population inferences from samples, contrast with modern statistical and machine learning methods that identify generalizable predictive patterns. These conventional methods depend on historical internal loss data, such as event databases that record loss amounts, business lines, risk types, and years, but often overlook related operational factors.

Consequently, these techniques are high-level, descriptive, and backward-looking, in contrast to the detailed and predictive capabilities that are currently required in risk management (Cornwell et al., 2023). Nowadays, companies' risk functions are thus increasingly required to harness the power of digital technologies, such as AI and Big Data.

6.3 AI Applications in Risk Management: Opportunities and Challenges

Big data is becoming increasingly important for risk analysis. To illustrate the rapid growth of Big Data and its application in risk analysis Choi and Lambert (2017) summarize research on this topic by identifying five different timeframes, that allowed to highlight a significant surge in academic interest on Big Data-based risk analysis since 2011. Further, their analysis pointed out that the most researched areas included transportation and logistics infrastructure, weather and natural resources, economics and industrial systems, and security and social concerns. On the same vein, Cornwell et al. (2023) reviewed the most relevant academics and practitioners' contributions on the use of data analytics in operational risk management, by focusing on financial and energy industries. Their research found that the application of data analytics to risk management increased from the 80s and accelerated from 2012, with a significant prevalence of studies focused on financial risk management domain (Dwivedi et al., 2023). Other relevant domains in which scholars and professionals have investigated the use of advanced analytics techniques to risk identification and assessment related to credit scores, default probabilities, and bankruptcy prediction. Further, non-financial risks also constitute a large portion of studies and include natural disasters, road traffic and transport risks, medical diagnosis, and disease prediction. Research on operational risks usually covered workplace safety, system and equipment disruption or failures, supply chain risks, fraud and money laundering, and improper or illegal business practices (Araz et al., 2020; Choi & Lambert, 2017; Dicuonzo et al., 2021; Lawrencia & Ce, 2019).

The first and foremost opportunity that the use of Big Data and AI technologies brings to risk management relates to the possibility to access and analyze alternative data sources in risk modeling, thus providing new shine to quantitative risk analysis (Nateghi & Aven, 2021). In this respect, Roberts and Tonna (2022, pp. 23–24) provide a useful overview of traditional and alternative data sources that can be employed to build risk models (see Table 6.1). According to the authors, risk models' development is increasingly involving various types of traditional and non-traditional data sources. A significant consideration also emerges from their analysis. When using alternative, new types of data as a relevant source for developing a risk model, regardless of the underlying techniques (i.e., whether traditional or based on AI technologies), risk managers must justify the reason why using that data source is appropriate for the model to be built. Data sources' justification implies that the resulting model will not lead to biased or unethical outcomes.

Moreover, by exploiting Big Data in building risk models offers companies the opportunity to benefit not only from its variety, but also from its velocity, volume, and granularity. This means that companies can mine highly dimensional, fast, and rich sources of data to conduct more real-time analyses of the dynamics in the system, thus uncovering new variables and complex dynamic causal relationships that would have remained unknown to domain experts adopting traditional risk models (Nateghi & Aven, 2021).

According to Zhu et al. (2024), the use of Big Data and AI techniques provides companies not only with more information, but also with more accurate information as compared to traditional risk management models, thus reducing risk exposure. Specifically, AI algorithms such as predictive analytics, anomaly detection algorithms, and semantic analyses can improve risk identification (Deiva Ganesh & Kalpana, 2022). Anomaly detection algorithms can be used to scan the risk register or other highly dimensional and granular data sources to identify outliers and other potential red flags for fraudulent activities or non-compliance. Moreover, by scanning the risk register maintained by the company, or other public or private databases, AI algorithms can identify other parameters which affect business processes' activities, that have been missed by human experts. AI can thus augment human experts' capabilities in searching for connections between historically manifested risks and the specific activities of each business process, thus enriching root-cause analysis(Griffy-Brown et al., 2020). With semantic analyses, AI may lead to the identification of additional risks relevant to the organization's business processes, thus supplementing human-based risk identification (Biolcheva, 2021).

During the risk assessment phase, Risk Scoring Models, Credit Risk Assessment tools, and Fraud Detection algorithms can work autonomously, without the need for human intervention to conduct an analysis related to the main factors and causal relationship characterizing

Table 6.1 Traditional and alternative data sources in risk modeling

Types of data	*Definition*	*Traditional sources*	*Alternative sources*
Transactional	Structured and detailed information on customer transactions' key characteristics that is stored in massive online transaction processing (OLTP) relational databases	Aggregated, structured, and typically summarized over longer-term horizons by aggregating into averages, etc	Vast amounts of granular data
Internal data	Customer, product, and transactional history	Stored in ERP, CRM, and SCM systems	Call center data Digital journeys Clickstream data App usage
External data	Data available from third-party data providers and public information (e.g., public data and open data)	Macro-economic information	Multiple sources of third-party data (e.g., bureau data, payment data from utilities, purchasing data from online platforms, subscription information, browsing history, weather, and location data) Public information Social media data
Unstructured data	Data not stored in a predefined structured format	Traditionally required human effort and intuition to analyze	Text documents (e.g., emails, web pages, claim forms) Multimedia content Network information (i.e., ownership structures, suppliers, liquidity, legal dependencies between counterparties)

Source Roberts and Tonna (2022, pp. 23–24)

each individual risk. Machine learning techniques can be used to automatically analyze risk frequency basing on historical data or to provide an estimation of the financial consequences related to risks' occurrence. Finally, deep learning algorithms and artificial neural networks constitute useful techniques to suggest organizations the most appropriate risk treatment/mitigation strategies that would give positive outcomes (Biolcheva & Valchev, 2022).

While the abundance of data offers numerous benefits in integrating AI in risk management practices, it also introduces significant practical challenges that need to be addressed, such as ensuring data quality, maintaining cybersecurity, and responsibly handling personal data. Robust data management is essential for the effective adoption of AI to support risk identification, assessment, and treatment as these modeling approaches rely heavily on data (Roberts & Tonna, 2022). That is to say that the reliability of risk analyses using Big Data is highly dependent on the quality and credibility of the data itself (Hirsch, 2023). Poor data quality, lack of representativeness, or credibility issues can lead to inaccurate risk identification and assessment. Integrating the strength of knowledge about the credibility and representativeness of input data into the risk management process is crucial. Without this, there could be suboptimal allocation of resources, poor predictions, and erroneous inferences about the impact of negative events (Nateghi & Aven, 2021). Additionally, poor data quality may also refer to data incompleteness, inaccuracies, or inconsistencies, which further affect the accuracy and reliability of algorithms (Zhu, 2024).

The sheer complexity of the data and methods used in Big Data risk analytics constitutes a strength and a weakness simultaneously. On the one hand, complex AI-based risk models involve greater flexibility, that makes them particularly suitable to detect nonlinear causal relationships among risk factors. On the other, they increase the difficulties in risk communication and the opacity of the model (Aziz & Dowling, 2019; Nateghi & Aven, 2021; Roberts & Tonna, 2022). Roberts and Tonna (2022) specifically refer to a trade-off between the opacity of the algorithm and its business benefits—e.g., those related to improved accuracy or efficiency.

6.4 Conclusions

The integration of AI into risk management processes marks a significant evolution in how organizations identify, assess, and mitigate risks. As highlighted in this chapter, the transition from silo-based risk management to a holistic ERM framework has paved the way for more comprehensive and resilient risk management strategies. AI's contribution to this transformation is profound, offering both opportunities and challenges that organizations must navigate carefully.

Historically, risk management was often compartmentalized, with different departments addressing their specific risks in isolation. This silo-based approach limited the organization's ability to understand and mitigate risks comprehensively. The emergence of ERM has shifted the focus toward a more integrated approach, where risks are viewed in relation to their impact on the entire organization. This holistic perspective enables better resource allocation, more informed decision-making, and a stronger alignment between risk management and organizational objectives.

Traditional risk models, both quantitative and qualitative, have inherent limitations. Quantitative models often rely on historical data and assume that future risks will resemble past events, which is not always the case. Qualitative models, on the other hand, depend heavily on subjective judgments, which can be biased and inconsistent. These shortcomings paved the way to the emergence of the need for more advanced approaches that can adapt to the dynamic and complex nature of modern hypercompetitive and turbulent environments.

In such a scenario, AI and Big Data offer several benefits for risk management. They can process and analyze large volumes of data at unprecedented speeds, uncover hidden correlations, and provide real-time risk assessments. This capability is particularly valuable in identifying emerging risks and making proactive decisions. Additionally, AI can enhance the accuracy and objectivity of risk assessments, reducing the reliance on human intuition and bias.

However, the implementation of AI in risk management also presents challenges. These include data privacy concerns, the need for substantial investment in technology and expertise, and the risk of over-reliance on automated systems. Ensuring the ethical use of AI and maintaining human oversight are critical to mitigating these challenges. Organizations must also address the potential for AI algorithms to perpetuate existing biases if not properly monitored and calibrated.

The future of risk management lies in the continuous integration of AI and other advanced technologies. The adoption of AI in risk management represents a paradigm shift that offers significant advantages in terms of efficiency, accuracy, and proactive risk mitigation. While challenges remain, the potential benefits far outweigh the risks. By embracing AI and integrating it into a robust ERM framework, organizations can better navigate the uncertainties of today's complex risk landscape and secure a more resilient and prosperous future. As AI algorithms become more sophisticated and capable of handling unstructured data, their application in risk management will expand. Organizations must invest in developing their AI capabilities while fostering a culture of continuous learning and adaptation.

References

Araz, O. M., Choi, T.-M., Olson, D. L., & Salman, F. S. (2020). Role of analytics for operational risk management in the era of big data. *Decision Sciences, 51*(6), 1320–1346. https://doi.org/10.1111/deci.12451

Arena, M., & Arnaboldi, M. (2014). Risk and performance management: Are they easy partners? In *Management research review* (Vol. 37, pp. 152–166). https://doi.org/10.1108/MRR-08-2012-0180

Aven, T., & Thekdi, S. (2019). *Enterprise risk management: Advances on its foundation and practice* (1st ed.). Routledge. https://doi.org/10.4324/978 0429425028

Aziz, S., & Dowling, M. (2019). Machine learning and ai for risk management. In *Palgrave studies in digital business and enabling technologies* (pp. 33–50). Scopus. https://doi.org/10.1007/978-3-030-02330-0_3

Baxter, R., Bedard, J. C., Hoitash, R., & Yezegel, A. (2013). Enterprise risk management program quality: Determinants, value relevance, and the financial crisis. *Contemporary Accounting Research, 30*(4), 1264–1295. https://doi.org/10.1111/j.1911-3846.2012.01194.x

Beasley, M. S., Clune, R., & Hermanson, D. R. (2005). Enterprise risk management: An empirical analysis of factors associated with the extent of implementation. *Journal of Accounting and Public Policy, 24*(6), 521–531. https://doi.org/10.1016/j.jaccpubpol.2005.10.001

Bertini, U. (1969). *Introduzione allo studio dei rischi in economia aziendale.* Colombo Cursi editore.

Biolcheva, P. (2021). The place of artificial intelligence in the risk management process. *SHS Web of Conferences, 120*, 02013. https://doi.org/10.1051/shs conf/202112002013

Biolcheva, P., & Valchev, E. (2022). Roadmap for risk management integration using AI. *Journal of Risk & Control*, 13–28. https://doi.org/10.47260/jrc/912

Choi, T.-M., & Lambert, J. H. (2017). Advances in risk analysis with big data. *Risk Analysis, 37*(8), 1435–1442. https://doi.org/10.1111/risa.12859

Committee of Sponsoring Organizations of the Treadway Commission (COSO), (2004). Enterprise risk management-integrated framework. *Committee of Sponsoring Organizations of the Treadway Commission, 2*(1), 6–10.

Cornwell, N., Bilson, C., Gepp, A., Stern, S., & Vanstone, B. J. (2023). The role of data analytics within operational risk management: A systematic review from the financial services and energy sectors. *Journal of the Operational Research Society, 74*(1), 374–402. Scopus. https://doi.org/10.1080/01605682.2022.2041373

Deiva Ganesh, A., & Kalpana, P. (2022). Supply chain risk identification: A real-time data-mining approach. *Industrial Management and Data Systems, 122*(5), 1333–1354. Scopus. https://doi.org/10.1108/IMDS-11-2021-0719

Dezzani, F. (1971). *Rischi e politiche d'impresa: Contenuto e relazioni*. Giuffrè editore.

Dicuonzo, G., Donofrio, F., & Galeone, G. (2021). Big data and artificial intelligence to support risk management: A systematic literature review. In *SIDREA series in accounting and business administration* (Vol. Part F23, pp. 119–130). Scopus. https://doi.org/10.1007/978-3-030-80737-5_9

D'Onza, G. (2008). *Il sistema di controllo interno nella prospettiva del risk management*. Giuffrè editore.

Dwivedi, D. N., Mahanty, G., & Pathak, Y. K. (2023). AI applications for financial risk management. In *The impact of ai innovation on financial sectors in the era of industry 5.0* (pp. 17–31). Scopus. https://doi.org/10.4018/979-8-3693-0082-4.ch002

Florio, C., & Leoni, G. (2017). Enterprise risk management and firm performance: The italian case. *The British Accounting Review, 49*(1), 56–74.

Gordon, L. A., Loeb, M. P., & Tseng, C.-Y. (2009). Enterprise risk management and firm performance: A contingency perspective. *Journal of Accounting and Public Policy, 28*(4), 301–327. https://doi.org/10.1016/j.jaccpubpol.2009.06.006

Grace, M. F., Leverty, J. T., Phillips, R. D., & Shimpi, P. (2015). The value of investing in enterprise risk management. *Journal of Risk and Insurance, 82*(2), 289–316. https://doi.org/10.1111/jori.12022

Griffy-Brown, C., Miller, H., Zhao, V., Lazarikos, D., & Chun, M. (2020). Making better risk decisions in a new technological environment. *IEEE Engineering Management Review, 48*(1), 77–84. Scopus. https://doi.org/10.1109/EMR.2020.2969121

Hirsch, P. B. (2018). Tie me to the mast: Artificial intelligence & reputation risk management. *Journal of Business Strategy*, *39*(1), 61–64. Scopus. https://doi.org/10.1108/JBS-11-2017-0160

Hirsch, P. B. (2023). At the crossroads: Generative ai and corporate risk management. *Journal of Business Strategy*, *44*(6), 426–429. Scopus. https://doi.org/10.1108/JBS-09-2023-0196

Holtz, N., Wittfoth, S., & Gomez, J. M. (2023). *AI meets risk management: A literature review on methodologies and application fields*. PICMET 2023—Portland international conference on management of engineering and technology: Managing Technology, Engineering and Manufacturing for a Sustainable World, Proceedings. Scopus. https://doi.org/10.23919/PICMET59654.2023.10216845

Knight, F. H. (1921). *Risk, uncertainty and profit* (Vol. 31). Houghton Mifflin.

Lawrencia, C., & Ce, W. (2019). *Fraud detection decision support system for indonesian financial institution* (pp. 389–394). Scopus. https://doi.org/10.1109/ICIMTech.2019.8843719

Misani, N. (1994). *Introduzione al risk management*. EGEA.

Nateghi, R., & Aven, T. (2021). Risk analysis in the age of big data: The promises and pitfalls. *Risk Analysis, 41*(10), 1751–1758. https://doi.org/10.1111/risa.13682

Presti, C., & Greco, G. (2019). L'esigenza di un'integrazione tra la gestione dei rischi e delle performance nel contesto italiano. In G. Greco & L. Marchi (Eds.), *Nuove prospettive su governance, audit, risk e performance*. Giappichelli Editore.

Roberts, T., & Tonna, S. J. (2022). *Risk modeling: Practical applications of artificial intelligence, machine learning, and deep learning* (p. 186). Scopus. https://doi.org/10.1002/9781119824961

Rodríguez-Espíndola, O., Chowdhury, S., Dey, P. K., Albores, P., & Emrouznejad, A. (2022). Analysis of the adoption of emergent technologies for risk management in the era of digital manufacturing. *Technological Forecasting and Social Change, 178*. Scopus. https://doi.org/10.1016/j.techfore.2022.121562

Sassi, S. (1940). *Il sistema dei rischi d'impresa*. Vallardi.

Scott, E. T., Stiles, P., & Debata, P. (2022). *Managing new technology: The combination of model risk and enterprise risk management*. University of Cambridge.

Selleri, L. (2006). *L'impresa e il rischio: Introduzione all'enterprise risk management*. EDUCatt Università Cattolica.

Zagaria, C. (2017). *L'Enterprise Risk Management. Gestione integrate del rischio, profili di comunicazione ed evidenze empiriche*. Giappichelli Editore.

Zhu, J. (2024). Application of artificial intelligence data mining algorithm in enterprise management risk assessment. *International Journal of Information Systems and Supply Chain Management, 17*(1), 1–19. Scopus. https://doi.org/10.4018/IJISSCM.342119

CHAPTER 7

AI for Financial Accounting

Mariarita Pierotti

7.1 Digitalization in Accounting

The accounting sector is experiencing growth and improvement. The range of tasks accountants handle is expanding due to technological advancements and changing customer expectations. With the current use of automated technologies in the accounting industry, the scope of an accountant's role should expand and become more adaptable to technological advancements and digitalization. The implementation of digitalization in the accounting sector has significantly changed the nature of accountants' jobs, making them increasingly reliant on modern equipment and technology (Fettry et al., 2019). The number of positions available for accountants with programming and analytical abilities is expected to decrease as technology becomes more prevalent in the accounting sector. Therefore, it is important for organizations to provide sufficient retraining to existing workers (Zhang et al., 2020). Adequate training boosts workers' confidence, helps them better understand their responsibilities, and equips them with the necessary knowledge and skills to perform their jobs.

Businesses planning to replace their old analog accounting and management information systems with new digital systems must first update their systems to keep up with rapid developments (Andreassen, 2020). The massive digital revolution in communications and Internet

M. Pierotti et al., *Artificial Intelligence in Accounting and Auditing*,
https://doi.org/10.1007/978-3-031-71371-2_7

networks has led to a significant and rapid transition in the business environment. We are not referring to information systems that are reliant on computers, software, or other traditional accounting tools, which have been around for a long time. Even after the emergence of digital entities, these systems have changed the way businesses operate by setting standards that allow each organization to select technologies suitable for their work. Some examples of such technologies include artificial intelligence, the Internet of Things, blockchain technologies, Big Data, and cloud computing, among others. According to Oncioiu et al. (2019), these technologies will increase operational efficiency, reduce costs, provide data access, secure data, and enhance transparency. Additionally, they will save time and effort.

1. Enterprises Resource Planning (ERP)

Enterprise Resource Planning (ERP) software is utilized by businesses to oversee fundamental business functions, including accounting, purchasing, project management, risk management and compliance, and supply chain management. A comprehensive ERP package includes enterprise performance management software, which assists with planning, budgeting, forecasting, and reporting an organization's financial achievements. ERP systems connect all the various business functions and facilitate data exchange. They prevent data duplication and ensure data integrity with a single source of truth by consolidating an organization's common transactional data from multiple sources. ERP systems are essential for managing thousands of enterprises today, regardless of size or industry. ERP is as indispensable to these businesses as the electricity that powers the lights.

2. Cloud Computing

Cloud computing is a type of digital transformation that improves the way accounting work is carried out, rather than just being a technical fix or a saved server with another purpose (Demiröz & Heupel, 2017). The main advantages of cloud computing include cost reduction through labor and time savings, faster processing and storage, scalability, and data protection.

The four primary categories of cloud deployment approaches are private clouds, public clouds, hybrid clouds, and multi-cloud. The three main categories of cloud service models are Infrastructure-as-a-Service (IaaS), Platform-as-a-Service (PaaS), and Software-as-a-Service (SaaS).

Choosing a cloud type or cloud service is a unique decision. While they may be of the same type, no two clouds are the same, and no two cloud services are used to address the same issue. By recognizing the similarities, you can better understand how the limitations of each type of cloud computing and cloud service might impact your business.

3. Big Data

It has an enormous volume of complex data that can't be stored, processed, or circulated using conventional computer programs and techniques (Yao & Gao, 2020). Big Data can be used in accounting because, by evaluating data from social media and financial markets, it enables businesses to classify their target market and estimate the results of their marketing and sales activities.

4. Block Chain

A blockchain is a shared distributed database or ledger among computer network nodes. It serves as an electronic database for storing data in digital form. The most well-known use of blockchain technology is for keeping a secure and transparent record of transactions in cryptocurrency systems such as Bitcoin. The innovation of a blockchain is that it fosters trust without the need for a trusted third party by ensuring the fidelity and security of a record of data.

One key difference between a typical database and a blockchain is how the data is structured. In a blockchain, data is gathered in groups called blocks, each including various sets of information. When a block is full, it is sealed and linked to the block before it to form the data chain known as the blockchain. Blocks have predefined storage capacities. When the chain is complete, a new block is created from each piece of information that follows the just-added block and added to the chain.

As its name suggests, a blockchain separates its data into pieces (blocks) that are joined together, as opposed to a database, which typically organizes its data into tables. When used in a decentralized manner, this data format inherently offers a timeline that cannot be changed. A completed block is wrapped indefinitely and added to the timeline. Every new block that is included in the chain receives its own unique timestamp on the block.

5. Artificial Intelligence

The term "artificial intelligence" refers to the practice of using technology to mimic human intelligence, particularly computer systems. Some examples of specialized applications of artificial intelligence include expert systems, machine learning, natural language processing, voice recognition, and machine vision (Sharida & Hashlamon, 2021; Sharida et al., 2020). This interesting topic will be thoroughly covered in the following chapter. In this section, we will confine ourselves to a preliminary discussion.

The digitalization of accounting is an ongoing process that has a significant impact on the Accounting Information Systems of organizations, the accounting sector as a whole, and the accounting profession itself. In this chapter, we will analyze the impact of digital transformation in the accounting sector, with a special focus on AI technologies. Among the emerging technologies, OCR, AI, and the cloud are the most widely adopted IT solutions. Resistance to change, organizational culture, and cost appear to be the main barriers to digitalization in accounting. On the other hand, the automation of routine tasks and the reduction of errors were universally recognized as advantages. These benefits free up time for accountants to focus on higher value-added services and eliminate paper-based processes. It is expected that the digital skills of accounting professionals operating in the digital era would complement the existing knowledge, competencies, and skills, in a way that adds and substitutes. Our main contribution is to provide a clearer discussion about the impact of digital transformation in the accounting sector, although it does not prove any causal effect. Nevertheless, the results can be of great interest to researchers, policymakers, educators, professional bodies, and accounting professionals.

7.2 AI in Accounting Environment

In the past decade, the use of artificial intelligence (AI) has significantly increased. AI has enhanced the capabilities of the computing world, taking it to the next level by improving predictions, assessing risks, and demonstrating appropriate reactions to them. This growth reflects a growing awareness of the importance of AI in accounting. Both regulators and clients are demanding that auditing firms adopt this new system to facilitate timely and accurate completion of work at reduced costs. It has been argued that accountants engaged in routine tasks in the accounting profession may eventually be replaced by AI to create a better future. Many auditing and business firms have already applied AI to analyze large volumes of data in a short time, a task that would be challenging for humans to accomplish without this technology. For example, the use of AI for administrative and accounting tasks has led to structural changes within firms. Furthermore, AI is an entirely automated process for generating data, which is utilized to prepare taxation reports accurately and in a timely manner. Additionally, AI can be used to automatically recognize and categorize both external (financial reports) and internal (managerial reports) resources within the firm, ensuring accurate submissions to department heads. AI is permeating every industry globally, making a significant impact on the accounting world by saving time, money, and providing accurate data to regulators and customers. However, previous studies have found that AI could lead to increased competitive disadvantages between auditing firms and businesses.

Agarwal and Gaur (2020) affirmed that artificial intelligence has quickly emerged as a disruptive force in the accounting field, transforming how accounting tasks are performed, from simple data entry to complex analysis, resulting in significant benefits for businesses. Zhang et al. (2019) asserted that artificial intelligence is a fast-growing technology that has the potential to revolutionize several industries, including accounting. Artificial intelligence can automate monotonous tasks, improve decision-making processes, and provide considerable insights that can lead to enhanced performance. There are several applications of artificial intelligence in accounting, such as automated data entry, financial statement analysis, fraud detection, and tax planning and compliance. Artificial intelligence-powered systems can automate data entry tasks, reducing the need for manual input and minimizing the risk of errors.

According to Gartner "Digitalization is the use of digital technologies to change a business model and provide new revenue and value-producing opportunities—the process of moving to a digital business (Gartner, 2024). As such, it has affected all kinds of business activities, including business models and supply chains, as well as support functions such as human resources and accounting. Digitalization enables various new forms of cooperation between companies, suppliers, customers, and employees, leading to new product and service offerings. At the same time, digitalization is a challenge for incumbent companies, as it requires them to reflect on their current strategy and to explore new business opportunities. In the finance function, digitalization has resulted in the automation and robotization of routine processes, the introduction of Business Intelligence, and the application of data analytics. Digitalization is affecting our daily lives as well as the role of controllers" (Möller et al., 2020).

AI systems play a crucial role in the accounting field by analyzing financial statements, identifying trends and patterns, and providing insights to help accountants make informed decisions. They can also analyze large amounts of financial data to detect potential fraud, guide compliance with tax laws, and identify opportunities to reduce tax liabilities. In the past, accounting tasks were done manually, which was time-consuming and prone to errors. However, with the introduction of AI, accountants can now use advanced technologies to automate tasks, reduce errors, and increase efficiency (Hasan, 2022).

Artificial intelligence in accounting dates back to the 1950s when computers were first used to automate routine accounting tasks. The development of accounting software in the 1970s allowed for the automation of bookkeeping tasks. However, these systems lacked intelligence and could not provide meaningful analysis and insights (Agarwal & Gaur, 2020). In the 1980s, expert systems using artificial intelligence were introduced to replicate human experts' decision-making abilities. These systems relied on rule-based approaches to accounting, using a set of predefined rules to make decisions (Vărzaru, 2022). In the 1990s, neural networks and fuzzy logic were used in accounting, providing more flexibility and the ability to learn from data, leading to more accurate decisions. However, these systems still had limitations in analyzing large amounts of data (Agarwal & Gaur, 2020).

The 2000s saw the emergence of machine learning and natural language processing, revolutionizing accounting. Machine learning algorithms could analyze vast amounts of data, learn from it, and make predictions. Natural language processing enabled computers to understand and interpret human language, automating tasks such as financial reporting (Agarwal & Gaur, 2020). Recent technological advancements have allowed accountants to process large amounts of data, analyze it in real time, and provide valuable insights to businesses, making the current use of AI in accounting possible (Agarwal & Gaur, 2020). Artificial intelligence has significantly advanced in accounting, from automating simple tasks to performing complex analyses and predictions. Technological advancements in expert systems, neural networks, fuzzy logic, and machine learning have driven the development of artificial intelligence in accounting. Big Data analytics, cloud computing, and the Internet of Things have also contributed to the current use of AI in accounting. These technological developments have transformed accounting, improving efficiency, accuracy, and decision-making. Accountants must embrace artificial intelligence technology to remain relevant in a digital economy (Askary et al., 2018; Berdiyeva et al., 2021; Chu & Yong, 2021).

Zhang et al. (2019) discussed how the use of artificial intelligence (AI), machine learning, and natural language processing tools can help automate accounting processes, enabling accountants to make better decisions. This accelerates the integration of accounting systems with intelligent logic. Exploring how AI can enhance accounting practices is therefore logical.

The advancement of technology has led to the automation of various accounting functions such as data input, bookkeeping, financial analysis, compliance monitoring, and cost analysis. Artificial intelligence (AI) has played a crucial role in reducing errors, increasing efficiency and accuracy, and providing valuable insights and recommendations for better decision-making in accounting.

One of the main benefits of AI in accounting is the automation of data entry and bookkeeping. AI can swiftly and reliably handle large volumes of data, minimizing the likelihood of errors and freeing up time for other essential tasks, which can save accountants a significant amount of time.

AI-powered software can also analyze financial data, offer insights and recommendations, and proactively detect errors or inconsistencies. This technology enables accountants to make well-informed decisions more quickly and improve overall financial performance.

Moreover, AI can enhance compliance by automating the monitoring process and identifying any regulatory issues by analyzing financial records for potential fraudulent behavior or noncompliance with applicable laws. It also helps ensure that financial reports are accurate and compliant with relevant standards, reducing the risk of fines or legal action.

Baldwin et al. (2006) emphasized the importance of the current audit and assurance environment in the accounting profession. They pointed out that audit failures have significant financial implications, leading to adjustments in regulations, rules, and accountant training by the government and professional bodies. Chu and Yong (2021) suggested that artificial intelligence (AI) could address these issues through Big Data analytics, helping auditors focus on exception reporting and improve the risk assessment process. AI can also assist in detecting potentially fraudulent transactions and conduct predictive analysis to understand future trends based on past data (Chu & Yong, 2021). Additionally, AI can be used to create data visualizations and dashboards, enhancing the efficiency and accuracy of traditional accounting activities.

While AI offers numerous benefits to the accounting industry, including increased efficiency, accuracy, and automation, it also presents challenges. It opens up new career opportunities for data analysts, data scientists, and software developers, who play crucial roles in developing AI-driven solutions for the accounting industry. However, it's important to note that AI is meant to assist accountants, not replace them. Human skills and judgment remain essential in accounting, but as AI technology advances, we can expect increasingly sophisticated uses of AI in this field.

7.3 AI Adoption: Challenges for the Accounting Profession

The adoption of AI applications brings both benefits and implications to the accounting profession. AI offers the ability to advance the industry while also requiring safeguards against potential negative effects.

Artificial intelligence (AI) involves applying science and engineering to make machines intelligent (Sutton, 2020). AI has numerous applications across many industries, yet there is a lack of sufficient research in the accounting industry. Many manual tasks traditionally carried out by human resources, such as accountants, auditors, and bookkeepers, are now being enhanced by applications like OpenAI's ChatGPT (Jammalamadaka & Itapu, 2022).

Technological advancements have brought transformative changes to the accounting profession, with AI emerging as a powerful tool with the potential to revolutionize accounting practices.

Askary et al. (2018) highlighted the significance of reliable accounting information, which can be achieved by establishing strong internal control systems. The accounting profession has long relied on time-consuming, error-prone manual operations. Consequently, the production of high-quality accounting information depends largely on the effectiveness of internal control systems within organizations. According to Askary et al. (2018), having competent management and auditors who analyze the company's financial reporting is essential for strengthening internal control systems. Findings from various studies (Askary et al., 2018) suggest that integrating modern technology, such as artificial intelligence, to address weaknesses in internal accounting control systems would be wise. By eliminating asynchronous data, digital technologies could enhance decision-making quality, transparency, and the speed of intra- and inter-organizational communication. This shift could enable accountants to concentrate on high-value activities such as analysis, problem-solving, decision-making, strategy development, and leadership (Vărzaru, 2022).

According to Rom and Rohde (2007), accounting's inner functions will change due to digitalization rather than its component parts. Robotic Process Automation (RPA), for example, will modify the jobs that need to be done by humans but won't completely eliminate them. Accountants will still have a place in businesses, but digitization will significantly change their role. Thus, the structure developed by Rom and Rohde (2007) is suitable for studying digitalization's effects on accounting.

Gulin et al., (2019a, 2019b) emphasized the importance of distinguishing between routine careers that are easy to automate and nonroutine tasks that are difficult for computers or software to perform. According to Oschinski and Wyonch (2017), jobs requiring creativity, critical thinking, training, and human contact won't be automated soon. However, routine jobs with little human interaction, expertise, and training may be easily mechanized (Kim et al., 2017). Many accounting operations, such as invoicing, payroll, and bookkeeping, are already automated in numerous firms, especially larger businesses (Arntz et al., 2017).

Moudud-Ul-Huq (2014) highlighted the support provided by digitalization and automation in various accounting processes, such as audit planning, analytical review procedures, materiality evaluation, internal control appraisal, risk assessment, and going-concern judgments. Surveys have shown that many organizations currently use digital solutions and plan to implement more in the coming years. According to KPMG (2020), major digital solutions used or soon to be used in German businesses include connections to internal or external systems, data quality management, process automation, system uniformity, integrated consolidation system, real-time reporting, transparency creation, Big Data analysis, visualization tools, and cloud computing.

PwC conducted research among large- and medium-sized enterprises with operations in Germany and found that the most intriguing uses of artificial intelligence are automated money transfers and automated reading of invoices and other accounting documents. The research also revealed that many businesses are planning to start using advanced technologies for tasks such as document recognition, direct exchange of information with clients and vendors, payment through transfers, and finding alternatives to Excel worksheets.

According to KPMG (2020), the majority of firms participating in the study will be using paperless accounting, standard system design, links to external systems, integrated consolidation systems, Big Data analysis, and data quality management. These findings indicate that companies are preparing for the adoption of digitalization and the changes it will bring to their sectors.

Implementing new software solutions requires time and money, especially if internal solution development is involved. This presents significant opportunities for companies providing services and developing cutting-edge accounting system solutions. However, smaller firms may struggle to afford such expensive solutions, leaving larger enterprises as the primary adopters.

Möller et al. (2020) emphasized the importance of making choices based on relevant and reliable information from a trustworthy, safe database. However, controllers' ability to develop and manage such systems is facing increasing pressure from data scientists and other departments like IT, as noted by Patra and Roy (2023).

Despite the many benefits, the adoption of AI in accounting also faces challenges and barriers. This section discusses these drawbacks. Several issues affect the application and implementation of AI in the accounting firm.

First, AI has been used in several industries, including banking, agriculture, mining, and manufacturing. Generally, the use of artificial intelligence in the accounting industry is in its infancy, implying a lack of experience. The application of automation is mainly focused on financial reporting, neglecting core areas of accounting such as financial analysis, and has not yet impacted the change of accounting standards. If AI is implemented in the accounting industry, it should cover almost all aspects of traditional accounting, including the formation of accounting information, report generation, and decision-making (Shaffer et al., 2020). This suggests that AI's capabilities in the accounting industry require further development of use cases across the financial preparation and reporting spectrum. AI tools, due to their perceived ease of use and value, will make this spectrum adoption possible over time (Goh et al., 2019).

Second, implementing AI requires a high initial investment with slow returns, and firms should be prepared to invest significant capital in the long term (Shin, 2021). Introducing AI also requires adjustments to a firm's daily operations, which can affect human resource management through job displacement. Therefore, the decision to introduce AI in the accounting industry should be long-term rather than short-term. Additionally, the quality of professional talent needs to be improved, requiring the reskilling or upskilling of a firm's staff to use the technology. Employees who cannot be upskilled might lose their jobs.

Challenges in AI adoption include the lack of market understanding and awareness of AI technology, particularly among small- and medium-sized enterprises. Data privacy and security concerns also arise due to the reliance of AI-powered solutions on large amounts of data. Firms must ensure that their solutions comply with data protection regulations and implement robust data security measures.

Jammalamadaka and Itapu (2022) emphasized the importance of explainable AI in the workplace to ensure accountability and transparency. They highlighted the critical need for objectivity, pointing out the potential for systematic errors in AI algorithms that could lead to unequal treatment of different populations. The authors stressed that AI used in accounting must be free of bias and should not perpetuate discrimination or unfairness.

The authors also emphasized the importance of maintaining trustworthiness in AI algorithms developed by firms, as they should be accepted based on the output or outcome of the completed activity.

Trust in the accounting profession is crucial, as financial results must be specified, measured, monitored, and evaluated in ways that lead to the achievement of desired objectives. AI firms need to develop platforms that align with acceptable moral behavior and ethical standards. Other ethical concerns regarding AI include result distortion, accessibility, expectation gap, and the competence of developers (Zhang et al., 2023).

7.4 ChatGPT in the Accounting Field

Historically, the accounting profession has been associated with labor-intensive tasks such as tax return compilation, financial reporting, and audits. However, the integration of AI has the potential to enhance productivity and success within the sector. Alshurafat (2023) asserts that ChatGPT is beneficial for accountants and financial specialists, enabling the comprehension of natural language queries and the provision of relevant answers.

The ChatGPT, developed by OpenAI, is a significant language model that holds promise as an artificial intelligence solution within the accounting industry. According to Alshurafat (2023), ChatGPT demonstrates the capability to comprehend natural language queries and provide accurate responses, potentially streamlining accounting processes and enhancing operational efficiency. Furthermore, the study addresses potential challenges and solutions involved in ChatGPT implementation.

Accountants often grapple with large volumes of data to discern trends, patterns, and anomalies that influence financial decisions. ChatGPT can aid in this process, called data analysis, by offering swift and accurate responses to financial data queries, provided that the financial dataset has been integrated with the system.

Many accounting tasks, like data entry and record-keeping, are repetitive and time-consuming. Utilizing ChatGPT can automate these processes by processing and categorizing financial data, generating reports, and issuing payment reminders to clients when provided access to the necessary data. Finally, ChatGPT has the potential to improve customer service by promptly addressing client queries related to account balances, payment due dates, and financial planning advice.

Integrating ChatGPT as a powerful tool can greatly improve productivity and efficiency in the accounting business, allowing professionals to concentrate on more valuable tasks such as financial planning and analysis. However, implementing ChatGPT also brings challenges, including ensuring response accuracy and securing financial data. This requires integrating it with a secure system to protect client information.

7.5 Conclusions

The incorporation of AI in the accounting industry offers substantial potential for growth and innovation. In the past, accounting processes relied heavily on manual methods, which were time-consuming and susceptible to errors. However, the advent of AI has radically changed accounting by facilitating task automation, thus enabling accountants to concentrate on more strategic endeavors (Zhang et al., 2019).

The use of AI in accounting is expected to open up new opportunities for accountants. In 2023, Alshurafat highlighted that AI firms in the accounting industry have used technology to create unique solutions for industry challenges. These firms are driving innovation in the accounting sector by developing AI-powered software that automates tasks, improves accuracy, and enhances decision-making. Furthermore, AI technology can help accountants offer additional value-added services such as business forecasting, risk management, and strategic planning.

The study's key findings suggest that using AI platforms can be beneficial for the accounting profession. AI can automate tasks such as data input, bookkeeping, expense reporting, auditing, fraud detection in financial transactions, tax preparation and filing, and financial analysis. This helps accounting professionals save time and money. Additionally, AI creates new job opportunities in accounting, such as in data science, software development, and machine learning.

In conclusion, the accounting profession will continue to benefit from the adoption of AI solutions, as they increase productivity by automating specific tasks traditionally performed by accountants and bookkeepers. The profession will also achieve cost savings in compiling financial statements and documentation. AI solutions aid decision-making by utilizing datasets for machine learning, supporting accountants in financial decisions. As the accounting industry embraces AI technology, AI is expected to become an integral component of accounting practices, leading to major and exciting developments. It is important to remain vigilant about the ethical implications of using AI in the accounting industry.

References

Agarwal, P., & Gaur, F. (2020). A historical perspective of artificial intelligence in accounting: Evolution, current developments, and future opportunities. *Journal of Accounting and Organizational Change, 16*(1), 1–12.

Alshurafat, H. (2023). *The usefulness and challenges of chatbots for accounting professionals: Application on ChatGPT*. Available at SSRN: https://doi.org/10.2139/ssrn.4345921

Andreassen, R. I. (2020). Digital technology and changing roles: A management accountant's dream or nightmare? *Journal of Management Control, 31*(3), 209–238.

Arntz, M., Gregory, T., & Zierahn, U. (2017). Revisiting the risk of automation. *Economics Letters, 159*, 157–160.

Askary, S., Abu-Ghazaleh, N., & Tahat, Y. A. (2018). Artificial intelligence and reliability of accounting information. In *Challenges and opportunities in the digital era* (p. 11195). Springer. https://doi.org/10.1007/978-3-030-02131-3_28

Baldwin, A. A., Brown, C. E., & Trinkle, B. S. (2006). Opportunities for artificial intelligence development in the accounting domain: The case for auditing. *International Journal of Intelligent Systems in Accounting, Finance and Management, 14*(3), 77–86.

Berdiyeva, O., Islam, M. U., & Saeedi, M. (2021). Artificial intelligence in accounting and finance: Meta-analysis. *NUST Business Review, 3*(1), 57–79.

Chu, M. K., & Yong, K. O. (2021). Big data analytics for business intelligence in accounting and audit. *Open Journal of Social Sciences, 9*(9), 42–52.

Demiröz, S., & Heupel, T. (2017). Digital transformation and its radical changes for external management accounting: A consideration of small and medium-sized enterprises. In *FDIBA Conference Proceedings*.

Fettry, S., Anindita, T., Wikansari, R., & Sunaryo, K. (2019). The future of accountancy profession in the digital era. In *Global competitiveness: Business transformation in the digital era* (pp. 8–14). https://doi.org/10.1201/978 0429202629-2

Gartner glossary. (2024). https://www.gartner.com/en/information-technology/glossary/digitalization. Acccessed 16 October 2024.

Goh, C., et al. (2019). *Charting the future of accountancy with AI*. https://ink.library.smu.edu.sg/cgi/viewcontent.cgi?article=2833&context=soa_research

Gulin, D., Hladika, M., & Valenta, I. (2019a). Digitalization and the challenges for the accounting profession. *Entrenova—Enterprise Research Innovation, 5*, 428–437.

Gulin, D., Hladika, M., & Valenta, I. (2019b). Digitalization and the challenges for the accounting profession. *IRENET—Society for Advancing Innovation and Research in Economy* (pp. 502–511).

Hasan, A. R. (2022). Artificial Intelligence (AI) in accounting & auditing: A literature review. *Open Journal of Business and Management, 10*(1), 440–465.

Jammalamadaka, K. R., & Itapu, S. (2022) Responsible AI in automated credit scoring systems. *AI Ethics Publication*, 1–11. https://doi.org/10.1007/s43681-022-00175-3

Kim, Y. J., Kim, K., & Lee, S. (2017). The rise of technological unemployment and its implications on the future macroeconomic landscape. *Futures, 87*, 1–9.

KPMG (2020). *Digitalisation in accounting*. https://hub.kpmg.de/digitalization-in-accounting-2020. Accessed on 16 october 2024.

Möller, K., Schäffer, U., & Verbeeten, F. (2020). Digitalization in management accounting and control: An editorial. *Journal of Management Control, 31*(1–2), 1–8. https://doi.org/10.1007/s00187-020-00300-5

Moudud-Ul-Huq, S. (2014). The role of artificial intelligence in the development of accounting systems: A review. *The IUP Journal of Accounting Research and Audit Practices, 12*(2), 7–19.

Oncioiu, I., Bîlcan, F. R., Stoica, D. A., & Stanciu, A. (2019). Digital transformation of managerial accounting—Trends in the new economic environment. *EIRP Proceedings, 14*(1), 266–274.

Oschinski, M., & Wyonch, R. (2017). *Future stock? The impact of automation on Canada's labour market*. Institute C.D. Howe Institute, Commentary No. 472. https://www.cdhowe.org/sites/default/files/attachments/research_papers/mixed/Update_Commentary%20472%20web.pdf

Patra, G., & Roy, R. K. (2023). Business sustainability and growth in journey of industry 4.0-A case study. In A. Nayyar, M. Naved, & R. Rameshwar (Eds.), *New horizons for industry 4.0 in modern business. Contributions to environmental sciences & innovative business technology*. Springer. https://doi.org/10.1007/978-3-031-20443-2_2

Rom, A., & Rohde, C. (2007). Management accounting and integrated information systems: A literature review. *International Journal of Accounting Information Systems, 8*(1), 40–68.

Shaffer, K. J., Gaumer, C. J., & Bradley, K. P. (2020). Artificial intelligence products reshape accounting: Time to re-train. *Development and Learning in Organisations, 34*(6).

Sharida, A., & Hashlamon, I. (2021). Real-time vision-based controller for delta robots. *International Journal of Intelligent Systems Technologies and Applications, 20*(4), 271–295.

Sharida, A., Hamdan, A., & Al-Hashimi, M. (2020). Smart cities: The next urban evolution in delivering a better quality of life. *Toward Social Internet of*

Things (SIoT): Enabling Technologies, Architectures and Applications: Emerging Technologies for Connected and Smart Social Objects, 287–298.

Shin, D. (2021). The effects of explainability and causability on perception, trust, and acceptance: Implications for explainable AI. *International Journal of Human-Computer Studies, 146*, 1–10.

Sutton, R. S. (2020). John McCarthy's definition of intelligence. *Journal of Artificial General Intelligence, 11*(2), 66–67. https://doi.org/10.2478/jagi-2020-0003

Vărzaru, A. A. (2022). Assessing artificial intelligence technology acceptance in managerial accounting. *Electronics, 11*, 1–13. https://doi.org/10.3390/electronics11142256

Yao, Q., & Gao, Y. (2020). Analysis of environment accounting in the context f big data. *Journal of Physics: Conference Series, 1650*(3), 032081. https://doi.org/10.1088/1742-6596/1650/3/032081

Zhang, Y., Xiong, F., Xie, Y., Fan, X., & Gu, H. (2020). The impact of artificial intelligence and blockchain on the accounting profession. *IEEE Access, 8*, 110461–110477.

Zhang, C., Zhu, W., Dai, J., Wu, Y., & Chen, X. (2023). Ethical impact of artificial intelligence in managerial accounting. *International Journal of Accounting Information Systems, 49*, 1–19. https://doi.org/10.1016/j.accinf.2023.100619

Zhang, Y., Xiong, F., Xie, Y., Fen, X., & Gu, H. (2019). The impact of artificial intelligence and blockchain on the accounting profession. *IEEE Open Access Journal, 8*, 110461–110477. https://ieeexplore.ieee.org/stamp/stamp.jsp?arnumber=9110603

CHAPTER 8

AI for Managerial Accounting

Mariarita Pierotti

8.1 Modern Managerial Accounting

Over time, the focus of managerial accounting has expanded to include identifying, measuring, and managing a company's key financial and operational drivers (Ittner & Larcker, 2001). Today, the main responsibilities of managerial accounting include preparing financial statements, budgeting for internal costs, implementing control for corporate performance, and facilitating strategic cost management to achieve long-term goals (Brands & Holtzblatt, 2015). To fulfill these duties, managerial accountants must analyze various data from both within and outside the company. Management accountants are involved in strategic cost management to achieve long-term goals, implement management and operational control for corporate performance measurement, plan for internal cost activity, and prepare financial statements. In order to effectively carry out these responsibilities, the primary obligations of management accountants can be categorized into (1) preparing financial statements, (2) measuring the company's performance, and (3) providing decision-related information (Cokins, 2013).

The field of managerial accounting has evolved from its traditional focus on financial decision analysis and budgetary control to a more strategic approach that concentrates on identifying, measuring, and managing the key financial and operational drivers of shareholder value (Ittner & Larcker, 2001). The primary aim of management accounting is

M. Pierotti et al., *Artificial Intelligence in Accounting and Auditing*, https://doi.org/10.1007/978-3-031-71371-2_8

to provide managers with both operational and financial accounting information. With the introduction of ERP systems and powerful business analytic tools, management accountants have demonstrated adaptability by adjusting their responsibilities to help companies gain a competitive advantage (Nielsen, 2015). In the preparation of financial statements, management accountants use historical values to report the financial situation of the company. However, as businesses require more timely and relevant information for decision-making, financial statements are not always an ideal source of information, since they are backward-looking and report on past events rather than providing the forward-looking data needed for running the business. Modern management accountants assist management by measuring firm performance using internal data and providing decision-related information from both internal and external sources. In addition to providing descriptive reports on prior events, management accountants also need to make predictions, including considering uncertainty and risk in decisions (Nielsen, 2015). To meet these challenging tasks and help businesses stay competitive, management accountants can now use business analytical tools to conduct prescriptive analysis to support decision-makers in uncertain situations. For example, an optimization model could allow accountants in a manufacturing company to choose among different raw material vendors, reducing costs and boosting revenue (Taleizadeh et al., 2015). It is suggested that management accountants should expand their role and interact with non-accountants to solve practical problems (Birnberg, 2009). Cokins (2013) highlights seven trends that are occurring in management accounting: expansion from product to channel and customer profitability analysis. An expanding role of management accounting in enterprise performance management (EPM). The shift to predictive accounting. Business analytics embedded in EPM methods. Coexisting and improved management accounting methods. Managing information technology and shared services as a business (Appelbaum et al., 2017). There is a need for better skills and competency in behavioral cost management. In summary, management accounting has broadened its focus from conventional financial reporting to include performance measurement and strategic decision-making. It has extended its traditional role to include identifying the drivers of financial performance, both internal and external to the business. New non-financial metrics and approaches have been added to management accounting functions, and their impact is still being studied by academics and practitioners (Silvi et al., 2010).

8.2 Business Intelligence and Analytics for Managerial Accounting

AI can enhance the efficiency of data analysis by identifying patterns from historical data. For instance, AI-powered systems can integrate and analyze internal and external data, as well as extract and analyze data from news articles and social media. However, the ethical impact of AI may only become apparent in the long term due to the complex nature of its design and implementation. Using AI for activities such as employee monitoring may raise legal and ethical concerns. It's important for managers and regulators to recognize and address these ethical risks. Business intelligence and analytics (BI&A) technologies are designed to support decision-making through data collection, analysis, and information delivery. There is a strong connection between BI&A and management accounting, as executives believe that better data analysis and decision support can create value for their companies. Therefore, successfully integrating BI&A techniques into managerial accounting tasks can greatly benefit management accounting.

The current business focus on business intelligence and analytics (BI&A) and its perceived management importance makes it an area of interest for Accounting Information Systems (AIS) research. However, scholars have pointed out the limited understanding of these developments in accounting academia (Granlund, 2011). In understanding management accounting, four main elements are defined to guide the literature review and discuss its links to BI&A (Rom & Rohde, 2007). These include the overall tasks of the management accounting function, specific management accounting techniques, the organization of management accounting, and the impact of management accounting on organizational behavior and management's perception of accounting issues. Firstly, the core tasks of the management accounting function include planning, control, performance measurement, transaction processing, reporting, and decision support. Second, specific management accounting techniques such as activity-based costing, balanced scorecard frameworks, volume-based allocation of costs, strategy maps, zero-based budgeting, and forecasting are used in carrying out these tasks. Management control, which is broader than management accounting, includes other controls, such as personal and clan controls, in addition to management accounting practices to achieve specific goals. Furthermore, the organization of management accounting includes the roles of management accountants in organizations and how these functions are organized across industries, cultures, and organizational types. Lastly, management accounting has an impact on organizational behavior and management's perception of accounting issues. Research has explored the impact of information technologies, such as Enterprise Resource Planning (ERP) systems, on all these elements. ERP systems have been found to increase the efficiency of collecting and reporting accounting data but often have stabilizing effects on management accounting practices rather than direct significant changes. Additionally, ERP systems enable better control and positively affect organizational performance. Studies have also looked at the changing role of the management accountant due to the digitization of accounting processes. Management accountants' roles have become more business-oriented and strategic, and greater access to information has led to the decentralization of the management accounting function within organizations.

The current business focus on business intelligence and analytics (BI&A) and its perceived management importance makes it an area of interest for Accounting Information Systems (AIS) research. However, scholars have pointed out the need for more understanding of these developments in accounting academia (Granlund, 2011). In understanding management accounting, four main elements are defined for guiding the literature review and discussing its links to BI&A (Rom & Rohde, 2007). These include the overall tasks of the management accounting function, specific management accounting techniques, the organization of management accounting, and the impact of management accounting on organizational behavior and management's perception of accounting issues. Firstly, the core tasks of the management accounting function include planning, control, performance measurement, transaction processing, reporting, and decision support. Second, specific management accounting techniques such as activity-based costing, balanced scorecard frameworks, volume-based allocation of costs, strategy maps, zero-based budgeting, and forecasting are used in carrying out these tasks. Management control, which is broader than management accounting, includes other controls, such as personal and clan controls, in addition to management accounting practices to achieve specific goals.

Furthermore, the organization of management accounting includes the roles of management accountants in organizations and how these functions are organized across industries, cultures, and organizational types.

Lastly, management accounting has an impact on organizational behavior and management's perception of accounting issues. Research has explored the impact of information technologies, such as Enterprise Resource Planning (ERP) systems, on all these elements. ERP systems have been found to increase the efficiency of collecting and reporting accounting data but often have stabilizing effects on management accounting practices rather than direct significant changes. Additionally, ERP systems enable better control and positively affect organizational performance. Studies have also looked at the changing role of the management accountant due to the digitization of accounting processes. Management accountants' roles have become more business-oriented and strategic, and better access to information has led to the decentralization of the management accounting function within organizations (Fig. 8.1).

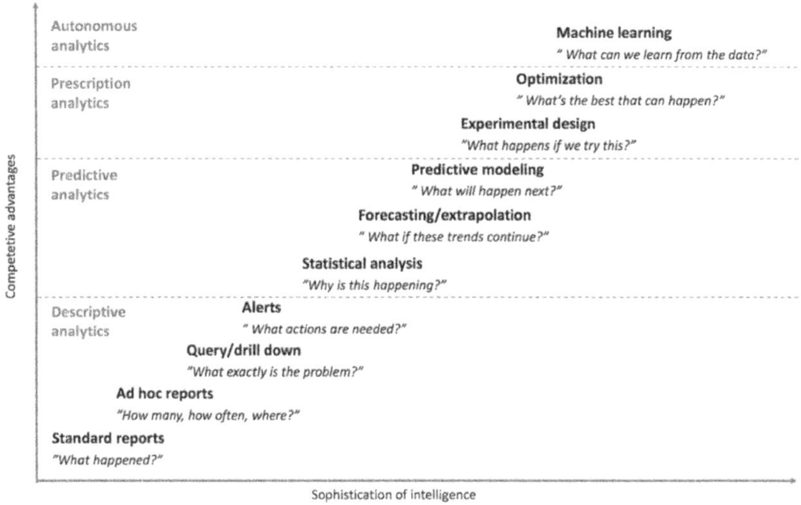

Fig. 8.1 Potential competitive advantage increases with more sophisticated analytics (Davenport & Harris, 2017)

8.3 Integration of Data Analytics in ERP Systems for Management Accounting

In the previous chapter, we discussed enterprise systems applications, which are software packages typically based on relational databases. These systems play a crucial role in business operations such as order capturing, accounting, and warehouse management (Edwards, 2001). All levels and sources of information are entered into the system once, at the time of occurrence, and the system's enterprise-wide scope enables instant access to this new data from anywhere within the organization. Enterprise systems emerged from the need for business management to plan, manage, and account for resources and activities in a real-time, relevant, and insightful manner (Edwards, 2001). Many businesses have replaced or connected previously separate legacy systems to integrated enterprise systems to enhance support for better insights and subsequent decisions and actions (Appelbaum et al., 2017). The cloud, Big Data, business analytics, and a competitive business environment are influencing the functions and scope of enterprise systems, compelling businesses to derive new "actionable insights," and improved outcomes from these new capabilities and capacities (Oracle, 2015). The integration of diverse external Big Data streams and the increasing volume of internal data in the enterprise environment may pose challenges. Without re-engineering the enterprise system to address the complexities arising from different data streams and advanced business analytics, the situation could become unmanageable. In a Big Data context, business analytics encounters several challenges, such as complex data extracts, data fluctuations, data duplications, data security weaknesses, and the potential use of multiple analytical tools and languages (such as SAS, SAP, R, SQL, Python, SPSS, and Tableau). Furthermore, traditional analytical and machine learning methodologies may present issues in the context of a Big Data enterprise system. For instance, typical data analysis involves extracting a representative sample or "training set" of the data to a separate "sandbox" environment where tools like SAS, R, Python, or SPSS may be utilized. Subsequently, a descriptive, predictive, or prescriptive model or solution is developed, which is deemed suitable and beneficial.

The model and all its associated data preparation and transformation steps will need to be translated into SQL for use in most enterprise systems. This process can be time-consuming and error-prone. However, enterprise system providers are starting to offer this functionality in

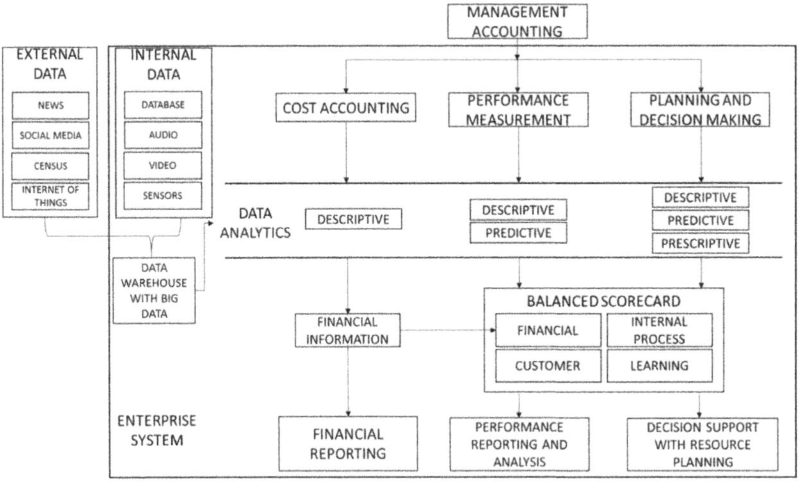

Fig. 8.2 The Managerial Accounting Data Analytics (MADA) framework, motivated from Cokins (2013, p. 27)

order to help businesses fully leverage the benefits of Big Data analytics (Oracle, 2015). These systems also prepare the data for analysis by cleaning, normalizing, and formatting it before extraction. They enable management accountants to access a wide range of internal and external information and make informed predictions using Big Data. Furthermore, modern enterprise systems now support R and other open-source applications like Python directly, allowing accountants to build automated analytical applications within the system once the tasks have been defined (Oracle, 2015). With these advancements in enterprise systems and the possibilities presented by Big Data and business analytics, management accountants can go beyond simply monitoring and tracking historical financial reports (Fig. 8.2).

The Managerial Accounting Data Analytics (MADA) Framework

The Managerial Accounting Data Analytics (MADA) framework has the potential to revolutionize management accounting by integrating data analytics into enterprise systems. According to Cokins (2013), management accounting can be classified into cost accounting, performance measurement, and planning and decision-making. In this framework, management accounting focuses on using internal and external data to generate financial reports, measure corporate performance, and provide relevant information for decision-making. The tasks described in the MADA framework are essential components of Business Intelligence (BI). Successful application of MADA relies on its seamless integration within the overall BI system and its ability to contribute meaningful insights. Business Intelligence is a management support system for gathering, storing, accessing, and analyzing data for decision-making. It is considered crucial for businesses to leverage their data sources and enterprise system capacities to realize a competitive advantage. Research shows that investment in BI infrastructure and functionality is associated with increased competitive advantage. BI systems lead businesses to evolve to fact-based decision-making from intuitive decision-making. The benefits of BI systems include time savings, improved information and business processes, and enhanced strategic decisions. Management accounting tasks align as an essential component of BI functionality and may require the usage of Big Data and advanced analytics. There has been explosive growth in the use of BI by enterprises, and several critical success factors have been formalized for the implementation of BI. Data is regarded as a highly valuable asset of an organization, and its value can be realized as a competitive advantage if the appropriate BI tools, expanded data sources, and systems are in place. Major software vendors have developed ETL and BI tools and applications.

Data analytics can be implemented to assist management accountants in all three aspects of management accounting. For financial reporting purposes, the most applicable type of data analytics is descriptive analytics, which helps to summarize and describe the financial situation of a business. In the field of performance measurement, management accountants can utilize predictive analytics, which can employ machine learning algorithms with inputs from descriptive analytics to provide prediction of future organization performance. With the results from both cost accounting and performance measurement, prescriptive analytics are incorporated into planning and decision-making to provide information regarding the optimized solution for decision-makers. Big Data serves as the data source of data analytics, and it is comprised of both internal and external data. Internal data represents data gathered inside the entity (i.e., the company's database). This type of data is generally structured and familiar to management accountants. On the other hand, external data represents data collected from sources outside the company, such as news, social media, or the Internet of Things (IoT). Usually, external data are unstructured data that can only provide information after being processed by analytics tools. Data types listed in both internal and external boxes represent only examples, not the inclusive list of all internal and external data types.

Similar to other analytical functions within an organization, MADA relies on system processes and functions to ensure high-quality data. MADA can be seen as an essential component of an enterprise Business Intelligence (BI) system. Although the MADA framework does not specifically define the processes for Data Consolidation and Data Quality, these are usually part of most corporate enterprise systems, emphasizing the strong connection between MADA and the broader enterprise system.

The MADA framework is envisioned to be integrated at the same level in the system as the other BI applications. The source systems are where all the business events and transactions take place, either inside or outside the system. In the conceptual MADA and BI integrated framework represented in Fig. 8.3, this is depicted in the upper left-hand quadrant as external and internal Big Data. However, this data is varied and messy, so it needs to be extracted, transformed, and loaded (ETL) before it can be stored or analyzed. This ETL process creates consolidation, consistency, convenience, and referential integrity of the data. This allows the third process of data storage in the enterprise system to occur, where data can be integrated with meta tags. Data Marts serve to facilitate the data for a particular MADA or BI analysis. The Data Marts contain a semantic layer (fourth layer) that allows MADA and business analytics to occur. The last layer allows for multiple ways for management accountants to consume the information provided by MADA at the previous layer.

The role of managerial accounting is changing from the traditional focus on financially oriented decision analysis and budgetary control to a more strategic approach that emphasizes the identification, measurement, and management of the key financial and operational drivers of shareholder value (Ittner & Larcker, 2001).With the advent of enterprise systems, management accountants now have unprecedented access to a wealth of data and data types, larger data storage, and enhanced computational power. These systems have the potential to leverage data analytics techniques to answer crucial questions. These include what has happened (descriptive analytics), what will happen (predictive analytics), and what the optimal solution (prescriptive analytics) is (Appelbaum et al., 2017).

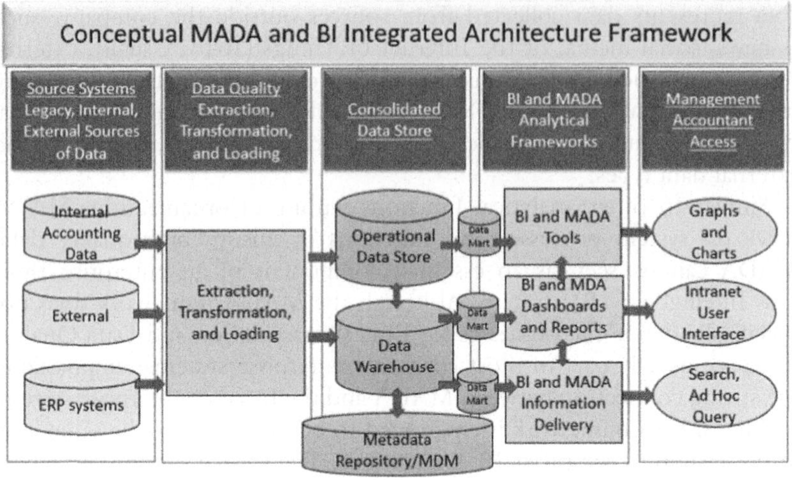

Fig. 8.3 Ideal enterprise system structure that supports management accountants in a BI system motivated from Chaudhuri et al. (2011, p. 90)

However, it is noteworthy that managerial accounting has yet to fully embrace these powerful techniques (Sangster et al., 2009).

Data analytics and managerial accounting tasks are integral parts of Business Intelligence (BI). The selection of appropriate analytical techniques and high-quality data for analysis, characterized by attributes such as relevance, timeliness, and accuracy, is crucial. This ensures the generation of useful and reliable information.

The use of enterprise systems by businesses has led to the emergence of continuous monitoring, facilitated by the decreasing computation and storage costs. The low incremental cost of repeating analytics procedures allows for more frequent application of analytics, leading to better-managed processes and highlighting the benefits of technological advancements.

We are interested in ascertaining whether commercial ERP providers offer training programs tailored to Master of Analytics and Data Analytics (MADA). Additionally, we are keen to explore the potential for companies to provide support for training in analytics, potentially through sponsoring their accountants' enrollment in online or on-campus courses offered by universities. We also seek to uncover the ways in which university programs accommodate and enhance the study of analytics and Big Data for accountants to prepare them for the evolving demands of the future.

These are the challenges facing the field of accounting and auditing as businesses transition toward the use of technology, analytics, and Big Data.

8.4 Machine Learning for Management Accounting

Machine learning (ML) has proven to be very valuable in handling unstructured data. This type of data doesn't have a predefined structure or organization and is often too complex or high-dimensional for traditional estimation methods. It includes information from language and images that we didn't previously consider workable for analysis. However, with ML, researchers can now explore these new types of data for traditional research questions in management accounting (MA). For example, researchers can use unsupervised ML to analyze complex and high-dimensional data like text, images, and video. They can identify similar patterns within this data and then create measures for these features using the ML model.

ML methods are capable of handling large datasets, reducing their dimensionality, and converting identified features into quantifiable values.

Deep learning, a flexible branch of ML that relies on neural networks, can be tailored to compute various measures from images, videos, speeches, and similar sources by adding an extra layer to the network. The initial layers, specializing in different types of unstructured data, extract pertinent features from the input. To generate the measure, an additional feed-forward layer is necessary in the neural network to quantify the extracted features. Deep learning can be adapted to produce numerical or classification measures to suit specific research requirements; however, training data requires fine-tuning the layer for accurate responses. For a more comprehensive understanding of the various architectures employed in deep learning (LeCun et al., 2015).

Research in management accounting typically focuses on internal company operations, like cost management, budgeting, and performance evaluation. One of the main challenges for researchers is obtaining quantitative data related to these functions, as much of it is proprietary or confidential. As a result, scholars are constantly exploring new ways to access this information, looking for alternative “signal sources.“ Incorporating machine learning methods can greatly assist in gathering and analyzing these new data sources, thereby creating fresh opportunities for management accounting research.

Creating Measures from Textual Data

Textual analysis tools leveraging machine learning (ML) can be highly valuable in empirical research in management accounting (MA). They can be utilized to construct outcome variables or explanatory variables, depending on the specific research context. Recently, advanced deep learning models have been employed in related studies to quantify corporate culture (Grennan, 2019) and develop a novel text-based measure of innovation (Bellstam et al., 2021). Although these examples are from different fields, they can be adapted for MA research. For instance, MA researchers can innovate new measures to complement traditional survey research or devise fresh approaches to measure outcome variables such as innovation. These tools can also be instrumental in defining measures pertaining to company strategy and organizational control, underscoring their versatility in our field.

Creating Measures from Other Than Textual Sources

Textual data continues to show potential as an unstructured data source for MA research, but it’s not the only avenue to explore. There’s a recent and intriguing approach that’s making strides by using ML models in face detection. This method enables the exploration of various facial appearance features in individuals, such as trustworthiness, beauty, and masculinity, thus presenting new and exciting possibilities for MA research.

MA research has a strong history of incorporating psychological theories in behavioral research settings, and the literature in psychology and neuroscience suggests that people can effectively judge the facial appearance of others and rapidly form perceptions of others’ facial trustworthiness (e.g., Mathur & Reichling, 2016; Todorov et al., 2009). For instance, previous studies have utilized ML to investigate the effects of facial trustworthiness across various business settings (Duan et al., 2020; Hsieh et al., 2020). An interesting example of this area of research is demonstrated in the work of Choudhury et al. (2019), where they combined the topical content and sentiment of CEO oral communication with CEOs' facial expressions to evaluate their unique oral communication styles.

The study by Hsieh et al. (2020) utilized an ML-based face detection algorithm to explore whether and how auditors integrate client firm executives' facial trustworthiness into their audit pricing decisions.

ML-based face detection models can introduce innovative approaches to studying individual behaviors and the role of facial appearance in the MA context. For example, prior research by Rouwelaar et al. (2021) has explored whether management accountants' (MAs) interpersonal, conceptual, and technical skills are linked to MAs' perceptions regarding their impact on management's decision-making and effectiveness in this role. Future research can integrate MAs' facial appearance to investigate, for instance, whether trustworthiness, masculinity, and attractiveness influence the extent to which MAs impact management's decision-making.

Another unstructured data source for new measurements is satellite data. While past research has primarily used satellite data for macro-level economic forecasting (Donaldson & Storeygard, 2016), advances in technology have made it possible to utilize this data to observe individual companies. For instance, individual factories can be monitored to estimate their emissions and output volumes (Scheibenreif et al., 2021). Also, timely forecasts of retail store performance can be estimated by analyzing parking space occupancy outside stores (Katona et al., 2018). A similar analysis could also be employed to estimate a company's environmental performance in ESG evaluation. For instance, in MA research, this approach could be leveraged to objectively assess the effectiveness of eco-control systems in companies.

Prediction Methods for MA

In addition to methodological advancements, the increasing availability of new data sources due to digitalization also strongly influences the success of ML. This is also true for MA research, which now has access to many new relevant data sources. MA research has a strong tradition of using different performance evaluation datasets that can be complemented in various ways. For example, digital performance monitoring involves the use of advanced tools to observe, record, and analyze information that directly or indirectly relates to employee job performance (Bhave, 2014). This method is commonly used in many organizations, with examples including call, email, and Internet usage monitoring, social media observation, and wearable sensors (Ravid et al., 2020). Such data can be analyzed using ML tools to predict employee personality or performance (Kosinski et al., 2014).

In research related to managerial accounting (MA), the focus is on understanding the relationships between variables such as leaders and employees in an MA context. Machine learning (ML) methods can be used to analyze data from social media websites like Facebook or Twitter to predict personality profiles. This approach offers new research opportunities compared to the traditional survey method.

ML methods can also be used for discovery-driven research, such as inductive or abductive research. ML algorithms can uncover complex patterns that are not predefined. Unlike traditional econometric analysis, where a model is tested deductively based on prior specifications, ML algorithms can inductively build a model from the data to reveal patterns. This approach aligns quantitative empirical research with the grounded theory tradition, where researchers identify data patterns to build theories.

Therefore, ML methods provide tools to generate new types of observations, aiding in the theory-building process in an inductive or abductive manner, depending on the context.

The predictive approach is essential in management accounting (MA), but research in MA has primarily focused on theory-driven explanatory modeling. There is a consensus among MA researchers that "theory comes first." However, despite the availability of statistical methods designed to discover causality, research in MA and related fields often relies on associative linear regression models, which cannot provide insights into causality. Furthermore, the assertion that machine learning is only suitable for prediction and that linear regression models are better for explanatory modeling is misleading. For instance, Lundberg et al. (2020) demonstrated in detail how the inadequacy of simple linear models can lead to serious problems in explanation and produce completely erroneous estimates of the importance of factors.

It has been argued that theories in the social sciences, such as MA research, are often more ambiguous compared to those in the natural sciences (see, e.g., Malmi & Granlund, 2009; Zimmerman, 2001). Nevertheless, theoretical development in MA should continuously progress. The theoretical frameworks of MA revolve around concepts in a dynamic corporate management environment. They are, or should be, constantly refined, and MA scholars should embrace new theories, refine them, and test them alongside traditional theories (Keating, 1995; Lukka & Vinnari, 2014; Malmi & Granlund, 2009; Mantere & Ketokivi, 2013; Zimmerman, 2001).

The predictive modeling approach offers researchers a valuable set of tools for the development and support of MA theory, as outlined by Shmueli (2010):

1. Exploiting new data: With new and extensive datasets containing intricate patterns difficult to hypothesize, predictive modeling helps unearth potential new causal mechanisms and contributes to both refining existing theories and devising new ones.
2. Comparative analysis: Predictive modeling assists in the comparison of different operationalizations of theoretical constructs, allowing for the creation of entirely new operationalizations.
3. Bridging theory and practice: Enabling the assessment of the distance between theory and practice, predictive modeling provides a practical evaluative tool.
4. Comparative theory analysis: Predictive modeling allows for the comparison of competing theories by measuring their predictive power.

It is essential to discern between "explanatory modeling" and "predictive modeling" in the empirical cycle. Explanatory modeling focuses on comprehending the underlying mechanisms and relationships between variables, whereas predictive modeling is primarily concerned with generating accurate predictions based on the available data. Predictive modeling plays a vital role in the empirical cycle, transitioning from observations to theory (Mantere & Ketokivi, 2013), as well as in testing theories on new data (Zimmerman, 2001). The rapid availability of new datasets for MA research and the accelerating pace of social and technological changes have significantly impacted the business environment. This has placed increased pressure on existing theories, and neglecting to incorporate predictive modeling and testing alongside explanatory modeling can result in the loss of the ability to test the relevance of existing theories and discover new causal mechanisms (Shmueli, 2010).

Machine learning (ML) algorithms are particularly effective in addressing problems where the relationships between variables and their impact on outcomes are not readily apparent. In such cases, the association between dependent and independent variables may not be straightforward, and the interactions between variables are not known beforehand (Bertomeu et al., 2021). Predictive modeling is especially valuable when there is no strong theoretical or empirical evidence indicating the superiority of one variable over another. By utilizing an ML approach, researchers allow the data to inform their understanding of variable importance and relationships, which is then interpreted within the framework of existing theory. ML methods provide powerful predictive tools for uncovering the functional relationships between variables from the available data. This is critical for refining theories, as the operationalization of a theory should closely align with the theory itself. Therefore, by design, ML methods are well-suited to contribute to empirical research aimed at refining existing theories and uncovering new ones; in essence, ML methods "lay the groundwork for explanatory research" (Shmueli, 2010).

Research in management accounting often involves studying how different management control practices affect the performance of individuals, teams, and companies. These research methods can benefit from using machine learning (ML) to build more accurate models. It's important to note that a model's ability to explain data does not guarantee its ability to make accurate predictions. To assess predictive power, cross-validation or metrics from a holdout dataset should be used, as performance measures from the same dataset used to train the model can overestimate predictive accuracy. However, integrating ML into management accounting research comes with challenges, such as the need for large and diverse datasets, potential biases in data, and the interpretability of ML models. Understanding and addressing these challenges is essential for successful integration.

Tidhar and Eisenhardt's (2020) study is an innovative example of how machine learning (ML) can be used by management accounting (MA) scholars to enhance research methods and advance theory. Their approach involved using a unique method to build theories and identify optimal revenue models by analyzing data from a variety of products on the App Store. They combined multiple-case theory building with ML analyses, initially using a multicase method to identify theoretical constructs and then employing a large-scale ML analysis to validate and extend these findings. The use of predictive approaches has gained traction in disciplines related to MA. Ding et al. (2020) demonstrated this by using various ML techniques to predict insurance losses for different business lines and comparing the predictions to managers' estimates. Their findings revealed that ML has the potential to significantly improve managerial estimates, suggesting that ML techniques could be valuable for refining accounting estimates, which are prevalent in accounting. Given the promising results of Ding et al. (2020) and similar studies, there is a need for further research to explore the potential superiority of ML models over human-generated accounting estimates in MA. This includes validating and generalizing findings and exploring the use of ML for different types of revenue, cost, and profit estimates. Moreover, economists have contributed to the development of ML for causal inference, which has the potential to improve causal estimates in MA research. New solutions, such as causal forests, counterfactual simulation, double ML, and ML for matching, are being developed to address control issues and improve causal inferences. Studies have also shown how ML methods can be combined with experimental designs to draw causal relationships in MA research.

In the preceding pages, we presented various examples of machine learning (ML) in different application areas, highlighting potential future opportunities for ML methods in management accounting (MA) research. Our illustrative examples were supported by recent research in accounting and related disciplines like finance, management, ML, and economics. It's important to acknowledge that our literature coverage was not systematic, and it may have been biased toward topics that we subjectively deemed most pertinent for future MA research. In conclusion, ML methods hold promise for advancing MA studies, despite being in the early stages of research. Other areas of accounting and related fields offer concrete research examples. Based on our review, the majority of ML research in accounting has focused on: (1) the impact of AI on the accounting field and the evolution of the accounting profession; (2) textual analysis of accounting data and reports; and (3) prediction methods, particularly in the fields of bankruptcy prediction and fraud detection. Although the utilization of ML and AI methods in MA research is still emerging, the existing research highlights numerous potential applications for advancing MA studies.

8.5 AI Ethics for Managerial Accounting

Managerial accounting processes, unlike financial accounting, are characterized by their flexibility and diversity due to the absence of widely accepted standards. This unique aspect poses a plethora of ethical challenges when it comes to the development and utilization of AI in managerial accounting.

The existing literature needs a precise definition and scope of AI ethics in managerial accounting; several studies provide some insights. First, the ethical impact of using AI in managerial accounting should focus on whether user behaviors harm people (Paul & Elder, 2013), organizations, or society (Dillard & Yuthas, 2002). The behaviors of AI users are attributed to their ethical considerations (Alles, 2020b). As a result, it is critical to identify ethical considerations that may lead to behaviors that harm others and society (Alles, 2020a) and to create a code of conduct to prevent them when using AI (Alles, 2020b). Second, the ethical foundation in the use of AI in managerial accounting should be related to the accountability of stakeholders (Dillard et al., 2005). This underscores the importance of each individual's role in ensuring ethical AI use, as the behaviors of accountants, managers, and other stakeholders will affect the results of AI, which will be used to make decisions that affect organizations and people (Guragai et al., 2017). Therefore, a mechanism that stipulates the accountability of each individual and his/her behavior must be established (Davern et al., 2019). Third, ethical risks may be widely exhibited throughout the AI system development life cycle: design, development, implementation, and use (Alles, 2020a). Therefore, identifying AI ethical impact in each stage can help managerial accountants and other stakeholders to avoid ethical challenges at a particular stage.

It has been observed that technologies like AI can significantly influence human ethical decisions, both positively and negatively, during their development and use. Understanding these effects, whether intentional or unintentional, is crucial as they can potentially harm users and associated entities, thereby impeding AI adoption. Therefore, a comprehensive and clear comprehension of AI ethics in managerial accounting is not just important, but also a pressing need, given the rapid advancements in AI technology and its widespread use across industries.

There is a pressing need for more research on the ethical impact of AI in the accounting profession. Munoko et al. (2020) provided a comprehensive list of ethical risks associated with the use of AI in auditing.

These risks include data security and privacy, expectation gaps, accountability, bias, auditor competency, and audit quality standards. However, their study focused solely on the ethical risks faced by auditors, which may not be the same as those encountered by managerial accountants. In this paragraph, we provide initial insights into identifying the ethical risks associated with the use of AI in managerial accounting. The findings of our analysis could serve as a starting point in guiding the accounting profession as it addresses the ethical challenges posed by AI.

References

Alles, M. G. (2020a). AIS-ethics as an ethical domain: A response to Guragai, Hunt, Neri and Taylor (2017) and Dillard and Yuthas (2002). *International Journal of Digital Accounting Research, 20*, 1–29.

Alles, M. G. (2020b). Business process "De-Engineering": establishing the value of the human auditor in an automated audit system. *Journal of Emerging Technologies in Accounting, 17*(1), 43–49.

Appelbaum, D., Kogan, A., Vasarhelyi, M., & Yan, Z. (2017). Impact of business analytics and enterprise systems on managerial accounting. *International Journal of Accounting Information Systems, 25*, 29–44.

Bellstam, G., Bhagat, S., & Cookson, J. A. (2021). A text-based analysis of corporate innovation. *Management Science, 67*(7), 4004–4031.

Bertomeu, J., Cheynel, E., Floyd, E., & Pan, W. (2021). Using machine learning to detect misstatements. *Review of Accounting Studies, 26*, 468–519.

Birnberg, J. G. (2009). The case for post-modern management accounting: Thinking outside the box. *Journal of Management Accounting Research, 21*(1), 3–18.

Brands, K., & Holtzblatt, M. (2015). Business analytics: Transforming the role of management accountants. *Management Accounting Quarterly, 16*(3), 1–12.

Chaudhuri, S., Dayal, U., & Narasayya, V. (2011). An overview of business intelligence technology. *Communications of the ACM, 54*(8), 88–98.

Choudhury, P., Wang, D., Carlson, N. A., & Khanna, T. (2019). Machine learning approaches to facial and text analysis: Discovering CEO oral communication styles. *Strategic Management Journal, 40*(11), 1705–1732.

Cokins, G. (2013). Top 7 trends in management accounting. *Strategic Finance, 95*(6), 21–30.

Davern, M., Gyles, N., Hanlon, D., & Pinnuck, M. (2019). Is financial reporting still useful? Australian Evidence *Abacus, Accounting Foundation, 55*(1), 237–272.

Davenport, T., & Harris, J. (2017). *Competing on analytics: Updated, with a new introduction: The new science of winning*. Harvard Business Press.

Dillard, J., Brown, D., & Marshall, R. S. (2005). An environmentally enlightened accounting. In *Accounting Forum 29*(1), 77–101.

Dillard, J. F., & Yuthas, K. (2002). Ethical audit decisions: A structuration perspective. *Journal of Business Ethics, 36*, 49–64.

Ding, K., Lev, B., Peng, X., Sun, T., & Vasarhelyi, M. A. (2020). Machine learning improves accounting estimates: Evidence from insurance payments. *Review of Accounting Studies, 25*(3), 1098–1134.

Donaldson, D., & Storeygard, A. (2016). The view from above: Applications of satellite data in economics. *Journal of Economic Perspectives, 30*(4), 171–198.

Duan, Y., Hsieh, T. S., Wang, R. R., & Wang, Z. (2020). Entrepreneurs' facial trustworthiness, gender, and crowdfunding success. *Journal of Corporate Finance, 64*, 101693.

Edwards, J. B. (2001). ERP, balanced scorecard, and IT: How do they fit together? *Journal of Corporate Accounting & Finance, 12*(5), 3–12.

Granlund, M. (2011). Extending AIS research to management accounting and control issues: A research note. *International Journal of Accounting Information Systems, 12*(1), 3–19.

Grennan, M. (2019). 1 Billion Citation Dataset and Deep Learning Citation Extraction.

Guragai, B., Hunt, N. C., Neri, M. P., & Taylor, E. Z. (2017). Accounting information systems and ethics research: Review, synthesis, and the future. *Journal of Information Systems, 31*(2), 65–81.

Hsieh, T. S., Kim, J. B., Wang, R. R., & Wang, Z. (2020). Seeing is believing? Executives' facial trustworthiness, auditor tenure, and audit fees. *Journal of Accounting and Economics, 69*(1), 101260.

Ittner, C. D., & Larcker, D. F. (2001). Assessing empirical research in managerial accounting: a value-based management perspective. J. Account. Econ. 32 (1), 349–410.

Katona, Z. (2018). *On the capital market consequences of alternative data: Evidence from outer space*. eScholarship, University of California.

Keating, P. J. (1995). A framework for classifying and evaluating the theoretical contributions of case research in management accounting. *Journal of management accounting research, 7*, 66–86.

Kosinski, M., Bachrach, Y., Kohli, P., Stillwell, D., & Graepel, T. (2014). Manifestations of user personality in website choice and behaviour on online social networks. *Machine Learning, 95*, 357–380.

LeCun, Y., Bengio, Y., & Hinton, G. (2015). Deep Learning. *Nature, 521*(7553), 436–444.

Lukka, K., & Vinnari, E. (2014). Domain theory and method theory in management accounting research. *Accounting, Auditing & Accountability Journal, 27*(8), 1308–1338.

Malmi, T., & Granlund, M. (2009). In search of management accounting theory. *European Accounting Review, 18*(3), 597–620.

Mantere, S., & Ketokivi, M. (2013). Reasoning in organization science. *Academy of Management Review, 38*(1), 70–89.

Mathur, M. B., & Reichling, D. B. (2016). Navigating a social world with robot partners: A quantitative cartography of the uncanny valley. *Cognition, 146*, 22–32.

Munoko, I., Brown-Liburd, H. L., & Vasarhelyi, M. (2020). The ethical implications of using artificial intelligence in auditing. *Journal of Business Ethics, 167*(2), 209–234.

Nielsen, S. (2015). *The impact of business analytics on management accounting*. Available at SSRN 2616363.

Oracle. (2015, July). *Big data analytics with oracle advanced analytics*. Oracle White Paper.

Paul, R., & Elder, L. (2013). Critical thinking: intellectual standards essential to reasoning well within every domain of human thought, part two. *Journal of Developmental Education, 37*(1), 32.

Ravid, D. M., Tomczak, D. L., White, J. C., & Behrend, T. S. (2020). EPM 20/20: A review, framework, and research agenda for electronic performance monitoring. *Journal of Management, 46*(1), 100–126.

ten Rouwelaar, H., Schaepkens, F., & Widener, S. K. (2021). Skills, influence, and effectiveness of management accountants. *Journal of Management Accounting Research, 33*(2), 211–235.

Rom, A., & Rohde, C. (2007). Management accounting and integrated information systems: A literature review. *International Journal of Accounting Information Systems, 8*(1), 40–68.

Sangster, A., Leech, S. A., & Grabski, S. (2009). ERP implementations and their impact upon management accountants. *Journal of Information Systems and Technology Management, 6*(2), 125–142.

Scheibenreif, L., Mommert, M., & Borth, D. (2021). *Estimation of air pollution with remote sensing data: Revealing greenhouse gas emissions from space*. arXiv preprint arXiv:2108.13902.

Shmueli, G. (2010). To explain or to predict? *Statistical Science, 25*(3), 289–310.

Silvi, R., Moeller, K., Schlaefke, M. (2010). *Performance management analytics—The next extension in managerial accounting*. Available at SSRN 1656486.

Taleizadeh, A. A., Noori-daryan, M., & Cárdenas-Barrón, L. E. (2015). Joint optimization of price, replenishment frequency, replenishment cycle and production rate in vendor managed inventory system with deteriorating items. *International Journal of Production Economics, 159*, 285–295.

Tidhar, R., & Eisenhardt, K. M. (2020). Get rich or die trying… finding revenue model fit using machine learning and multiple cases. *Strategic Management Journal, 41*(7), 1245–1273.

Todorov, A., Pakrashi, M., & Oosterhof, N. N. (2009). Evaluating faces on trustworthiness after minimal time exposure. *Social Cognition, 27*(6), 813–833.

Zimmerman, J. L. (2001). Conjectures regarding empirical managerial accounting research. *Journal of Accounting and Economics, 32*(1–3), 411–427.

CHAPTER 9

Artificial Intelligence in Auditing

Federica De Santis

9.1 Introduction

As underlined in previous chapters, we know that todays' competitive environment has become more and more dynamic, requiring companies to spur productivity growth and to speed up their decision-making processes, also by means of cognitive technologies (Kokina & Davenport, 2017). The world's increasing "datafication" (Cao et al., 2015) provides a high volume, a high velocity, and a high variety of data—the Big Data—that offers opportunities to innovate several business processes (Tang & Karim, 2017), including accounting and auditing (Bhimani & Willcocks, 2014; Vasarhelyi et al., 2015). The audit environment is "a unique and highly complex decision-making environment," which presents distinctive sources of errors and inconsistencies. As compared to any other businesses' decision-making processes, in fact, financial statements audit is process-oriented and not results-oriented activity, since its quality is determined basing on the record of the process as summarized in the work papers rather than on its results, represented by the audit opinion (O'Leary & Watkins, 1989).

With the spread of AI technologies, academics, and professionals underline that cognitive technologies can act as a game changer also in innovating auditing practice and in improving financial audit quality (Ackerman, 2023; AICPA, 2015; Dickey et al., 2019; IAASB, 2016; Seethamraju & Hecimovic, 2022; Vasarhelyi & O'Leary, 2000). Over

M. Pierotti et al., *Artificial Intelligence in Accounting and Auditing*,
https://doi.org/10.1007/978-3-031-71371-2_9

the last decade, scholars, practitioners, and representatives of regulators and standard setters intensely debated on the potential that AI and its related technologies can have on financial auditing (Dai & Vasarhelyi, 2016; Gepp et al., 2018; Krahel & Titera, 2015). In addition, the Big Four audit companies are claiming heavy investments on the development and implementation of AI systems within the auditing activities. As a way of example, KPMG and Microsoft recently announced a multibillion-dollar global relationship that will "reshape professional services across a number of business-critical areas including workforce modernization, safe and secure development, and use of AI solutions for clients, industries and society more broadly".[1] Further, PwC and Deloitte are integrating a variety of cognitive capabilities from diverse vendors to enhance the quality of their audit and assurance services.

This debate deals with the various facets of the connection between financial statements audit and AI, but at its core, it raises two fundamental questions: Does the introduction of AI represent a genuine revolution, or is it just an evolution of the way in which financial auditing is performed? Can AI and related technologies really enhance the efficiency and effectiveness of external audit processes? These questions appear to be highly relevant not only to understand the possible future developments of the audit activities, but they can also have an impact from the perspective of academic research.

The auditing field has a long history of AI applications, dating back more than three decades (Baldwin et al., 2006; Hansen & Messier, 1982; Murphy & Brown, 1992). However, many of these technological aids have evolved as fads without determining any real developments of the profession. The potential of technologies such as the Computer Assisted Audit Techniques (CAATs) and the Continuous Auditing (Curtis & Payne, 2008) has remained largely unrealized (Vasarhelyi & O'Leary, 2000). Despite these failures, scholars and practitioners believe that AI will have a more substantive impact on audit practice when compared to earlier technologies, due to the characteristics of the current digital environment. Firms can access and transform huge volumes of structured and unstructured data from a variety of sources through software and hardware solutions with unprecedented opportunities to perform cognitive tasks (Kokina & Davenport, 2017; Seethamraju & Hecimovic, 2022).

[1] https://kpmg.com/xx/en/home/media/press-releases/2023/07/kpmg-and-microsoft-enter-landmark-agreement.html.

It would be misleading, however, to assume that the mere introduction of AI technology will automatically lead to an increase in audit efficiency and effectiveness. As any other investment, it brings both opportunities and challenges for auditors. To determine a paradigm shift for the audit profession, it is necessary that technological advancements lead to significant improvements of the assurance activities (Fischer, 1996; Issa et al., 2016). Otherwise, the overall costs to be paid to employ cognitive technologies, which include those related to the provision of the necessary education and training for the involved professionals, will substantially exceed the attainable benefits. If this would be the case, the AI phenomenon would assume a marginal role within the external audit domain (De Santis, 2018).

This chapter starts from these considerations and reviews current literature on the application of AI in the audit field with the aim of provide an in-depth understanding of how AI can impact on auditing processes, both in terms of opportunities and challenges.

9.2 The History of Digital Technologies in Auditing: An Overview

The history of digital technologies in financial audit is marked by significant advancements and changes in the way auditing is conducted. After the emergence of computers in the 1950s and 1960s, the introduction of mainframe computers in large organizations enabled the automation of data processing tasks. During this period, technology was used primarily for data processing and record-keeping tasks, thus supporting auditors to perform calculations and automate certain aspects of their work.

Computer Assisted Audit Techniques (CAATs) were introduced during the 1970s with the diffusion of batch processing systems to support data analysis, extraction, and testing, thus allowing auditors to run automated data analysis overnight. By means of CAATs, auditors were able to perform substantive testing and analyze large datasets more efficiently and effectively (Curtis & Payne, 2014).

Since the establishment of CAATs, the widespread use of spreadsheet software, such as Microsoft Excel during the 1980s, greatly enhanced auditors' ability to perform financial analysis and create custom audit work papers.

Over the same timeframe, expert systems, which consisted in a preliminary form of AI, were developed using mostly a rule-based approach to support auditors in making decisions and providing expertise in complex financial audits (O'Leary & Watkins, 1989). Early expert systems also comprised a wide variety of prototypes including knowledge representation schema, learning and natural language understanding so that numerous scholars underlined that these technologies had the potential to improve the accuracy, objectivity, efficiency, consistency, and transparency of audit judgements (Brown, 1991; Dowling & Leech, 2014; Hunton & Rose, 2010). Nonetheless, extant literature demonstrates that they were often misused and that their recommendations were frequently ignored by auditors, who manifested a leery posture toward technologies that appeared to take the decisions out of their control (Bierstaker et al., 2014; Davis et al., 1997). As also Brown (1991) underlined, one of the major challenges that hindered a successful utilization of knowledge-based expert systems such as natural language understanding or artificial neural networks[2] to accounting problems was related to the fact that these systems did not explain how decisions were reached.

During the last two decades, the concepts of Big Data, Data Analytics, AI, and cognitive technologies have become widespread within a variety of business and research fields, including accounting and auditing (Kloviene & Dagiliene, 2018). Following the advancements of technology, auditors are starting to exploit audit data analytics and Robotic Process Automation to improve audit risk assessment, to collect evidence from entire population of company data and exogenous information, to automate repetitive audit procedures, and to increase the frequency of performing the audits from yearly to near real time (Dai & Vasarhelyi, 2020). Notwithstanding the labor-intensive nature of the audit work, the repetitiveness of the tasks composing the auditing process, and the need to comply with a mandatory set of standards that make auditing an ideal field for the introduction of digital technologies in general, and AI in particular (Issa et al., 2016; Seethamraju & Hecimovic, 2022), the financial statements audit was not immediately at the forefront of the digital transformation of society, as it was for other business fields. Moreover, several contributions by both professionals and researchers reveal that the adoption and use of AI technology in audit are substantially below

[2] Here, the reference is to the so-called shallow machine learning algorithms. See Chapter 5, Sect. 5.2 for a more detailed explanation of the difference between shallow and deep machine learning.

expectations (AICPA, 2015; Alles & Gray, 2016; Dai & Vasarhelyi, 2020; IAASB, 2016; KPMG, 2020; Li et al., 2018).

The incorporation of the AI technologies into financial statement audits has the potential to extend the scope of data collection and analysis beyond financial data to encompass non-financial ones and would make it possible to consider both structured and unstructured data. Consequently, this would prompt auditors to effectively tailor the engagement basing on a very robust picture of their clients, by accessing a diverse range of data sources that goes far beyond small samples of transactional data when formulating their audit opinions (Appelbaum et al., 2017; De Santis, 2018; De Santis & D'Onza, 2021).

9.3 Opportunities and Challenges of Introducing AI in the Audit Process: A Literature Review

Consistently with extant literature, we assumed that AI can significantly transform the way in which financial statements audits are performed, making them more efficient and effective (Arnold, 2018; Gepp et al., 2018; Krahel & Titera, 2015; Zhang et al., 2015). Scholars and practitioners, indeed, believe that the utilization of AI would be more revolutionary for the audit profession than other technologies introduced over time to improve the audit process—e.g., Excel, ACL, or the Internet itself. As per other business fields, the convergence of substantive advancements in data science, increases in computer power, and the opportunity to access huge amounts of data and information from a variety of internal and external sources, created also for the audit profession an environment that is ripe for the application of AI (AA. VV., 2015; De Santis & D'Onza, 2021). Simultaneously, regulators are increasingly aware of the growing use of AI technology in audit, so that they are attempting to figure out what is the impact of this trend and stimulate standard setters to regulate the use of technology (e.g., IAASB, 2016).

Since the earliest developments of AI with expert systems, scholars recognized their potential within the financial statements audit domain. The characteristics of auditing work make it particularly suitable for the application of artificial intelligence tools and techniques. The solution of audit problems hardly requires the identification of a single best alternative. Rather, they often require the adoption of heuristic approaches, based on the rules of thumbs of experienced auditors. Knowledge-based systems, machine learning algorithms, and other AI systems can include these rules of thumb, thus offering an alternative and feasible solution methodology to auditing situations (O'Leary & Watkins, 1989; Vasarhelyi & O'Leary, 2000). Nonetheless, investments in AI-based technologies cannot be considered risk free. On the one hand, audit firms must harness the power of such technologies. On the other, they must also clearly understand the challenges that such an investment poses to the profession (Alles & Gray, 2016; Hunton & Rose, 2010).

Opportunities of Using AI in Financial Statements Audit

According to Fedyk et al. (2022) the audit procedures directly derive from the available technologies and data analytics represents the most used AI-based technology in financial statements audit. Specifically, data analytics represents "the science and art of discovering and analyzing patterns, identifying anomalies, and extracting other useful information in data underlying or related to the subject matter of an audit through analysis, modeling, and visualization for the purpose of planning or performing the audit" (AA. VV., 2015).

The current literature on AI's use in auditing mostly discusses how this technology could impact the audit process, conceptualizing the opportunities, potential applications, trends, and challenges that such technologies could contribute to the audit profession (Ackerman, 2023; De Santis, 2018; Haugh, 2023; Issa et al., 2016; Lehner et al., 2022; Lin & Hazelbaker, 2019; Munoko et al., 2020; Omoteso, 2012; Salijeni et al., 2019; Seethamraju & Hecimovic, 2022; Zhang et al., 2022).

First of all, the use of AI technologies provides auditors with the opportunity to make the audit work more proactive than reactive. Following this perspective, scholars underline that AI is helping auditors to remain timely and useful for investors, creditors, and other stakeholders that base their decision-making processes on entities' financial statements. Before smart technologies' advent, periodic (audited) financial statements were the prime source of information about a company's financial situation. Nowadays, instead, companies are able to share their financial information with the public in real time, thus making it increasingly necessary for auditors to provide "on-demand audit services" to maintain their relevance in ensuring financial markets' stability and stakeholders' trust in corporates' financial information (Lombardi et al., 2015; Vasarhelyi et al., 2010).

Second, AI-related technologies' introduction into the audit process can change the trade-off between the audit tasks' speed, costs, and quality, but also to enhance audit work's effectiveness, efficiency, and quality (Dickey et al., 2019; Greenman, 2017; Issa et al., 2016; Raphael, 2017). In this respect, scholars underline that AI has the potential to substitute traditional audit trails, thereby radically changing how the audit process occurs (Omoteso, 2012).

When making client acceptance decisions, auditors can use text mining and sentiment analysis techniques to examine press releases and social networks to assess the reputation of potential clients and that of their key people (e.g., the CEO, the CFO, and the members of the Board of Directors) (Hunton & Rose, 2010). AI technologies can be helpful also in conducting preliminary analytical procedures, since auditors can compare a potential client's financial statements with industry reports or data from other competitors to form a first opinion regarding the company's financial health conditions through clustering techniques (Appelbaum et al., 2018; De Santis & D'Onza, 2021).

During the planning phase, data analytics technologies enable auditors to efficiently navigate high-volume, and unstructured data to identify patterns and trends that provide a more detailed understanding of the auditee's inherent risks and assist in setting materiality thresholds (Cao et al., 2015; Earley, 2015; Salijeni et al., 2018). Moreover, process mining techniques can help auditors during the risk assessment phase, and particularly in control risk's assessment. Process mining tools consist in the analysis of a so-called event log, that is defined as "a chronological record of computer system activities which are saved to a file on the system" (Jans et al., 2013, p. 2). By analyzing event logs, process mining techniques enable auditors to discover process models, thus increasing the accuracy and effectiveness of the preliminary assessment of Internal Controls over Financial Reporting.

Further, process mining offers a superior alternative to the traditional walkthrough audit procedures, usually performed during the interim phase of the audit engagement in order to assess the client's accounting controls and identify potential weaknesses. Process mining is far more insightful than a "regular" walkthrough for two main reasons: The auditor can examine the entire population of transactions and not just a sample, and the auditor can validate transaction entries with the metadata reported in the event log rather than relying only on data entered by the auditee.

On the same vein, the use of AI technologies enables auditors to test entire populations of transactions, and to overcome sampling limitations when performing substantive and analytical procedures, thus increasing audit efficiency and effectiveness (Dai & Vasarhelyi, 2016, 2020). In this regard, auditors can benefit from IoT-equipped goods to improve asset examination or inventory testing and to enhance their ability to detect mismatches between financial statements' sales data and physical products' movement in the client's warehouse. This opportunity is mostly helpful in circumstances in which inventories or assets are less accessible through traditional audit methods, such as physical count or observation (Dai & Vasarhelyi, 2020). The case of a Chinese seafood company is a particularly insightful example of the IoT's potential benefits in substantive testing. As Dai and Vasarhelyi (2020) report, the Zhangzidao Group Co. Ltd. perpetrated a major fraud by asserting that the frequent dramatic changes in its financial statements were because a massive scallops' leak from its farms. The auditors would have hardly discovered that fraud due to the difficulty of examining inventories underwater. Such difficulties could have been overcome by placing IoT devices to monitor the scallops' quantity and conditions.

Fraud detection is the audit activity that may benefit the most from the introduction of AI technologies, such as text mining to analyze contracts, email, and other written communications both inside and outside the organization, thus allowing more targeted tests for fraud and accounting discrepancies (Dechow et al., 2011; Gray & Debreceny, 2014; Hunton & Rose, 2010). More broadly speaking, auditors can exploit text mining techniques to determine writers' attitudes about specific topics such as to analyze email and discussion groups to evaluate corporate culture and assess management's risk appetite or tone at the top (Hunton & Rose, 2010; Li & Wu, 2010).

Lastly, extant research underlines that data analytics techniques can complement traditional sources by delivering sufficient, appropriate, and real-time audit evidence at reasonable costs (Brown-Liburd & Vasarhelyi, 2015; Moffitt & Vasarhelyi, 2013; Yoon et al., 2015).

Challenges Related to the Use of AI in Financial Statements Audit

There is large consensus among academics and practitioners that the audit profession can benefit from AI's potentialities in terms of improved understanding of auditees' operations and associated risks, increased potential for detecting fraud and misstatements, and improved communications with those charged with governance of audited entities (Fedyk et al., 2022). Specifically, large datasets available from a variety of sources, combined with unprecedented analytics opportunities, allow auditors to collect more, and new types of evidence, and to perform audit procedures far more efficiently and effectively (Dai & Vasarhelyi, 2020; Issa et al., 2016; Omoteso, 2012). Notwithstanding, using AI to revolutionize the audit work could be a "double-edged sword" that could create new challenges or exacerbate existing ones for audit professionals (Goto, 2022; Munoko et al., 2020).

We know that AI could be highly beneficial with regard to increasing audit evidence's sufficiency (i.e., the quantity) by allowing auditors to test full transaction populations and to access new sources of financial and non-financial data (Zhang et al., 2022). However, it is still unclear whether these benefits also extend to audit evidence's appropriateness, i.e., their relevance and reliability (ISA, 500; PCAOB AS 1105). Several commentators underline that a major challenge for audit professionals relates to the difficulty of appreciating the reliability of such new sources of evidence, with specific regard to non-financial, external, and unstructured data that auditors can use to confirm financial statement information in the specific audit engagement (Appelbaum, 2016; Appelbaum et al., 2017; De Santis & D'Onza, 2021).

Another big challenge relates to the AI algorithms' increasing complexity, which also corresponds to a decrease in their explainability. A growing body of literature underlines that, despite the growing accuracy of AI's predictive capabilities, auditors find it increasingly hard to explain why certain transactions are identified as outliers and what they should look for in their further investigation to base their opinion (Zhang et al., 2022). We know that financial statements audit is a process-oriented, rather than results-oriented activity, whose quality depends on the professionals' ability to record and explain the process in their work papers (O'Leary & Watkins, 1989). The opacity of AI-based algorithms, that is often referred to as AI's "black-boxing effect" (Adadi & Berrada, 2018; Appelbaum, 2016; Miller, 2019), contrasts with audit standards' requirements. Auditors, in fact, are required to explain and document the rationale for their decisions by documenting the procedures they apply, the evidence they obtain, and the conclusions they reach on the basis of such evidence (Munoko et al., 2020; Zhang et al., 2022).

Stemming from these considerations, scholars also point out that auditors, especially those from small audit firms or operating in less-developed countries, are discouraged from exploring and exploiting the benefits of AI due to lack of skills and experience in data analysis, and inadequacy of audit firms' resources and IT infrastructures. Professionals that are new to those data-driven technologies may not be able to create effective models, thus failing to detect misstatements or confronting with overwhelming false alerts (Dai & Vasarhelyi, 2020; Munoko et al., 2020).

Finally, literature has amply highlighted that another obstacle to the adoption of AI technologies for financial statements audit derives from the fact that standard setters do not explicitly recognize or regulate the utilization of new techniques in financial statements auditing, thus concerning auditors about the potential legal liabilities deriving from a departure from accepted audit standards (Austin et al., 2021; Cao et al., 2015; Salijeni et al., 2018).

9.4 Conclusions

This chapter's main purpose was to provide an in-depth overview of the potentialities and challenges of integrating AI technologies into financial statements audit. The analysis of extant literature on this topic revealed that AI can represent a revolutionary paradigm shift for the audit profession, as compared to earlier expert systems technologies, as it gives auditors access to new sources of audit evidence and to new ways of performing audit procedures thus making the audit work more efficient and effective (Dai & Vasarhelyi, 2020; Issa et al., 2016; Omoteso, 2012).

Scholars and practitioners recognize that the use of AI to perform audit engagements allows auditors to act more proactively than reactively. By means of AI, auditors can provide "on demand audit services" so that they can maintain their relevance in today's highly dynamic competitive environment, where companies are able to share financial information with stakeholders close to real time thus heightening the latter's need for timely audit opinion about the fairness of this information.

AI technologies proved to be beneficial in almost every phase of the audit process, by enabling new ways of collecting and analyzing audit evidence. Nevertheless, the complexity of ensuring the reliability of new data sources and the increasing complexity and opacity of AI algorithms combined with the persistent lack of professionals adequately skilled and experienced in data analysis seem to hinder a full adoption of AI technologies in audit.

Finally, the need for huge investments in IT infrastructure and employees' education while an explicit recognition of AI algorithms as acceptable audit techniques by regulators and standard setters is lacking constitutes a significant obstacle that prevents audit professionals to reap the benefits of advanced technologies in auditing.

References

AA. VV. (2015). *Audit analytics and continuous audit: Looking toward the future.* American institute of certified public accountants, Inc. (AICPA).

Ackerman, J. L. (2023). Artificial intelligence may be coming sooner than expected. *The CPA Journal*, *93*(5–6), 72–74.

Adadi, A., & Berrada, M. (2018). Peeking inside the black-box: A Survey on explainable artificial intelligence (XAI). *IEEE Access*, *6*, 52138–52160. https://doi.org/10.1109/ACCESS.2018.2870052

AICPA. (2015). *Audit analytics and continuous audit: Looking toward the future.* https://www.aicpa.org/interestareas/frc/assuranceadvisoryservices/downloadabledocuments/auditanalytics_lookingtowardfuture.pdf

Alles, M. G., & Gray, G. L. (2016). Incorporating big data in audits: Identifying inhibitors and a research agenda to address those inhibitors. *International Journal of Accounting Information Systems*, *22*, 44–59. https://doi.org/10.1016/j.accinf.2016.07.004

Appelbaum, D. (2016). Securing big data provenance for auditors: The big data provenance black box as reliable evidence. *Journal of Emerging Technologies in Accounting*, *13*(1), 17–36. https://doi.org/10.2308/jeta-51473

Appelbaum, D., Kogan, A., & Vasarhelyi, M. A. (2017). Big data and analytics in the modern audit engagement: Research needs. *Auditing: A Journal of Practice & Theory*, *36*(4), 1–27. https://doi.org/10.2308/ajpt-51684

Appelbaum, D., Kogan, A., & Vasarhelyi, M. A. (2018). Analytical procedures in external auditing: A comprehensive literature survey and framework for external audit analytics. *Journal of Accounting Literature*, *40*(September 2016), 83–101. https://doi.org/10.1016/j.acclit.2018.01.001

Arnold, V. (2018). The changing technological environment and the future of behavioural research in accounting. *Accounting & Finance*, *58*, 315–339. https://doi.org/10.1111/acfi.12218

Austin, A. A., Carpenter, T. D., Christ, M. H., & Nielson, C. S. (2021). The data analytics journey: Interactions among auditors, managers, regulation, and technology. *Contemporary Accounting Research, 38*(3), 1888–1924.

Baldwin, C., Hienerth, C., & Von Hippel, E. (2006). How user innovations become commercial products: A theoretical investigation and case study. *Research Policy, 35*(9), 1291–1313. https://doi.org/10.1016/j.respol.2006.04.012

Bhimani, A., & Willcocks, L. (2014). Digitisation, big data and the transformation of accounting information. *Accounting and Business Research, 44*(4), 469–490. https://doi.org/10.1080/00014788.2014.910051

Bierstaker, J., Janvrin, D., & Lowe, D. J. (2014). What factors influence auditors' use of computer-assisted audit techniques? *Advances in Accounting, 30*(1), 67–74. https://doi.org/10.1016/j.adiac.2013.12.005

Brown, C. E. (1991). Expert systems in public accounting: Current practice and future directions. *Expert Systems with Applications, 3*(1), 3–18.

Brown-Liburd, H., & Vasarhelyi, M. A. (2015). Big data and audit evidence. *Journal of Emerging Technologies in Accounting, 12*(1), 1–16. https://doi.org/10.2308/jeta-10468

Cao, M., Chychyla, R., & Stewart, T. (2015). Big data analytics in financial statement audits. *Accounting Horizons, 29*(2), 423–429. https://doi.org/10.2308/acch-51068

Curtis, M. B., & Payne, E. A. (2008). An examination of contextual factors and individual characteristics affecting technology implementation decisions in auditing. *International Journal of Accounting Information Systems, 9*(2), 104–121. https://doi.org/10.1016/j.accinf.2007.10.002

Curtis, M. B., & Payne, E. A. (2014). Modeling voluntary CAAT utilization decisions in auditing. *Managerial Auditing Journal, 29*(4), 304–326. https://doi.org/10.1108/MAJ-07-2013-0903

Dai, J., & Vasarhelyi, M. A. (2016). Imagineering audit 4.0. *Journal of Emerging Technologies in Accounting, 13*(1), 1–15. https://doi.org/10.2308/jeta-10494

Dai, J., & Vasarhelyi, M. A. (2020). Continuous audit intelligence as a service (CAIaaS) and intelligent app recommendations. *Journal of Emerging Technologies in Accounting, 17*(2), 1–15). https://publications.aaahq.org/jeta/article-abstract/17/2/1/9307

Davis, J. T., Massey, A. P., & Lovell, R. E. R. (1997). Supporting a complex audit judgment task: An expert network approach. *European Journal of Operational Research, 103*(2), 350–372. https://doi.org/10.1016/S0377-2217(97)00125-2

Dechow, P. M., Ge, W., Larson, C. R., & Sloan, R. G. (2011). Predicting material accounting misstatements. *Contemporary Accounting Research, 28*(1), 17–82. https://doi.org/10.1111/j.1911-3846.2010.01041.x

De Santis, F. (2018). *Auditing and management control systems in the age of big data*. Franco Angeli.

De Santis, F., & D'Onza, G. (2021). Big data and data analytics in auditing: In search of legitimacy. *Meditari Accountancy Research, 29*(5), 1088–1112. https://doi.org/10.1108/MEDAR-03-2020-0838

Dickey, G., Blanke, S., & Seaton, L. (2019). Machine learning in auditing. *The CPA Journal, 89*(6), 16–21.

Dowling, C., & Leech, S. a. (2014). A big 4 firm's use of information technology to control the audit process: How an audit support system is changing auditor behavior. *Contemporary Accounting Research, 31*(1), 230–252. https://doi.org/10.1111/1911-3846.12010

Earley, C. E. (2015). Data analytics in auditing: Opportunities and challenges. *Business Horizons, 58*(5), 493–500. https://doi.org/10.1016/j.bushor.2015.05.002

Fedyk, A., Hodson, J., Khimich, N., & Fedyk, T. (2022). Is artificial intelligence improving the audit process? *Review of Accounting Studies, 27*(3), 938–985. https://doi.org/10.1007/s11142-022-09697-x

Fischer, M. J. (1996). "Real-izing" the benefits of new technologies as a source of audit evidence: An interpretive field study. *Accounting, Organizations and Society, 21*(2–3), 219–242. https://doi.org/10.1016/0361-3682(95)00005-4

Gepp, A., Linnenluecke, M. K., O'Neill, T. J., & Smith, T. (2018). Big data techniques in auditing research and practice: Current trends and future opportunities. *Journal of Accounting Literature, 40*, 102–115. https://doi.org/10.1016/j.acclit.2017.05.003

Goto, M. (2022). Accepting the future as ever-changing: Professionals' sensemaking about artificial intelligence. *Journal of Professions and Organization, 9*(1), 77–99. https://doi.org/10.1093/jpo/joab022

Gray, G. L., & Debreceny, R. S. (2014). A taxonomy to guide research on the application of data mining to fraud detection in financial statement audits. *International Journal of Accounting Information Systems, 15*(4). https://doi.org/10.1016/j.accinf.2014.05.006

Greenman, C. (2017). Exploring the impact of artificial intelligence on the accounting profession. *Journal of Research in Business, Economics and Management, 8*(3), 1451.

Hansen, J. V., & Messier, W. F. (1982). Expert systems for decision support in EDP auditing. *International Journal of Computer & Information Sciences, 11*(5), 357–379. https://doi.org/10.1007/BF01001957

Haugh, J. R. (2023). Is AI a threat or helper? Let's chat about it. *Pennsylvania CPA Journal, 94*(2), 14–15.

Hunton, J. E., & Rose, J. M. (2010). 21st century auditing: Advancing decision support systems to achieve continuous auditing. *Accounting Horizons, 24*(2), 297.

IAASB. (2016). *Exploring the growing use of technology in the audit, with a focus on data analytics* (pp. 1–24). International Auditing and Assurance Standards Board. https://www.iaasb.org/publications/exploring-growing-use-technology-audit-focus-data-analytics

Issa, H., Sun, T., & Vasarhelyi, M. A. (2016). Research ideas for artificial intelligence in auditing: The formalization of audit and workforce supplementation. *Journal of Emerging Technologies in Accounting, 13*(2), 1–20. https://doi.org/10.2308/JETA-10511

Jans, M., Alles, M., & Vasarhelyi, M. (2013). The case for process mining in auditing: Sources of value added and areas of application. *International Journal of Accounting Information Systems, 14*, 1–20. https://doi.org/10.1016/j.accinf.2012.06.015

Kloviene, L., & Dagiliene, L. (2018). Motivation to use big data and big data analytics in external auditing. *Managerial Auditing Journal, 34*(7), 750–782. https://doi.org/10.1108/MAJ-01-2018-1773

Kokina, J., & Davenport, T. H. (2017). The emergence of artificial intelligence: How automation is changing auditing. *Journal of Emerging Technologies in Accounting, 14*(1), 115–122. https://doi.org/10.2308/jeta-51730

KPMG. (2020). *Audit data & analytics—KPMG global*. https://home.kpmg/xx/en/home/services/audit/audit-data-analytics.html

Krahel, J. P., & Titera, W. R. (2015). Consequences of big data and formalization on accounting and auditing standards. *Accounting Horizons, 29*(2), 409–422. https://doi.org/10.2308/acch-51065

Lehner, O. M., Ittonen, K., Silvola, H., Ström, E., & Wührleitner, A. (2022). Artificial intelligence based decision-making in accounting and auditing: Ethical challenges and normative thinking. *Accounting, Auditing & Accountability Journal, 35*(9), 109–135. https://doi.org/10.1108/AAAJ-09-2020-4934

Li, H., Dai, J., Gershberg, T., & Vasarhelyi, M. A. (2018, January). Understanding usage and value of audit analytics for internal auditors: An organizational approach. *International Journal of Accounting Information Systems, 28*, 59–76. https://doi.org/10.1016/j.accinf.2017.12.005

Lin, P., & Hazelbaker, T. (2019). Meeting the challenge of artificial intelligence: What CPAs need to know. *The CPA Journal, 89*(6), 48–52.

Li, N., & Wu, D. D. (2010). Using text mining and sentiment analysis for online forums hotspot detection and forecast. *Decision Support Systems, 48*(2), 354–368. https://doi.org/10.1016/j.dss.2009.09.003

Lombardi, D. R., Bloch, R., & Vasarhelyi, M. A. (2015). The current state and future of the audit profession. *Current Issues in Auditing, 9*(1), P10–P16. https://doi.org/10.2308/ciia-50988

Miller, T. (2019). Explanation in artificial intelligence: Insights from the social sciences. *Artificial Intelligence, 267*, 1–38.

Moffitt, K. C., & Vasarhelyi, M. A. (2013). AIS in an age of big data. *Journal of Information Systems, 27*(2), 1–19. https://doi.org/10.2308/isys-10372

Munoko, I., Brown-Liburd, H. L., & Vasarhelyi, M. (2020). The ethical implications of using artificial intelligence in auditing. *Journal of Business Ethics, 167*(2), 209–234. https://doi.org/10.1007/S10551-019-04407-1/TABLES/6

Murphy, D., & Brown, C. E. (1992). The uses of advanced information technology in audit planning. *Intelligent Systems in Accounting, Finance and Management, 1*(3), 187–193. https://doi.org/10.1002/j.1099-1174.1992.tb00020.x

O'Leary, D. E., & Watkins, P. R. (1989). Review of expert systems in auditing. *Expert Systems Review, 2*(1), 3–22.

Omoteso, K. (2012). The application of artificial intelligence in auditing: Looking back to the future. *Expert Systems with Applications, 39*(9), 8490–8495. https://doi.org/10.1016/j.eswa.2012.01.098

Raphael, J. (2017). Rethinking the audit. *Journal of Accountancy, 223*(4), 29–32.

Salijeni, G., Samsonova-Taddei, A., & Turley, S. (2018). Data analytics in auditing: Opportunities and challenges. *Accounting and Business Research, 49*(1), 95–119.

Salijeni, G., Samsonova-Taddei, A., & Turley, S. (2019). Big data and changes in audit technology: Contemplating a research agenda. *Accounting and Business Research, 49*(1), 95–119. https://doi.org/10.1080/00014788.2018.1459458

Seethamraju, R., & Hecimovic, A. (2022). Adoption of artificial intelligence in auditing: An exploratory study. *Australian Journal of Management, 48*, 780–800. https://doi.org/10.1177/03128962221108440

Tang, J. J., & Karim, K. E. (2017). Big data in business analytics: Implications for the audit profession. *The CPA Journal, 87*(6), 34–39.

Vasarhelyi, M. A., Alles, M., & Williams, K. T. (2010). *Continuous assurance for the now economy*. Institute of Chartered Accountants in Australia Sydney.

Vasarhelyi, M. A., Kogan, A., & Tuttle, B. M. (2015). Big data in accounting: An overview. *Accounting Horizons, 29*(2), 381–396. https://doi.org/10.2308/acch-51071

Vasarhelyi, M. A., & O'Leary, D. (2000). Artificial intelligence in accounting and auditing—Creating value with AI. *Rutgers Series in Accounting Information Systems, 5*(October 2015), 10–17.

Yoon, K., Hoogduin, L., & Zhang, L. (2015). Big data as complementary audit evidence. *Accounting Horizons, 29*(2), 431–438. https://doi.org/10.2308/acch-51076

Zhang, C., Cho, S., & Vasarhelyi, M. (2022). Explainable artificial intelligence (XAI) in auditing. *International Journal of Accounting Information Systems, 46*. https://doi.org/10.1016/J.ACCINF.2022.100572

Zhang, J., Yang, X., & Appelbaum, D. (2015). Toward effective big data analysis in continuous auditing. *Accounting Horizons, 29*(2), 469–476. https://doi.org/10.2308/acch-51070

CHAPTER 10

Using AI in the Business Context: Initial Applications in the Italian Business Environment

Mariarita Pierotti

10.1 Introduction

Artificial Intelligence (AI) has emerged as one of the most groundbreaking and transformative technological advancements of the twenty-first century. It has successfully revolutionized numerous industrial sectors, fundamentally altering the landscape of how companies operate and compete. AI has found applications across various fields, but its impact on business accounting is particularly noteworthy and dynamic. This is due to the escalating complexity of tax and accounting regulations, the substantial volume of data that requires analysis, and the imperative need to ensure transparency, traceability, and accuracy in financial activities, all of which have made the integration of AI an essential requirement. Especially in the realm of finance, accounting, and controlling, AI holds great potential for redefining processes and enabling more precision and efficiency. In particular three main application macro-areas can be identified:

M. Pierotti et al., *Artificial Intelligence in Accounting and Auditing*, https://doi.org/10.1007/978-3-031-71371-2_10

1. Compliance and legal aspects, where digitalization and the use of AI for developing tools to comply with regulations play a fundamental role, both in the fields of national and international taxation, as well as in contract procedures and bidding with suppliers.
2. Standardization of procedures and automation of repetitive tasks, where the steps of activities and the logic of data extraction and reprocessing are clear and defined.
3. Reporting, both strategical-managerial and operational. In this context, business decisions are increasingly driven by data.

In this chapter, the applications highlighted and analyzed were developed in collaboration with the AI-LOG consulting company, with the invaluable contributions of Maria Picciotti, Leonardo Vitali, and Claudia D'Addiego. These applications represent authentic scenarios encountered in a consulting setting and have been carefully tailored to balance the requirements of exposition and privacy.

10.2 The Application of AI in Italian Business Environment

In Italy, the Artificial Intelligence market has established fertile ground for growth. It is rapidly expanding and has garnered substantial interest from investors. According to a report from the Observatory of the School of Management at Politecnico di Milano,[1] the AI market in Italy is now valued at approximately 500 million, marking significant growth compared to previous years. This growth can be attributed to the increased adoption of AI-based solutions by companies and the growing investments in research and development. The impact of AI on various application sectors primarily revolves around operational efficiency, data analysis, and personalized services. The leading segment is forecast solutions, particularly in the context of Intelligent Data Processing, with high demand for activities such as business planning, investment management, and budgeting due to current geopolitical conditions. Language AI and Recommendation Systems closely follow in terms of demand. Although there is a rising interest in AI-based solutions across diverse industries, a considerable gap in adoption has been observed between large companies

[1] Sources on the website: https://www.som.polimi.it/en/labs-centers/observatories/.

and SMEs. Data indicates that 61% of large companies have launched AI projects, compared to only 15% of SMEs. The main contributors to this gap are the challenges related to securing a budget and the lower level of digitalization in SMEs.

Despite the challenges, the latter have shown a strong interest in the subject, partly influenced by the incentives provided by the PNRR (National Recovery and Resilience Plan) and the opportunity to develop straightforward projects with a promising chance of success. In summary, the high enthusiasm of Italian companies for Artificial Intelligence solutions is evident in the significant percentage of organizations that are in the early stages of adoption or experimentation on the adoption curve. The history and evolution of Artificial Intelligence dates back to the 1950s, when programs capable of perception, reasoning, action, and adaptation started to emerge. During this time, algorithms such as Genetic Algorithms, Intelligent Agents, Symbolic Programming, and Nearest Neighbor were developed, which later contributed to the advancement of anti-spam filters, forecasting methods, and expert systems. Subsequently, in the 1980s, algorithms for learning patterns in data, known as machine learning, were developed. Techniques such as Random Forest or Support Vector Machines have led to the creation of tools for fraud and anomaly detection, as well as customer segmentation. Finally, in recent decades, multilayered neural networks have become proficient in learning from Big Data, paving the way for AI applications such as Chatbots, image diagnostics, and language translation.

10.3 Artificial Intelligence Solution Classes

The solutions based on Artificial Intelligence are divided into different classes:

- Intelligent Data Processing and Analytics: Solutions that use AI algorithms on structured data to extract useful information. Methodologies can be descriptive, predictive, or prescriptive.
- NLP (Natural Language Processing): NLP solutions are extremely varied. For example, for a company with websites localized in different countries, it is possible to automatically translate customer reviews. Another example is the ability to analyze customer feelings through comments, thus feeding the marketing campaign.

- Recommendation system: The Recommendation System is a subclass of machine learning tools designed to suggest relevant items to users by analyzing interests and preferences.
- Computer vision: Computer Vision is one of the most used solutions, for example, through facial recognition solutions.
- Intelligent RPA (Robotic Process Automation): Intelligent RPA is software that mimics the steps humans take to perform repetitive tasks.

Classes of solutions for physical systems include:

- Autonomous Robot: Collaborative Robot, Humanoid Robot, etc.
- Autonomous Vehicle: Self-driving car, Self-driving boat, etc.
- Intelligent Object: Smart Camera or Smart Speaker.
- Virtual Assistant/Chatbot: Tools capable of interacting with the user.[2,3]

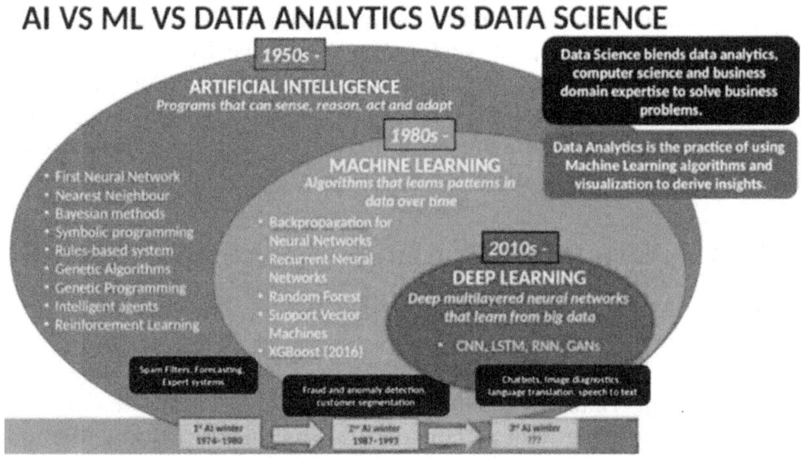

[2] Source from document of "MIT Professional Education" Data Science & Machine Learning, Making Data-Driven Decisions Program.

[3] Source from document of "MIT Professional Education" Data Science & Machine Learning, Making Data-Driven Decisions Program.

10.4 AI to Support Business Decisions

Artificial Intelligence, when strategically applied, has the potential to unlock untapped opportunities for businesses, propelling them toward tangible growth and innovation. Through the integration of AI solutions across the company, businesses can harness the power of data, setting the stage for a future of unprecedented possibilities.

The integration of Artificial Intelligence into a company can follow two paths:

1. Internally developing a model, referred to as proprietary technology.
2. Leveraging existing products or models that are easily implementable due to their scalability.

In relation to the second point, businesses can integrate Artificial Intelligence into their operations by using specific solutions developed within their respective ERP systems. These solutions harness the power of AI and machine learning, enabling companies to navigate process complexities, tackle challenges, and modernize their operations.

In the ERP environment, there is a cloud tool designed to fully capitalize on investments in mission-critical business applications and important data sources. This tool, powered by Generative Artificial Intelligence, enhances decision-making processes by providing reliable and efficient data analysis, risk assessment, and scenario modeling. With this tool, businesses can confidently make informed decisions knowing they have the best possible insights at their disposal.

An example of the value of implementing a cloud tool developed within the ERP environment can be seen in the case of a leading company in the construction industry that aims to pioneer green development by effectively managing carbon assets. The company turned to these solutions to advance its sustainable development strategy.

10.5 AI for Managerial Accounting Embedded in an ERP Solution

The case study in this paragraph is based on a real case that has been modified for demonstrative purposes. Enterprise Resource Planning (ERP) solutions in managerial accounting utilize Artificial Intelligence (AI) ensuring integration across different business areas. For example, a company in the Food & Beverage market can benefit from implementing an AI solution embedded in the ERP system, which allows for the adoption of a common model for industrial accounting and product costing across all production plants. The ultimate goal is to increase agility and improve business performance. For such a solution to be effective in a managerial accounting model, it must have uniform and harmonized processes. This means standardized and consistent data across the organization, with procedures, processes, metrics, and KPIs applied uniformly across all functional areas. If these characteristics are not met, the organization may face weaknesses such as lack of process governance, inconsistent data model, and complex processes requiring significant effort. In a case similar to the one discussed, the company underwent a transformation from unstructured processes and inconsistent information to a unified model. This transformation involved redesigning the organizational model, building a unified data model, costing model, operating model, analysis model, and reporting tools across different legal entities. The management control model typically revolves around process redesign, organizational mapping, technology coverage, and data model definition. Strategic decision-making is crucial in redesigning the organizational model, data model, and process. The adoption of AI solutions in managerial accounting brings several advantages, including greater efficiency, increased precision, improved quality of strategic decisions, reduced operating costs, scalability, continuous monitoring, and predictive analysis. These benefits are particularly valuable for companies operating across countries, as AI allows for the optimization of operations through the standardization of processes and effective management of large volumes of data.

Target Process Model and Technical Solution

The implementation of a cloud-based Enterprise Resource Planning (ERP) system has significantly improved the managerial accounting model by serving as a robust tool for Planning and Reporting. This sophisticated solution, incorporating artificial intelligence, ensures seamless integration and real-time processing of pertinent data, leading to a transformative impact on our operational methodologies. Within the realm of managerial accounting, the cloud-based ERP system offers diverse functionalities. It excels in integrating and consolidating financial and management data from multiple production plants into a singular centralized database. This system facilitates a comprehensive and harmonized perspective of business activities, resulting in enhanced transparency, consistency, and timeliness in managerial decisions. The structured, standardized, and centralized data can be effectively leveraged by Business Intelligence (BI) tools to optimize planning and reporting processes. The strategic implementation of Business Intelligence tools plays a pivotal role in enhancing an organization's planning and operational control. These BI reporting solutions, whether strategic or operational, are not only instrumental but also inspirational in propelling the organization forward. The subsequent Table 10.1 illustrates the Process Model, delineated into its respective steps.

The technical solution entails the execution of several activities. Specifically, Business Intelligence solutions are created within the organization through tasks such as connecting data sources, data integration and modeling, dashboard and report creation, KPI implementation, and predictive analysis and simulation. Table 10.2 provides a summary of the main activities.

In relation to the utilization of the ERP system, BI tools have improved reporting and planning. The solutions, whether strategic or operational, enhance account management activities by calculating KPIs. Table 10.3 outlines the main strategic and operational KPIs for various company departments.

10.6 AI for Financial Accounting: Main Solutions

In the realm of AI in financial accounting, the impactful capabilities of Robotic Process Automation (RPA) and Computer Vision are truly remarkable. These innovations not only improve process efficiency and route optimization but also introduce new opportunities for functionality. Cloud ERP solutions for managerial accounting span a broad spectrum of areas, ranging from working capital to compliance optimization, underscoring the extensive potential of AI in our industry.

AI is more than just a trendy term in the realm of managerial accounting; it is a valuable tool that can greatly enhance efficiency. The ERP system, serving as a holistic solution for analysis and planning, fully harnesses the potential of corporate investments. The capabilities of

Table 10.1 Macro-phases detail's process model

Macro-Phases	*Details*
Data Collection	The first step involves gathering data from various systems, such as Enterprise Resource Planning (ERP), Supplier Relations Management (SRM), Customer Relations Management (CRM), Human Resources (HR) management systems, and other enterprise applications. Most Business Intelligence (BI) tools allow direct connectivity to these sources to extract real-time data
Data Integration	Once collected, the data needs to be integrated and transformed for usability. This process may involve data cleaning, normalization, and aggregation
Data Modeling	The integrated data is then modeled to create analytical structures representing various business functions such as sales, finance, human resources, manufacturing processes, and inventory. This process involves defining hierarchies, metrics, and specific Key Performance Indicators (KPIs)
Data Analysis & Visualization	Using Business Intelligence (BI) tools, users can create interactive dashboards and reports to visualize data and key metrics. Modern BI tools integrate machine learning algorithms to enable predictive analysis and scenario simulation, providing more detailed insights
Planning	Once analytical data is obtained, advanced BI tools also provide support for planning processes, allowing users to set goals, budgets, and forecasts. When these planning tools are integrated, they foster collaboration between departments and functions, ensuring optimal alignment of strategic objectives
Monitoring & Control	The implementation of real-time monitoring dashboards enables constant operational control. Users can configure alerts and notifications to inform designated stakeholders if certain KPIs exceed predefined thresholds

Generative Artificial Intelligence are especially promising, as it can automate reporting to extract critical insights and formulate business plans, thereby saving time and resources.

This tool serves as a valuable asset for:

Table 10.2 Main activities of the technical solution

Macro-Phases	*Main Activities*
Connecting Data Sources	• Connecting the BI tool to various corporate data sources using so-called connectors; • Configuring data extraction in real-time or via scheduled batch processing, depending on operational requirements
Data Integration & Modeling	• Using data wrangling tools to normalize and clean the data. Below are the steps of data wrangling: – Discovery: conceptualizing the data to make it usable. Identifying trends and patterns – Structuring: transforming raw data to make it usable – Cleaning: removing errors from the data that could distort the analysis or make it less valuable – Enriching: selecting the data that is actually necessary for the final purpose – Verifying: ensuring that the data available, after the previous phases, is consistent and of high quality – Publishing: making the data available to the rest of the organization for analysis • Creating complex data models that include hierarchies, custom calculations, and aggregations to support required analyses
Dashboard & Report Creation	• Utilize the features of the BI tool for data visualization through interactive charts
KPI Implementation	• Define specific KPIs for each business area, such as sales, production, finance, and human resources
Predictive Analysis & Simulation (What-if Scenarios)	• Implement predictive models using machine learning algorithms; • Simulate future scenarios to support strategic and operational planning;

Table 10.3 Main KPIs of account management activities

Department	*Strategic KPI*	*Operational KPI*
Sales	***Revenue Growth Rate***: revenue growth percentage over a specified time period **Method of Calculation**: comparative analysis of Monthly/Annual revenues based on historical sales data It is important to note that many companies are currently shifting toward sustainability-related issues. Thus, there is an increasing demand for KPIs concerning the pricing and sales of sustainable products compared to those that don't meet sustainability criteria	***Confirmation of the first date in sales order***: time between the first delivery date in the sales order that the sales office has confirmed to the customer vs the last delivery date **Method of Calculation**: the difference between the confirmation date of the first delivery and the confirmation date of the last delivery
Warehousing	***Inventory Turnover***: inventory turnover measurement over a specified time period **Method of Calculation**: ratio of cost of goods sold to average inventory value	***Pick Pack Time***: average time taken by employees to pick and pack order items **Method of Calculation**: tracking of start and end times of the picking and packing process
Finance & Controlling	***Return On Investment (ROI)***: measures the return generated by investments **Method of Calculation**: percentage ratio of profit earned compared to invested capital	***Accounting Close Time***: time taken to complete the accounting closure process **Method of Calculation**: tracking of start and end times of the accounting closure process
Purchasing	***Total Purchasing Cost vs Budget***: monitoring the ratio between actual purchasing costs and the planned budget helps identify any discrepancies and take corrective actions to ensure cost control and achieve financial objectives **Method of Calculation**: the ratio is calculated by dividing the total purchasing cost by the budgeted amount	***Procurement lead time***: the duration from purchase request to goods receipt **Method of Calculation**: determine the time elapsed from purchase request to goods receipt
Human Resources	***Employee Turnover Rate***: the frequency at which employees leave a company within a specific period **Method of Calculation**: calculation of the number of employees leaving the company relative to the total number of employees	***Average Hiring Time***: average Time to Hire **Method of Calculation**: number of days from posting the job announcement to hiring the candidate

- Reliable integration of Artificial Intelligence: The solution facilitates the generation of insights using natural language, simplifies complex tasks, and automates workflow.
- Deployment of mission-critical analysis tools, thereby accelerating time-to-insight, disseminating insights comprehensively, and accessing insights in a decentralized manner.

- Transformation of corporate planning through the integration of different functions, enabling data-based simulations and forecasts, enhancing cross-functional planning across the entire organization, and implementing an extended planning and analysis solution.

ERP system solutions in the financial accounting domain enable:

- Automation of VAT declaration and quarterly settlement through Robotic Process Automation (RPA).
- OCR for the automatic reading of supplier invoices.
- Automatic reconciliation of customer-supplier and receivable-payable accounts using RPA.

Robot Process Automation (RPA) Business Case

The case study provided below pertains to an actual company in the Energy and Utilities Industry, which is a leading player in the energy transition. This particular case has been suitably adapted for illustrative purposes.

The real-world application of RPA-based solutions in financial accounting is undeniably compelling. These solutions have facilitated the automation of VAT Declaration and quarterly settlement, showcasing the tangible benefits of AI in our industry.

Let's consider the business case of a company operating in the Energy and Utilities Industry, where it's a market leader in the energy transition.

The company, which has been active in Italy since 2015, has leveraged Artificial Intelligence (AI) for automatic VAT Declaration and quarterly settlement.

The main factors driving the company to embrace an AI solution were the imperative to save time, reduce manual errors, and achieve real-time data management, allowing for immediate decision-making based on the most up-to-date financial data.

In relation to the VAT Declaration project, the advantages of automation are immediately apparent when we consider that the manual process consumes three weeks per year and necessitates 3 Full-time Equivalent (FTE) to handle activities such as:

Table 10.4 Effort and main pain points of quarterly VAT settlements and VAT declaration

Manual Process AS-IS	*Quarterly VAT Settlements*	*VAT Declaration*
Effort	2 FTE per year 44 annual process	3 FTE per year 1 annual process with 3 weeks of full effort by the reference of Tax
Key Pain Points	• Manual errors; • Disaggregated data that is not available in real time but collected and reprocessed offline; • Long process execution times, involving multiple functions such as the Tax & Legal, Accounting, Finance, and Administration departments. This results in difficult governance of the entire cross-functional process as well as challenging traceability of data and executed operations	

1. Extracting data from different transactions (reports) on the ERP system.
2. Collecting offline data and reprocessing it using disparate Excel spreadsheets that are not integrated with each other.

The introduction of automatic data extraction and reprocessing reduces the time required to half a day per year, eliminating manual errors and enabling real time, seamless accounting record management (Table 10.4).

The IT landscape chosen by the company was the following core modules of the ERP system (Table 10.5).

The VAT declaration and quarterly settlement manual workflow included the following steps (Picture 10.1).

Target Process Model and Technical Solution

The implementation of our automated solution for VAT declaration and quarterly settlement, utilizing RPA technology, has introduced a new level of convenience. This program can automatically generate a report, available for download as both an Excel and XML file, significantly reducing the manual workload involved in the process. The main goal was to create an artificial intelligence algorithm capable of automating the manual tasks necessary for preparing the VAT Declaration and quarterly settlement.

The process has been segmented into several key phases: Retrieval of data from the structured tables of the ERP system database. Retrieval

Table 10.5 ERP system core modules

ERP system	Finance (FI)	Asset accounting Account payables & receivable Invoicing & payments Banks managements Overdue & aging analysis
	Controlling (CO)	Costing based on cost centers Margin and profitability analysis
	Plan Maintenance (PM)	Management of corrective managements for equipment
	Materials Management (MM)	Procurement Materials & inventory management

of data related to adjustments needed to rectify errors or add subsequently recorded data. Calculation of the total VAT taxable amount and VAT amount by integrating the extracted system values with the adjustments. Creation of an Excel file for historical data tracking. Generation of an XML file for electronically submitting the Declaration to the Italian Revenue Agency. At the core of the solution lies a sophisticated AI algorithm.

This algorithm extracts data related to VAT taxable amounts, VAT amounts, and adjustments from the sales and purchase VAT registers, as well as adjustments related to the disposal of assets from the standard ERP system database. It follows a structured process: initially, it extracts the data from the ERP system and then calculates the total VAT taxable amount and VAT amount for each value, summing the data extracted from the VAT registers with those of the adjustments. Once all the necessary data is obtained, the algorithm produces two files: an Excel file that enables the creation of a historical record of the data for each fiscal period and an XML file that allows the submission of the data to the Italian Tax Agency (Picture 10.2).

After the introduction of the automated flow, the company has realized several benefits.

Specifically, the automated flow has resulted in a 95% reduction in time, allowing manual efforts to be redirected toward value-added tasks

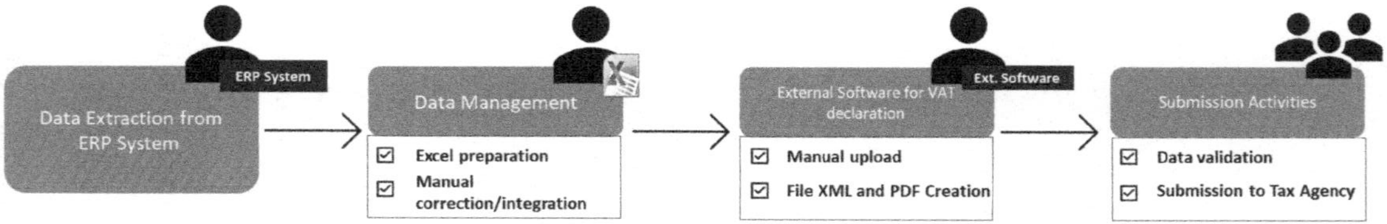

Picture 10.1 VAT Declaration and Quarterly settlement's manual workflow (AS-IS)

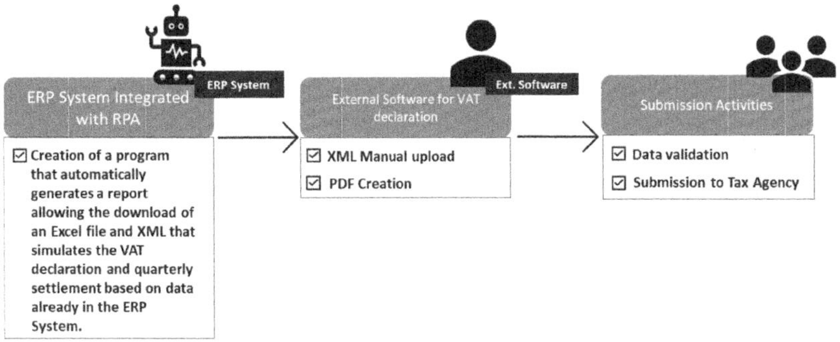

Picture 10.2 Automatic Flow Diagram (TO-BE)

like updating rules and conducting checks on the files generated by the program.

Additionally, the automated flow has established a standardized process, improving traceability and control. Most importantly, it has eliminated manual errors, ensuring a high level of accuracy and reliability.

Methodology

The chosen project governance and management approach for implementing an RPA solution for VAT Declaration and quarterly settlement is the agile methodology, involving incremental releases in sprints. The key phases include the kick-off meeting, business requirements gathering, solution development, user training, user acceptance testing (UAT), go-live, and post-go-live support. The kick-off meeting phase encompasses the presentation of the AS-IS and TO-BE processes, the system solution, and the RACI matrix of BPO and KU. Business requirements gathering involves analyzing the information to be submitted to the Italian Tax Agency and entails the drafting of approved functional analysis and technical specifications. Concurrently, the technical team develops the system solution, beginning with a simulation tool and then modularly constructing the solution and ensuring alignment with business and regulatory needs. User training aims to prepare Key Users to use the new tools through comprehensive training sessions. UAT is a critical step where users conduct tests on the system to ensure its functionality and reliability. The go-live phase involves deploying new functionalities to the production environment, which in this case includes Development,

Test, and Production environments within the ERP system. Lastly, post-go-live support provides technical and procedural assistance to users, including troubleshooting and guidance on system usage. Overall, the agile methodology is employed to facilitate the efficient and effective implementation of the RPA solution, ensuring alignment with business and regulatory requirements while providing support to users both during and after the deployment of the new system.

Optical Character Recognition (OCR) Solutions Business Case

The provided case study depicts a real-life scenario that has been modified for illustrative purposes. The case revolves around a manufacturing company established in 1948, which has adopted an Optical Character Recognition (OCR) solution for processing invoices from vendors. The company's primary goal is to streamline the acquisition and processing of vendor invoices through the integration of OCR technology. The project, which focuses on automating supplier invoice processing, offers immediate benefits for activities such as invoice control, verification, and data entry into Enterprise Resource Planning (ERP) systems. The adoption of automated invoice processing leads to advantages such as reduced processing times and minimized manual errors. The incorporation of OCR technology has enabled the company to automate payment reconciliations with vendor accounts, reconcile general and analytical accounting entries, and carry out real-time inventory evaluations. These automation objectives have been successfully realized through the implementation of the ERP system. In terms of resource allocation, the company estimates the requirement of one full-time equivalent (FTE) responsible for managing the posting of incoming invoices and reconciling them with supplier accounts. The posting of incoming invoices is expected to consume 0.5 FTE, while the reconciliation of payments with supplier accounts will also necessitate 0.5 FTE.

The company chose the following core modules of the ERP system.

In this scenario, Optical Character Recognition (OCR) was not embedded within the ERP system but integrated through an interface. Although the ERP system does offer some built-in functionalities, an external specialized tool was utilized. This tool seamlessly integrates with the ERP system to manage vendor invoices and streamline the approval workflow for any value discrepancies within the vendor invoices, as compared to the goods receipt postings in the ERP system.

Target Process Model and Technical Solution

The implementation of an OCR solution for handling supplier invoices has been completed, along with the creation of a tool that automatically scans invoices and processes the data for transmission to the ERP system. The artificial intelligence solution, which can automate the manual acquisition and validation of supplier invoices, encompasses a process that progresses through the following stages (Picture 10.3).

The process involves the use of several key software solutions, each serving a specific function within the supplier invoice management process. Firstly, the External Software for Invoice Reception is utilized for the reception of supplier invoices submitted in XML format. Subsequently, an External Software with Integrated OCR Solution is employed to capture supplier invoices using Optical Character Recognition (OCR) technology, facilitating automated data extraction from the invoices. Notably, discrepancies with the goods receipt are addressed in the downstream validation stage of the approval workflow. The ERP system plays a crucial role in managing various operations related to supplier invoice management, including the handling of Business Partners' and General Ledger (G/L) accounts' master data, as well as VAT codes. This system is also responsible for generating and posting accounting documents associated with vendor invoices. Finally, the Treasury Software is engaged in treasury management, overseeing the payment process of validated invoices and managing banking operations to ensure effective financial management.

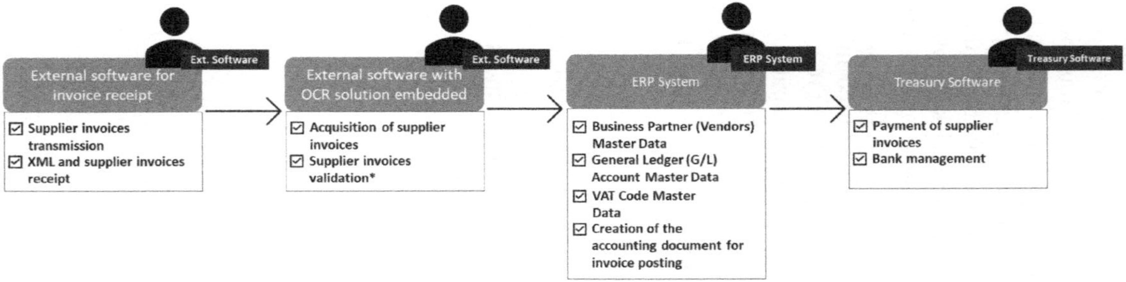

****The posting of the vendor invoice, in case of value discrepancies between goods receipt and invoice posting, is subject to validation through an approval workflow.**

Picture 10.3 Automatic Flow Diagram

Index

M. Pierotti et al., *Artificial Intelligence in Accounting and Auditing*, https://doi.org/10.1007/978-3-031-71371-2

U

SPRINGER NATURE

GPSR Compliance

The European Union's (EU) General Product Safety Regulation (GPSR) is a set of rules that requires consumer products to be safe and our obligations to ensure this.

If you have any concerns about our products, you can contact us on ProductSafety@springernature.com

In case Publisher is established outside the EU, the EU authorized representative is:

Springer Nature Customer Service Center GmbH
Europaplatz 3
69115 Heidelberg, Germany

The manufacturer's authorised representative in the EU is Springer Nature Customer Service Centre GmbH, Europaplatz 3, 69115 Heidelberg, Germany. If you have any concerns regarding our products, please contact ProductSafety@springernature.com

Printed and bound by CPI Group (UK) Ltd, Croydon, CR0 4YY
30/09/2026
02225502-0006